Administrative Theories

Changing Contours of Administration Since Independence
Golden Jubilee Volume Series - 7

Administrative Theories

Approaches, Concepts and Thinkers in Public Administration

Editors
RAKESH HOOJA
RAMESH K. ARORA

Series Editor
Rakesh Hooja

The HCM Rajasthan State Institute of Public Administration
Jaipur

RAWAT PUBLICATIONS
Jaipur • New Delhi • Bangalore • Guwahati • Kolkata

ISBN 978-81-316-0160-0 (HB)
ISBN 978-81-316-0346-8 (PB)

Reprinted, 2020

Published by
Prem Rawat for **Rawat Publications**
Satyam Apts, Sector 3, Jawahar Nagar, Jaipur 302 004 (India)
Phone: 0141 265 1748 / 7006 Fax: 0141 265 1748
E-mail: info@rawatbooks.com
Website: www.rawatbooks.com

New Delhi Office
4858/24, Ansari Road, Daryaganj, New Delhi 110 002
Phone: 011 2326 3290

Also at *Bangalore, Guwahati* and *Kolkata*

Typeset by Rawat Computers, Jaipur
Printed at Nice Printing Press, New Delhi

Contents

Section II
THINKERS AND THEIR THOUGHTS

Section III
COMPARATIVE AND DEVELOPMENT DIMENSIONS

Section IV
ORGANIZATIONAL CHANGE

Series Editor's Introduction

Rakesh Hooja

It is most likely that all possible types of developmental, governmental, regulatory and administrative initiatives have been tried out in some part or the other of India over the last 60 years since the country gained independence. With governments of different ideological hues having remained in power at different points of time in different states of the Indian Union and at the Centre, and with different ideas about development, governance, planning, state welfarism, market-orientation, administration, nation-building, etc., having been fashionable or accepted in different time-frames, as well as a willingness to try out and emulate what was being attempted in countries of the West, or of the Soviet bloc, or in other developing areas, all forms of administrative and governmental action and all types of development schemes, as well as types of organizational arrangements, have been tried out somewhere or the other in India and have been commented upon by experts, scholars, researchers, practitioners, journalists and the ordinary laymen. In fact, Public Administration is a well-established discipline in India and has been regularly analysing changes in the field, as also in administrative thinking, and in policy making, over the years. These debates, discussions, descriptions, analyses, comments, opinions, findings and administrative prescriptions have been duly covered in the various articles published in the two journals of the HCM Rajasthan State Institute of Public Administration (HCM RIPA), which contain useful and valuable reference material.

It is in this context that we have undertaken this project of preparing thematic volumes, which would indicate some of the important "Changing Contours of Indian Administration Since Independence". We wanted to look at how concepts, approaches, organizational structures, procedures, policies, programmes, projects, working styles, and modes of observation, analysis and evaluation, have all emerged and undergone change over time.

Accordingly, to celebrate 50 years of HCM RIPA, we felt it appropriate to select the best and most appropriate articles from the issues of *Prashasnika* which is being published for the past 33 years and from *Development Policy and Administrative Review* that was brought out for 11 years. Deliberately wanting the articles selected for inclusion in this series to retain the flavour of the period in which they were written and to reflect the thinking and practice of that time, we have chosen not to modify the selected articles, except in some cases to slightly change the titles of the articles. The words, descriptions and analyses are of the authors as they had originally written the pieces. However, the articles selected have their intrinsic value, and by putting them together into separate thematic volumes, we have, hopefully, enabled readers to visualize how certain administrative concepts, or governmental and developmental programmes (or experiments) and policies, have been initially conceptualized and implemented, and have subsequently evolved over time. We have also attempted to provide a judicious blend of the theoretical and the practical in each book as also in the series as a whole.

Having gone through the back issues of *Prashasnika* and of *Development Policy and Administrative Review*, we have selected the following as the themes for each of the separate volumes:

1. Development Administration and Rural Development
2. Training, Civil Services and Personnel Administration
3. Panchayati Raj, Participation and Decentralization
4. Administration of Health and Education Sectors
5. Welfare and Tribal Development Administration
6. Administration of Public Sector Enterprises and Industrial Development: Changing Trends Since Independence.
7. Administrative Theories: Approaches, Concepts and Thinkers in Public Administration
8. *Prashasnik Parivartan* or Administrative Change (in Hindi)
9. Plan and Project Formulation and Implementation: Theoretical and Applied Aspects
10. Urban Development and Administration
11. Governance and Reforms
12. District Level Administration and the Role of the Collector
13. Administration of Desert, Drought-prone and Dry Farming Areas
14. Administration of Water Management and Command Area Development
15. Administration for the Empowerment and Welfare of Women
16. Managing Change, Organizational Behaviour and Human Resource Development
17. Land Use, Revenue Administration and Land Reforms

Other titles may be added as we go along.

I have received able support from my colleagues on the Series Editorial Board, namely, Suneel Dhariwal, Sandeep Verma and K.K. Parnami in finalizing the themes for the individual volumes and identifying the possible thematic volume editors. Mr. Parnami got a cumulative index prepared of all matter published in our two journals without which this exercise could not have been started. We are also gratified that the two publishers Subodh Bhushan Gupta of Aalekh Publishers and Pranit Rawat of Rawat Publications respectively agreed to jointly co-publish the books with HCM RIPA at no cost to HCM RIPA, and to distribute them. The editors of each volume also are to be thanked for their efforts at meticulously culling out and selecting the best and most relevant articles for our consideration for inclusion in the respective volumes, and for their writing appropriate volume introductions.

It is hoped that this series of volumes shall prove to be a useful source of reference contributing to better understanding of the themes covered and acting as a stimulus for further reflection to all those interested in Indian administration, and that readers shall enjoy and appreciate reading the books as much as we in the Series Editorial Board, and the volume editors did, while preparing the books for publication.

1 Introduction: Ideas and Issues in Administrative Theory

Rakesh Hooja and Ramesh K. Arora

Public Administration is an applied science. It is transdisciplinary in its orientation and has borrowed extensively from a number of other disciplines and sciences including Management Sciences, Psychology, Sociology, Political Science, Economics and even Natural Sciences. It is a truism that an applied science is in a constant state of flux, for it continues to transform itself in the light of new experiences and insights from the empirical world. That makes the task of theory-building in Public Administration a complex phenomenon. Little wonder, theories in Administrative Sciences lack the empirical rigour that is characteristic of Psychology and Economics amongst the Social Sciences.

The strength of Administrative Sciences (including Public Administration) lies in their *approaches* to the understanding of and to explaining the complex administrative phenomena. While a theory is descriptive and analytical, an approach, is a conceptual construct to help design a theory. An approach is a *way* or a *method* of studying reality. Its focus is not so much on the 'is' dimension of truth, but on the 'how' aspect of creating systematic knowledge. The realm of Administrative Sciences is inundated with approaches which vary in their methodological rigour. And with each 'theory' or 'approach' are associated certain prominent thinkers who have made a signal contribution to the evolution of administrative thought. This anthology looks at a few eminent conceptual constructs (approaches and theories) and the contribution of prominent thinkers who have made possible these constructs. The word 'theory' is being used in this volume as a synonym of 'model' or 'approach' for such constructs cannot be ideally categorized on the basis of the intensity of their methodological rigour.

In many ways the articles provided in this volume provide an overview of the development of public administration which owes its origins to Woodrow Wilson's well-known article "The Study of Administration" written in 1887. Important stages in the journey of the discipline of public administration from the Scientific Management Movement of F.W. Taylor, the classical school of public administration (White, Willoughby, etc.), Max Weber's bureaucratic model, the human relations researches of the late 1920s and early 1930s, the introduction of decisional analysis into administrative theory by writers like Chester Bernard and Herbert Simon, the evolution of 'developmental administration' and the comparative administration movement in the decades after the Second World War, Fred Rigg's Prismatic Sala model, the movement in the late 1960s and early 1970s, which while drawing upon early American writings on public administration became known as 'New Public Administration' and which received a fillip from the Minnowbrook Conference organized at Syracuse University in 1968 by Dwight Waldo, the Public Policy approach, the second look at New Public Administration by the second Minnowbrook Conference of 1988, moves at Reinventing Government spurred by David Osborne and Ted Gaebler's book of the same name, the espousal of the concept of good governance, post-modern public administration, the short lived Public Choice theory, and New Public Management

(or NPM) which some scholars have dubbed 'neo-Taylorism' have all been reflected in some way or the other directly or somewhat tangentially in the articles compiled in this volume.

Concerns and Orientations

In his essay that starts of the first section of this volume, Ramesh Arora has undertaken a brief survey of the salient foci of a few eminent approaches to administrative analysis has been made. The classical approach, it is argued, is rational and structural in its orientation and concentrates on the attributes of efficiency and economy as the twin goals of administration. Max Weber's model of ideal type, though dominantly classical in its approach, is not a 'principle'-based prescriptive model. It is an ideal type construct that is rooted primarily in historical sociology and on the extrapolation regarding the likely structure of the fully developed future bureaucratic systems.

F.W. Taylor's scientific management, Henri Fayol's guidelines on management and the principles of administration highlighted by Luther Gulick and Lyndal Urwick represent the orthodoxy of the classical school. This orthodoxy was criticized by Herbert Simon and other behaviouralists for being unscientific and inconsistent.

What the Human Relations school did was not designed to supplant the classical school but instead to supplement it. Both the approaches believed in the 'goals' of efficiency and economy. Nonetheless, the Human Relations School (Elton Mayo, F.J. Roethlisberger, William J Dickson, et al.) discovered that these twin goals could not be achieved merely through structural designing and re-designing but that they also required the inputs of human relations' skills like leadership, motivation, communication and group dynamics.

The decision-making schema, introduced by Herbert Simon, through his monumental work, *Administrative Behavior* was the convergence point of the classical and the behavioural schools. It underscored the stark administrative truth that decision-making was the 'heart' of administration and it permeated and penetrated all the components and actors of the administrative system. The decisional approach focuses on the 'behaviour' of administrative organizations that can be observed and analysed through a study of the process of decision-making and the respective roles of various actors involved in it.

Mohammed Mohabbat Khan in his essay, "American Public Administration: A Critique" argues that most of the theories developed in the United States are culture-bound and do not have a universal application. The applied world of administration revealed that there was a noticeable chasm existing between the classical or traditional principles of administration and their relevance to the real world. The need, therefore, is to bridge the gap between the study and the practice of public administration. This would require intensive efforts on the part of contemporary scholars.

Amer Al-Koubaisy in his essay, "The Classical vs Modern Organization Theories" endorses the views of behaviouralists that the classical approach, including the Weberian model of bureaucracy, is inappropriate in explaining the administrative reality. Apropos, Theory X and Theory Y of Douglas McGregor, it is difficult to prefer any approach one over the other in all situations. Both these approaches are necessarily contextual and would be found relevant only in specific situations. Yet, one finds Douglas McGregor, Rensis Likert, Chris Argyris and other behaviouralists quite exciting, for they have highlighted the human aspect of organizational behaviour.

Amer Al-Koubaisy, despite recognizing the positive aspects of the classical as well as the modern organization theories, argues that both of these constructs are not unconditionally relevant and useful to developing nations. Favouring an 'ecological' approach, he suggests that the cultural milieu of a developing nation will decide the relevance and utility of a particular theory. Thus, the need for specific models of leadership, motivation and communication for developing nations is more than obvious. In fact, there should be constant churning of ideas in developing nations on the value and relevance of distinct conceptual constructs in the field of administration (and management).

An approach that is 'holistic' and comprehensive in its scope is the Systems Approach, the pros and cons of which have been examined by Sangeeta Sharma in her essay. During the 1950s and 1960s, the systems approach had emerged as a popular construct, primarily because of the efforts of David Easton. But at best, it remained an 'approach' to the study on a variety of social phenomena and their interrelationships. It also considered the dynamic interaction between a system and its external environment. But, because of an absence of any inherent 'explanatory power' it could not be accepted as an instrument of empirical analysis and theory-building and, little wonder, its glory waned by the end of 1960s. The post-behavioural revolution could not develop any sync with this 'grand' theory.

In the last one and half decades, there have emerged a number of conceptual constructs that have varying degree of application and relevance to administrative systems functioning in divergent environmental contexts. The concept of Good Governance, propounded by the World Bank, has as its major concerns, effectiveness, responsiveness, accountability and ethics. But good governance can hardly be treated as a theoretical construct with well-knit propositions. Alongwith good governance emerged the notion of New Public Management (NPM) which is based on the premise that the application of modern management techniques can augment the effectiveness of public systems. Notably, NPM does not focus on the goals and the environmental context of public systems, but only on their internal dynamics. Its main concern is to strategize the internal structural design and processes of a government administrative system in such a manner that its performance and output are augmented.

Conceptually speaking, NPM represents the continuity of a tradition. Certain scholars perceive in NPM the resurrection of Taylorism. Even when broad generalizations are hazardous to make, one cannot but see broad similarities of concerns in the traditional efficiency-oriented Scientific Management which had become a part of traditional public administration and the contemporary effectiveness-based NPM. This only underscores the perennial significance of professional management which has given a fillip to the notion of result-oriented progressive leadership at the macro as well as micro levels.

Before ending our introductory review of the first section of this book, it would also be pertinent to point out that there are many who believe that NPM is more germane to the milieu in developed countries, while for developing countries like India traditional public administration continues to be more relevant with the concerns of new public administration and NPM somewhat re-energizing both the academic discipline and administrative profession of public administration.

In fact as Raghavulu (in Hoshiar Singh (ed.) *Expanding Horizons of Public Administration,* Aalekh 2005) reminds us that good governance and NPM which try to apply principles of business management to the management of government has led to mixed results in developed countries and has not fared any better in developing countries.

Thinkers and Their Thoughts

More than four decades ago, eminent administrative thinker, Dwight Waldo, had observed that if there was one 'paradigm' in administration, it was Max Weber's bureaucratic model. Perhaps no other theoretical framework has influenced the discipline of public administration so much as has Max Weber's bureaucratic model. Weber was a keen observer of administrative systems in their historical and contemporary settings. He adopted ideal-type methodology while explaining the characteristics of modern bureaucracy. An ideal type bureaucracy is an imaginary system of fully developed bureaucracy which would be characterized by hierarchy, specialization, recruitment by merit, promotion by merit and seniority, career system, ethical behaviour, discipline, written rules, records, compensation by cash, regular training and other well-known attributes of the administrative system functioning in a legal-rational authority system. Weber's model is not an empirical model and it is not designed to explain any real world administrative phenomena. And yet it has been very often used for analysing empirical bureaucratic systems in the framework of certain parameters. The model does not have any empirical power, nor is it prescriptive in its overtones, yet it is a very handy instrument for understanding bureaucracies in a proper contextual framework.

T.K. Jain in his essay "Utility of Max Weber's Concept of Ideal Type Bureaucracy in Public Administration" observes that this concept is of great utility in the study of organizations - whether public or business - since it comprises characteristics that are shared by most bureaucracies. The ideal type model brings together certain relationships into a complex whole which makes it an internally consistent system. One is reminded of Peter Blau who had suggested that we should try to look at the functional relationship among various features of bureaucracy.

As already mentioned, the classical thinkers in Public Administration were descriptive, analytical and prescriptive while formulating various 'principles' of administration which, in turn, provided guidelines of action to the practitioners of administration. R.M. Khandelwal and Pushpa Khandelwal in their essay present a list of twenty-nine classical principles of organization given by Lyndal Urwick and ten such principles given by Luther Gullick. Most well known of these principles are hierarchy, division of work, unity of command, staff and line, span of control, coordination, delegation, decentralization and matching authority with responsibility. Khandelwal and Khandelwal refer to Simon's criticism of these principles. In fact Simon branded them as 'proverbs'. One major criticism against Gullick and Urwick is that they underemphasized the information dimensions of organizational analysis. One may not totally defend the classical thinkers but it must be recognized that most of the conceptual constructs designed in the period before the emergence of the Human Relations approach – which was inspired by the disciplines of psychology and sociology – could not have systematically used the knowledge of behavioural science in the understanding of organizational behaviour.

The scholar who was instrumental in synthesizing the classical school with the human relations school was Chester Barnard whose eminent treatise, *The Functions of the Executive* (1938) heralded a new era of synthesis in the study of administrative systems. As Purushottam Nagar explains, Barnard viewed organizations as cooperative systems and he underscored the coexistence of formal and informal organizations. His 'acceptance' notion of authority was Weberian in spirit, while his notion of responsibility had a moralistic fervour. Barnard looked at the process of administrative behaviour from a decisional perspective seven years before Herbert Simon's first limited edition of *Administrative Behavior* (1945) was published. In a way, the pioneer in decisional analysis was Chester Barnard who later wrote the foreword to Simon's *Administrative Behavior*.

Another scholar who has substantially influenced contemporary management thought is Peter Drucker who passed away only recently. Drucker, as Rakhi Pardarsani observes, was the father of modern management. It is well known that he gave the concept of 'Management by Objectives' in 1955 and he has been instrumental in providing fresh perspectives to the whole discipline of management and its application in cross-cultural settlings.

Drucker viewed management as a liberal art – liberal because it deals with the fundamentals of knowledge, self-knowledge, wisdom and leadership, and art because it is concerned with the practice and application of this knowledge in achieving the desired result effectively. Both 'management' and 'entrepreneurship', averred Drucker, have to be viewed in an integrated manner. He was right when he remarked that lack of the innovative strategy is the single largest reason of failure of existing organizations and lack of knowledge about management is the single largest reason of failure of a new venture. While discussing entrepreneurship strategies, Drucker advocates the adoption of creative strategies for promoting effectiveness in an organization. A good leader is one who is a visionary and focuses on the mission and purpose of the organization. He is expected to concentrate on developing the character of his team members. Drucker was a futurist. He wanted modern organization to respond to the rapidly changing environment and even be proactive in redesigning the future.

Comparative and Developmental Dimensions

The emergence of a host of developing nations after the Second World War propelled the study of Development Sciences. There was thus a visible emphasis on Economic Development, Political Development, Social Change, Cultural Regeneration and, of course, on Development Administration. S.L. Meena in his essay, "Development: A Contradictory Discipline" reviews the heterogeneity of approaches to the understanding of the development process in its wider manifestation and notes certain obvious inconsistencies in the various associated premises. In fact, he is not focusing as much on 'inconsistencies' as on the complexity of the development process. Hence, recommending the abandonment of a segmented or disciplinarian approach to development, he favours a transdisciplinary orientation which endorses Spengler's view that development takes place " when an index of that which is deemed desirable and relatively preferable increases in magnitude". This is a purely normative notion but may not be disputed even by the empiricists, though they would like the concept to be operationally viable.

Meena also subscribes to the Riggsian view of 'diffraction' being the indicator of development. Accordingly, an increasing specificity of functions performed by various structures is a prominent parameter of development. Such a differentiation (or specialization) can facilitate the diffraction process only when it is synthesized with an adequate amount of integration (or coordination).

Fred Riggs remarks that the relationship between development administration and administrative development is like the relationship between "chicken and egg". What comes first is extremely 'quizzotic'. There is a circular causation between the two phenomena, and it is difficult to develop consensus on the point of the initiation of either of the two. Yet the lesson is clear that a developing society ought to simultaneously give a fillip to the processes of economic, political, social, cultural and administrative development. Waiting for one category of development to take place before initiating the other category will only delay the process of comprehensive transformation of a society.

The differences between development and non-development administration, projected by certain scholars, are at best ideal-typical and therefore should not be accepted in an absolute sense. Nevertheless, public administration in developing countries is closer to the notion of development administration than would be the administrative systems of developed nations, for in the former, one notices the prominent place accorded to progressivism, innovation, flexibility, decentralization and goal-orientation.

'Formalism' is a marked characteristic of the administrative systems in developing countries – a concept propounded by Fred W. Riggs who views it as the gap between what is constitutionally prescribed and what is actually practiced in a governance system. This denotes the chasm between principles and their application and between what is proclaimed by the politico-administrative leadership and what is actually achieved. B.S. Bhargava in his essay, "Riggs's Concept of Formalism", points out that formalism is not confined to developing nations. It is prevalent even in developed societies.

The impact of formalism on the process of administrative reforms is dysfunctional. Reforms are introduced but rarely implemented effectively; and rules are violated and ethical norms nonchalantly violated, leading to endemic corruption. Therefore, the ruling elites as well as the people should try to contain formalism for a more effective socio-political order, observes Bhargava.

How can the activity of managing the development process be made more effective? The answer is found in the essay, "Development Management" by Hans C. Blaise. It would appear that Blaise was applying the precepts of what is now called "New Public Management" to the development process. He advocates rigorous setting of objectives, examining feasible alternatives in decision-making, making the most rational choices, undertaking systematic planning, effecting proper time-scheduling, ensuring an appropriate cost-benefit equation, setting satisfactory performance standards, focusing on results, measuring performance and taking corrective action, whenever and wherever required. Blaise provides most useful directions for making the administrative system in developing countries increasingly effective by adopting systematic managerial strategies.

Are there any flaws and foibles in the administrative systems that are prevalent in most developing countries? The answer is provided by B.L. Jacobs in his essay "Public Administration in Developing Countries: Some Observations". He points out that occasionally one finds civil servants who are less responsive to people's aspirations, and hence they do not respond positively to the demands of people-centred development. On account of their attitude, the process of administrative reforms has been woefully slow and the steps to combat corruption have been tardy, halting and wobbly. The generalist administrators rule the roost in most developing nations, while specialists are marginalized with the result that the quality of policy-making and decision-making lacks in professional profundity.

What is glaring in civil service management in developing countries is a low reward structure prescribed for civil servants. In the post-economic reform era, this observation of Jacobs is highly pertinent. Currently, civil services are unable to attract and retain the best talent, while the private sector offers most attractive service conditions to young and bright graduates. The traditional salary structure in government, therefore, must give way to more innovative strategies in compensation management.

Jacobs advocates a continuous open dialogue between all the major actors involved in the process of nation-building. Such a dialogue on improved governance should take place between politicians and civil servants; between legislators and the judiciary; and between civil servants and the people. And, then there is need for a closer rapport between academicians and policy makers. The world of ideas and the world of action must develop a collaborative relationship.

R.B. Jain in his essay, "Comparative Aspects of Public Administration" provides a gist of the Weberian model of bureaucracy, Riggs's prismatic model, John T. Dorsey's information-energy model and the development administration approach. He finds the operational aspects of comparative research nebulous and lacking in rigour. In India, for instance, very little genuine comparative administrative research has taken place. Yet, one cannot deny the potential value of cross-institutional, cross-national, cross-state and cross-temporal research. Such research can help in strengthening the conceptual base of administrative sciences and even in providing guidance and innovative perspectives to the practicing administration. What is problematic however, is scarcity of comparative data and lack of expertise in conducting comparative research. Hence, efforts should be made to initiate researches at the cross-national and cross-state levels in the realms of critical socio-economic policies and their implementation.

That the comparative approach can be helpful in opening new vistas of thought and action is also highlighted by K.D. Trivedi and Ravindra Sharma who in their essay "New Dimensions in Management Theory: The Japanese Contribution" highlight some of the pronounced features of the Japanese managerial ethos that, among other factors, have been responsible for making Japan a world economic power. Trivedi and Sharma showcase Theory Z of William Ouchi which goes beyond McGregor's Theory X and Theory Y. Ouchi's theory Z assumes that organization structures would be highly productive if they are built around a powerful bonding between workers and their firms, where everyone from top to bottom plays one's part in an integrative unity of business and in the long-range planned growth of an organization. Trivedi and Sharma find merit in the Japanese management system in the form of lifetime employment, organizational loyalty, consensual decision-making, participative management, innovative learning, collaborative strategies, team building, people's development and responsiveness.

It is remarkable that what the behavioural scholars of the USA, such as Douglas McGregor, Chris Argyris, Warren Bennis, and Rensis Likert advocated have been skillfully advanced and adopted by the Japanese. Developing countries like India and Sri Lanka can learn amply from the Japanese innovations in managerial practices. That is the beauty and utility of the comparative approach.

Organizational Change

Theories become meaningful in case they generate implementable ideas for organizational change and development. Udai Pareek in his essay, "Introducing Change in Bureaucracy: A Framework" mentions that in the Indian politico-administrative system, there are three interrelated systems –

the focal system, the proximate system and the political system. All of them are equally important for making organizational change effective. Further, all changes have to pass through various stages – the stage of acceptance, the stage of action and the stage of stabilization. All the three systems have a role in these three stages of the change process. Their respective roles and influence will depend upon their capabilities and competencies to generate a climate of responsiveness. At the applied level, the significance of power, monitoring, punishment, motivation and creativity becomes prominent. What Pareek advocates is developing a vision for a transformed system and a rational selection of strategies – structural as well as behavioural – to achieve them.

In a similar vein, though more at the empirical level, K.B.C. Saxena in his essay "Re-engineering Public Administration" advocates the adoption of Business Process Re-engineering for enhancing the effectiveness of the government systems. Business Process Reengineering refers to an integrated programme and perspective on organizational change focusing on 'business process' rather than 'business functions', in order to significantly improve their performance. Thus a set of interrelated work activities and value-added tasks can help convert business inputs into business outputs. Saxena extrapolates the concept of Business Process Re-engineering to Public Administration. Re-engineering which would involve a total planning and concurrent redesign and implementation of administrative processes, organizational structures and the supporting information system in direct or indirect response to external forces in order to achieve the objectives, among others, of cost-effectiveness, time service quality and customer satisfaction.

At the operational level, Public Administration Re-engineering will focus on the customer value-adding services for clients, simplification of procedure, result-orientation, performance management, employees' empowerment, application of information technology, etc. Citing examples from various countries, Saxena reflects that the success of Public Administration Re-engineering will depend upon the desire to change the status quo, sustained drive, commitment, patience, long term vision, sound planning, participatory management, effective communication and continuous feedback and evaluation.

Some observers have now started talking of a concept of Government Process Re-engineering.

Much of the success in organizational change would depend upon the fructification of the creative urge among men who initiate, sustain and monitor the process of change and development. This aspect of creativity has been dealt with in an essay on the same theme by Pradip N. Khandwalla. Creativity has to do with the "employment of playful and exploratory, rather than a mechanical process of problem solving, by a person who is open, curious and imaginative, rather than by a person who is inhibited and conventional, to find solutions or designs that are novel (and yet useful) rather than merely run-of the-mill". Khandwalla thus values inquisitiveness, imagination, intuition and out-of the box thinking. Creativity involves a cluster of abilities that include ideational fluency (ability to come up with a number of solutions to a particular problem), flexibility, originality, problem-sensitivity (what Simon would call 'intelligence'), ability to go to the roots of a problem (call it profundity), elaboration and the competence to restructure problems.

Khandwalla observes that brainstorming and attribute analysis are useful tools for generating a battery of solutions to a problem. In this category also belongs the 'syncretics' technique of Gordon which involves the explanation of a problem by the group members, formulations of pertinent analogies and development of empathy through identification of personal analogies. Syncretic problem solving is based as the process of imaginative exploration. Khandwalla underscores the point that in doing something creative, one needs to be very open to ideas and a seeker of information. "Creation requires an ability to visualize a new order of things, ability to intuit or grasp the basics, a capacity to be moved by higher emotions, the endless search for the elusively aesthetic or true or good."

What is particularly significant in the essays by Khandwalla and Saxena is the critical role of leadership in initiating and inspiring change. It is this leadership that is the core of Asha Hingar's essay, "Theories of Leadership: A Conceptual Overview". Leadership, as Keith Davis observes, "is the ability to persuade others to seek defined objectives enthusiastically". Truly, it is the human factor that binds a group together and motivates it towards the achievement of organizational goals. Hingar refers to a variety of leadership theories, including sociometric theory, situational theory, general interaction theory, contingency model and other associated conceptual constructs. She rightly observes that the presence of some basic personality traits and behavioural characteristics is helpful to the development of effective leadership but it is neither a necessary nor a sufficient condition for the success of a leader. The most appropriate leadership technique probably is the one which recognizes the importance of systematic interaction among styles, groups and situations. This presents a cogent lesson for administrative leadership in government systems.

The last essay of this anthology deals with a critical component of administrative system – administrative efficiency. Efficiency has numerous synonyms in contemporary parlance – ability, capability, adeptness, competence, economy, effectiveness, efficacy, productivity, proficiency and skillfulness. Herbert Simon comments that the criteria of efficiency dictates the choice of alternatives which produces the largest results for the given application of resources.

Efficiency has been the core concept in all administrative theories – classical, human relations, neo-classical, development administration, good governance and NPM. Little wonder, all the reports of the Central and state governments on administrative reforms and innovation have highlighted the need for enhancing efficiency in public systems. This is true of the first Administrative Reforms Commission as well as of the second Administrative Reforms Commission in India.

It would be relevant to, at this point, refer to the somewhat different views of Uma Medury, Dolly Arora and Mohit Bhattacharya (all three in Ramesh K. Arora (ed.), *Public Administration: Fresh Perspectives*. Aalekh, 2004). Medury opines that the prominence of the citizen appears to have been diluted by NPM whose emphasis on efficiency is negating the values of social justice and equity, accountability, participation, etc., and that the accountability concerns of NPM are more managerial than political. Dolly Arora stresses that efficiency and citizen's empowerment cannot be reduced to being a matter of more management reforms. Mohit Bhattacharya indicates that the big questions of public administration must go beyond the big questions of public management. Bhattacharya states that two contrasting visions have guided administration analysis: the managerial vision and the democratic vision. Both are required in a liberal democratic society. But some administration analysts have often been tempted to over-emphasize managerialism with its predilection for efficiency, economy and effectiveness. He adds that other more central pursuits of public administration like achieving a democratic polity, improving the instruments of collective action, creating conditions for good citizenship are of no concern for public management advocates. He adds that the anti-bureaucratic ideology of NPM defines managerial rationalism.

In the wake of the adoption of the maxims of good governance and the canons of NPM, there is a need for rightsizing the government at all levels (what is important is not less government, but better government), minimizing bureaucratic delays, augmenting the application of technology in administrative processes, introducing creativity and innovation in administrative structuring, promoting work culture and heightening a concern for value for money in the public system. In sum, the theoretical postulates of good governance have a perennial pertinence, while the operation or practice of good governance would be contextual in character.

As an applied science, public administration should constantly endeavour to apply the ideal and idealize the practical. This is the substance of the present anthology.

Section I

CONCERNS AND ORIENTATIONS

2 Organization Theories: Concerns and Orientations

Ramesh K. Arora

Any discussion on 'organization theories' per se would require at the outset an explication of the terms 'organization' and, 'theory', In simpler terms, organizations are those collectivities (human groups) that are engaged in the achievement of certain specific goals. Thus, an organization is a 'human' organization, which involves all the complexities associated with the interactions between the human groups and the individuals on the one hand and the goal-structures and the mechanisms designed to achieve these goals on the other. Although organizations can be small or large, unifunctional or multifunctional (depending on the number of activities they are involved in), in organizational analysis, generally the problems of large scale organizations are examined.

The term, theory is considered to be a set of generalizations, arrived at through a process of testing and verification of certain hypotheses. A theory describes and analyses certain empirical phenomena and helps in the prediction of future action. These functions of a theory are possible only if rigorous scientific method is applied in its formulation. We can easily conceive of such theoretical formulations and 'laws' in the domain of natural sciences, where adequate methods and facilities exist for testing, controlling and experimenting with variables. Conversely, in the realm of social sciences, such rigour may not be possible, since the most significant problem in social sciences relates to the difficulties associated with the prediction of human behaviour. It is a truism to state that human behaviour is an upshot of an interaction among a myriad of factors such as personality, environment and situation and it is not always possible to predict the relationship between stimulus and response in various settings involving socio-human interaction. Therefore, in social sciences, the search is not for 'theories' in the sense this term is used in natural sciences, but for 'models' and 'approaches' which focus upon the logical relationships existing among different variables of a given phenomenon, or on methods of studying the empirical reality from several possible angles. In fact, in a social science like Public Administration, the terms 'models', 'approaches' and 'theories' are used interchangeably.

Variety of Foci

In the field of organization theory, there are a number of foci on the basis of which numerous schools of thought have emerged. However, for the purpose of the present analysis, it would be pertinent to classify the major organization theories as follows:

- Theories which focus upon the structural configuration or the formal aspects of an organization – these are generally placed under the rubric of 'classical' or 'structural' theories.
- Theories which place human being in the centre of an organization and examine important aspects of human behaviour in organizational settings.
- Theories which consider decision-making to be the heart of administration and therefore prefer to view the whole

organization from the angle of the decision-making process. These are generally known as decision-making theories.

- Theories which are 'holistic' in nature, focussing on almost all the significant components of an organization and their mutual interactions. These theories, popularly known as, 'system' theories, also examine the interlinkages between the organizational system and its external environment.
- Recent interpretive and critical theories that are grounded in the ideas of 'action'.

In the following pages, a brief analysis of the above five major theoretical foci has been attempted. Notably, instead of the term, theory, it has been preferred to use the term approach, which actually represents, the level of conceptual development in the contemporary organizational studies. Further, it may be pertinent to mention that ever since the publication of *Organizations* by James G. March and Herbert A. Simon in 1958, the terms 'organization' and 'administration' are used interchangeably and therefore, since then, administrative theory, and organization theory are viewed as synonyms.

The Classical Approach

Variously known as the Classical approach, the Structural approach, the Formal Organization approach, the Engineering approach, the Mechanistic approach or even the Traditional approach, this school has the following important premises:

1. Efficiency and economy are the universal goals of all organizations.
2. In order to achieve efficiency and economy, the need is to design and re-design organizational structures in such a manner that the various structural parts of an organization function with coordination and harmony.

3. With a view to develop greater rational structures, an organization should follow certain 'principles' of formal designing and re-designing various organizational parts so that the goals of maximizing efficiency and economy are achieved with least effort and resources.

The Classical Organization approach, developed in the West during the end of the nineteenth century and the beginning of the twentieth century when the Industrial Revolution in the western industrial countries had reached a stage of maturity and most of the economic enterprises were struggling to enhance their productivity, to attain a relatively more advantageous position vis-à-vis their competing firms. The basic goals were, as already pointed out, enhancing efficiency and increasing economy. Thus, the stress was on effecting maximum possible utilization of human and non-human resources. Interestingly, the governmental systems during this period were also involved in the process of enhancing rationality and efficiency in their functioning. This was evident in the studies of bureaucracy conducted by the famous sociologist Max Weber. Though, technically, Weber's bureaucratic theory would not fall within the parameters of the classical approach, yet the commonality of orientations between the two, brings them nearer to each other. It should be interesting, therefore, to have a brief review of Max Weber's model of bureaucracy.

Max Weber's Model of Bureaucracy

An analysis of Weber's model of bureaucracy should be preceded by an understanding of the, 'ideal-type' methodology employed by Weber in his social analysis and of the authority systems that be formulated. An ideal-type formulation is based on the one-sided accentuation of certain characteristics of individual phenomena. It is a utopian model based on the imagined state of the fullest development of a phenomenon in its evolutionary process. On this premise, it becomes clear that the ideal-type formulation of bureaucracy is not intended to describe any empirical administrative system. Instead, it is a conceptual construct with the help of which comparative analysis of bureaucracies can be undertaken.

In the analysis of authority systems, Weber has used the ideal-typical methodology. Authority in Weberian sense is, "the probability that a command with a given specific context will be obeyed by a given group of persons". Thus, the authority seems to lie in the receiver of an order. Weber was interested in exploring the sources of legitimacy of authority, i.e., the reasons why people obey commands. On the basis of his socio-historical analysis, he classified authority systems into the following three categories:

1. *Traditional authority* resting on the established belief in the sanctity of traditions and the legitimacy of the status of those exercising authority under them.
2. *Charismatic authority* based on devotion to the specific and exceptional sanctity, heroism or exemplary character of an individual person and of the normative pattern or order revealed or ordained by him.
3. *Legal-rational authority* resting on a belief in the legality of patterns of normative rules and the right of those elevated to authority under such rules to issue command.

It may be mentioned that Weber was clear in. his conceptualization that bureaucracy as an administrative system exists *only* in a legal-rational authority system and not in the other two patterns of authority, viz., traditional and charismatic. The prominent features of bureaucracy, in fact, are derived from the nature of legal-rational authority systems. In sum, the main characteristics of ideal-typical bureaucracy are as follows:

1. It is organized in a hierarchy of offices.
2. Each office has specific sphere of responsibilities and tasks.
3. Specialized knowledge in organizations is indispensable.
4. Bureaucrats are subject to authority only in official capacities.

5. Personnel are appointed through a system of free selection.
6. Officials are appointed on the basis of technical competence.
7. Personnel are paid in money; they are placed in fixed graded salary scale and are paid pensions after retirement.
8. Office is the primary occupation of a person working in a bureaucratic system.
9. There is a career system; advancement in the career is by seniority and/or achievement.
10. Officials are separated from means of administration; in other words, an official, does not appropriate his office.
11. Officials are subject to discipline in conduct of office.
12. A system of rules guides the functioning of administration.
13. Written documents are the heart of the process; all decisions are in writing; written records form the memory of the system.

Weber observed that bureaucracy is the most rational means of administering affairs in the public or the private sector. Interestingly, the most developed system of bureaucracy, according to him, was the Roman Catholic Church.

Weber's model of bureaucracy has been criticized for ignoring the non-rational and the non-formal aspects of administration and for overlooking the possible conflicts between hierarchy and specialization and between rules and efficiency. Further, it has been pointed out that in the empirical world, Weber's bureaucracy is not found in its entirety. These criticisms generally emanate from an inadequate understanding of the Weber's ideal-typical formulation which, as already pointed out, is only a utopian model, and yet which can be extremely helpful in empirical analysis. The need is to move further from where Weber left and use his construct for culling out hypotheses for testing and verification in cross-cultural, cross-national and cross-institutional settings.

Taylor's Scientific Management and other Constructs on Formal Organizations

Towards the end of the nineteenth century, F.W. Taylor, an engineer in a steel company in the United States, was conducting continuous experiments to discover scientific methods for enhancing the productivity of workers. His researches were based primarily on the studies undertaken on the shop floor. Although Taylor's principles of scientific management had already been formulated by the year 1900, his monumental work, *Principles of Scientific Management* was published in 1911. Taylor believed that management was a true science, resting upon clearly defined laws, rules and principles. He argued that there "is one best way" for doing anything and, therefore, efforts must be made to identify this best way in the performance of any managerial task. Taylor conducted time and motion studies with a view to reduce the time involved in undertaking different activities in industrial organizations.

Taylor stressed considerably upon the physical layout of the plant and explored the impact of various structural configurations, lighting arrangements, etc., on the efficiency of the workers. Advocating specialization in the techniques of supervision, Taylor recommended a system of 'functional foremanship' under which a worker was to be supervised by eight foremen belonging to different specialized areas. Further, he introduced the system of intervals in the working day in order to reduce the fatigue of the workers. He also underlined the importance of offering monetary incentives to the workers and recommended the use of piece-rate system of wage-payment.

Taylor's scientific management was applied in a large number of industrial organizations in the USA, the continent and even in the Soviet Union. He was, however, criticized for understressing the human aspect of administration; but this criticism would seem to be less than justified, if one examines Taylor's philosophy more profoundly. In fact, Taylor never believed in the exploitation of individuals for the organizational ends. He showed considerable awareness in his analysis of the human dimension of administration. Despite the passage of more than eight decades, Taylor's insights into the process of management appear to be extremely perceptive and even pertinent to contemporary situations.

Besides Taylor, other eminent classical theorists have been Henri Fayol of France, L.D. White, W. F. Willoughby, James D. Morney and Luther Gulick of the USA and Lyndal Urwick of Great Britain. These scholars belonged to a variety of professions, including academic, military, engineering, business and government. Like Weber and Taylor, their main stress was on the formal structure of an organization. The underlying assumption was that economy and efficiency in an organization depended considerably upon designing and re-designing of formal structures.

As already pointed out, an eminent contribution of classicalists has been the formulation of certain principles of organization. Briefly, these principles are as follows:

1. An organization is a system of hierarchy under which there is a vertical division of authority and a definite assignment of duties in various organizational units.
2. For a clear-cut line of authority relationship, unity of command should exist, under which a person in the performance of his official duties, receives orders only from one superior.
3. There should be a rational division of work among various positions and persons working in the organizations.
4. There should be a limited number of immediate subordinates working under an executive, so that an effective supervision may be exercised over them.
5. There should be delegation of authority and responsibility among the various levels of an organization.
6. Authority and responsibility should be commensurate with each other, i.e., there should be a balance between the two at all organizational levels.

7. There should be coordination amongst the various parts of the organization, which would provide unity of action in pursuit of a common purpose.

The classicalists made a distinction between the line and staff, with the former representing authority and the latter advice and ideas. Besides, the acronym POSDCORB, propounded by Gulick, points out the major functions of the chief executive in an organization viz., planning, organizing, staffing, directing, coordinating, reporting and budgeting. In addition, Gulick classified the bases of departmentalization as purpose, process, clientele, and place.

It is obvious that the principles of classical theories are relevant to a variety of organizational settings even today. However, these conceptual constructs lack a rigorous scientific base and it is in this context that Herbert Simon argued that the principles of organization were no more than 'proverbs'. Simon's opinion is based on certain internal contradictions among the classicalists themselves. For instance, while a majority of classicalists favour unity of command, Taylor, on the other hand, advocates 'functional foremanship'.

It has also been argued that the classicalists have understressed the non-formal and irrational elements in an organization. Likewise, little attention has been paid to the individual and his personality, informal groups, conflicts and decision-making process in the analysis of organizations. However, the contribution of a conceptual construct should be viewed in the context of the period in which it evolved and from that specific perspective, the classical approach was indeed a path-breaking development in the evolution of administrative thought. The need is to further refine the concepts of the classical approach and use them more meaningfully in the contemporary settings.

The Human Relations Approach

The well-known researches undertaken at the Western Electrical Company at Hawthorne (1928-33), paved the way for the emergence of a radically new approach to organizational analysis, These researches conducted by Elton Mayo. F.J. Roethlisberger, T.N. Whitehead and others are known as the human relations researches. Others who have contributed significantly to this approach are George C. Homans, W. Lloyd Warner, W.F, Whyte and Chester Barnard. The last, however, is widely known for his perspicacious study, *The Functions of the Executive* (1938), which, till today, is the finest synthesis of the classical and the human relations approaches.

Essentially, the classical and the human relations approaches shared certain common premises. Both considered efficiency and economy as the implied goals of an organization and were thus engaged in search of variables or their combinations which would help achieve these twin goals. The human relationists accepted the existing organizational structures and did not question the premises and conclusions of the classicalists. But they went a few steps further and *supplemented* the classical theory by focussing on areas that were relatively understressed, if not ignored, by the classicalists. And this new area was the human behaviour in an organizational setting.

Studying the situation resulting from the division of labour, the human relationists examined the problems of fatigue and monotony. Besides, they paid attention to the problem of isolation of the worker, and his feeling of anonymity resulting from the insignificant jobs which contributed insignificantly to the final product. Interestingly, the human relationists studied a number of 'human tools' which would facilitate the functioning of an organizational structure. The major findings of this school can be summarized as follows:

1. Alongwith a formal organization evolves an informal organization which considerably influences the total work culture.
2. Human groups are a natural outcome of interpersonal social relationships and these groups influence the attitude and behaviour of its members.

3. Man is not just an economic man, he is also a social man. His motivation is influenced substantially by the social groups of which he is a part.
4. Conflict in interpersonal relationships within an organization is a natural phenomenon and there should be adequate mechanisms in an organization to tackle situations resulting from this conflict. Notably, conflict was not always considered dysfunctional by the human relationists
5. Span of control cannot be mechanically determined. Managerial abilities, the quality of persons supervised, the nature of work and the effectiveness of communication, would collectively determine the extent of span of control in an organization.
6. Besides the formal authority in an organization, there exists the phenomenon of leadership through which a leader influences the followers for the achievement of specific organizational objectives.
7. Morale is a state of mind in relation to life and work and it is influenced by a number of internal and external environmental factors.
8. Communication is the key to interpersonal relationships and to organizational dynamics. There are certain factors which promote positive communication and others that hinder it.
9. Organization should be viewed as a social system comprising of various parts, which are interacting with each other dynamically, and which interacts continually with its environment.

It is well known that the human relations researches created a revolution in organizational thinking. This approach proved to be a precursor to the behavioural, decision-making and systems approaches. Despite the fact that in the early stages of its formulation, the human relations theory was utilized for narrow organizational ends by certain managers, the fact remains that these researches opened wider vistas of understanding the nuances of organizational dynamics.

An important contribution of the human relations school has been in the sphere of promoting researches which accord a more central place to the individual in an organizational setting, than did the earlier theories. The 'Fusion' theory of Chris Argyris, the Democratic Managerial Style advocated by Rensis Likert, 'Theory X' and 'Theory Y' of Douglas McGregor, whose preference for Theory Y is well known and the 'Organic Populism' of Warren Bennis, are among the few efforts, which have indirectly been inspired by the Human Relations School. The difference between the 'old' Human Relations School of Elton Mayo, et at., and the 'new' Human Relations School of McGregor Likert, Argyris, Bennis et al., pertains to the relative stress placed on the individual goals and the organizational goals. While the old school appeared to focus more upon the organizational goals, the latter theorists seem to favour a fusion or a balance between the individual and the organizational objectives. More significantly, the contemporary human relationists are deeply committed to the fulfilment of organizational responsibilities towards the enhancement of the happiness of individuals, who are members of the organization.

The Decision-making Approach

The decisional approach, powerfully advocated by Herbert Simon, considers decision-making as the key activity of any human organization. In fact, 'decision-making' is not confined just to the 'formulation' of decisions, but extends to the realms of their implementation and feedback.

While criticizing the Formal Organization School, Simon, in his classic, *Administrative Behaviour*, published in 1947, had proclaimed that decision-making was the 'heart' of administration and thus was the key process which united all human and non-human components of an administrative system. In a similar vein, Jacob Marchack views the decision process as an independent variable upon which the survival of an organization is based.

According to Simon, a decision has two premises – facts and values. While values affect the choice of goals, facts relate to the means to achieve the goals. Rationality, Simon adds, can be exercised in the case of choice of means for achievement of given ends; while conversely, in the choice of goals or ends, values of decision-makers or policy makers gain prominence and thus, do not fall strictly under the purview of rationality.

In any case, man has only 'bounded' rationality. His knowledge of all the possible internal and external environmental factors, influencing decisions is generally incomplete and he cannot foresee the possible consequences of all his decisions. Even Robert Merton has talked of unintended consequences of 'rational' action and his conceptualization in this respect, appears to be relevant in the analysis of decision-making process. Simon stresses that man *intends* to be rational. In other words, he is 'intendedly rational' and not actually rational. The reasons lie in the perceptual and cognitive limitations referred to above. It is in this backdrop itself that Charles Lindbloom's view of decision-making as the "Science of muddling through" can be appreciated.

Simon opines that all decisions involve three basic processes. First, *intelligence* activity that relates to the identification of the problem areas which require decisions to be made. This process is based on the survey of the environment by a decision-maker, who uses his experience and other 'signals' to identify issues requiring decisions.

Following the intelligence activity is the *design* activity, which involves a critical analysis of the pros and cons of each possible alternative, or a set of alternatives for the solution of a problem. While examining the consequences of each alternative, the experience and the analytical ability of a decision-maker will influence his judgement.

And then comes the *choice* activity, which relates to the actual selection of the alternative that appears to be the most rational to the decision-maker. Simon notes, that while making a choice, a decision-maker generally acts as a 'satisfying' man and not a 'maximizing' man. Accordingly, he stops examining alternatives when he hits a solution that appears to be satisfying to him and once he does so, he refrains from examining the pros and cons of other remaining alternatives. Thus, man's nature is not to 'maximize' the decisional output but to be content or 'satisfied' with the choice that appears to be the best in a given situation.

Once a choice has been made, the decision is implemented. The feedback received by the decision-maker on the implementation of a decision, forms an additional input for the decisional system in an organization. The intelligence process thus goes on, followed by the successive activities in an ongoing sequential circle.

The decisional activity, according to Simon, can use traditional methods like habits and precedents or become innovative in the application of techniques. Certain decisions can be programmed through computers, while others cannot be treated in the like manner. The role of intuition cannot always be ruled out in the decisional process.

Notably, Simon's stress is on the socio-psychological factors involved in decision-making. He is not much concerned with the nature of bureaucratic structures and their influence on the decisional process. This makes Simon's approach a 'partial' approach to organizational analysis; though, his emphases are crucial to the understanding of organizational dynamics.

The Systems Approach

While the classical approach stresses the formal structure of an organization, the human relations approach emphasizes the human element in an organization, and the decisional approach focuses upon the socio-psychological components of the decisional process; it is the systems approach which views an organization in its entirety and in the context of its environment. Katz and Kahn, Kast and Rosenzweig and a few other organization theorists have further developed the social systems approach, once propounded by the human relationists. The central premise of the systems approach is that any organization can be viewed as a system, Thus, the systems approach helps promote unity of knowledge by providing a common framework for analysing a number of phenomena in diverse settings.

The essential features of the systems approach are as follows:

1. A system is composed of several parts which are known as subsystems.
   An organization has the following parts:
   (i) Individuals, their personalities, motives, attitudes, etc.
   (ii) Formal organization
   (iii) Informal organization
   (iv) Status and role patterns
   (v) Physical setting
2. All the parts of a system are dynamically interrelated with each other. The linking mechanisms in an organization are: (i) roles, (ii) decisions, and (iii) communication. There is a 'dynamic equilibrium' established among various parts through these linking mechanisms.
3. An organization has an artificial boundary, which separates it from its external environment.
4. There is a continuous flow of environmental influences on the system. These influences are known as 'inputs'.
5. A system prepares itself internally to respond to the inputs. This internal processing is called 'withinputs' or 'throughputs'.
6. A system responds to the inputs through its decisions and actions, which form a part of its 'outputs'.
7. Through the 'feedback' process, the 'outputs' generate new 'inputs', thus, causing a circular sequence of environment-system interactional activities.

8. There is a dynamic equilibrium between the environment and the organization system.
9. Each system has a specific set of goals towards the achievement of which it functions.

It is clear that the systems approach to organizational analysis is in striving to create a science of organizational universals. It is a unifying approach, holistic and ecological. However, in operational terms, it poses difficulties in research. It is not possible to identify all the components of an organizational system or of its environment, much less to observe the inter-linkages among various variables and their reciprocity. Besides, a concept such as 'dynamic equilibrium' is abstract and difficult to be operationalized. Moreover, at the mathematical level, the systems approach tends to emphasize those variables which are linearly measurable.

Despite its limitations, the systems approach does provide a framework of analysis which makes a student of organizations become aware of a number of variables that are crucial to the structural arrangement and functioning of an organization. It raises questions which can help formulate a comprehensive research design. True, resource limitations would not permit the application of systems approach at a macro level, but this framework can be very helpful and feasible in understanding organizational subsystems.

Interpretive and Critical Theories

Following the New Public Administration Movement, initiated in 1968, a number of new foci have been added to the battery of conceptual constructs in organization analysis. Though variations exist in the dominant concerns of respective schools belonging to this emergent stream, there are a few unified perspectives in such theories. The main premises and themes of these theories, as pointed out by Michael M. Harmon and Richard T. Mayer, are as follows:

1. Individual and organizational interests exist in a state of mutual tension. The principal concern of organization theory is not the integration between the individual and the organization, but with how the individual may transcend the organization.
2. The rational model of action, limits the understanding of action in individual, social and organizational contexts.
3. Social science should be grounded in the ideas of action that direct attention to the subjective meaning of people's everyday social experience.
4. The traditional dichotomy between empirical and normative theory is misleading and unproductive. Empirical concerns are intertwined with normative evaluation and social ethics.
5. Organization theory should help in understanding the ways, in which bureaucracy serves to reinforce social processes of domination, which in turn lead to individual alienation.
6. The administrative theories should fundamentally be practical, facilitating comprehension and leading to responsible and autonomous action.

Robert Denhard, a well-known contributor to the Critical Theory of Public Organization, observes that distorted communication between the bureaucracy and the public is essentially the source of apparent contradictions of interest between the two. The need is to provide the citizen with an opportunity for participation in administrative processes, through open communication.

A few eminent administrative thinkers, essentially adopting a psychological orientation, and broadly contributing to 'Theories of Emergence' focus on social and psychic dynamics that affect the unfolding of individual energy and the discovery of a shared purpose. An administrator's task is to facilitate self-awareness and the consequent responsible action in himself and in others. Change, according to these theorists, is more natural than stability in organizations. The main concern of people in organizations is to identify and remove the barriers and resistance to change, and not to try to create change.

Conclusion

In the preceding pages, a brief review of the essential features of classical, human relations, decisions, systems, interpretive and critical approaches has been attempted. These, however, do not exhaust the catalogue of organization theories or approaches that are in use in the contemporary administrative literature. Nevertheless, the above approaches are considered to be more well known and besides they focus on the most crucial components of an organization. They are neither mutually exclusive nor mutually competing. In fact, they are complementary to each other, with their own respective dominant foci. The most comprehensive among them is the systems approach.

Presently, we are in a poly-paradigmatic state in organizational analysis. There is a continuing need to evaluate the existing approaches with a view to update them and develop their fitness with the contemporary complex organizational reality. The process of learning and creation of knowledge goes on endlessly.

3 American Public Administration: A Critique

Mohammad Mohabbat Khan

American Public Administration (APA), as a conscious field of study, is not as yet hundred years old. Woodrow Wilson's famous essay entitled, "The Study of Administration"[1] (1887) is unanimously regarded as the first publication in the field. Throughout its development, APA has witnessed and has been influenced by changes in the American society. It is the product of American culture, ideology, and beliefs. With the exception of Max Weber, few, if any, other foreign scholars had substantial impact in the development of APA.

The discussion in this paper concentrates on the negative aspects of APA and the unintended consequences of those negative aspects. For the convenience of this discussion selected areas of APA have been chosen to illustrate its negative aspects and the resultant/unintended consequences. These are: the controversies surrounding the politics-administration dichotomy, the legacy of universal principles, the culture-bound character of APA, the impact of behaviouralism, lack of effort to synthesize the ideas in the field, and incoherence between theory and practice.

Politics-Administration Dichotomy

The attempts to demarcate rule-making (politics) and rule-implementation (administration) is found in the writings of Wilson,[2] Goodnow,[3] White,[4] and Willoughby.[5] They maintained that politics and administration are two distinct functions of government. The doctrine of separation of powers provided the basis for this distinction. However, it can be argued that this distinction is fallacious and gives an erroneous impression about the real world of governmental operations where politics and administration merge. Though it has been claimed[6] repeatedly that the dichotomy is dead, yet some of the unintended consequences of the dichotomy keep recurring which create outdated logic. In this regard two errors are detected.

First is the logical fallacy of assuming that if a boundary cannot be precisely drawn, no distinction can be asserted. Second is the overemphasis on the political process thereby either ignoring the administration altogether or giving it scant attention. Another unintended consequence of criticisms of the dichotomy led to the increasing influence of political science on public administration. The logic frequently advanced for such dominance is like this: If there is no distinction between politics and administration, and especially if it is argued that the latter can be included within the former then there is little rationale for a distinct and self-conscious discipline of public administration.

Legacy of Universal Principles

The search for 'universal principles' began in earnest in the late 1920s with the publication of Willoughby's book.[7] It was assumed that certain scientific principles exist and should be discovered and taught to administrators to make them more efficient. Gullick and Urwick,[8] Mooney and Reiley,[9] represent this school of thought. Critics like Simon,[10] Waldo[11] and Dahl[12] literally demolished the efficacy of universal principles. Simon dubbed them contradictory and inconsistent principles as mere proverbs. Waldo pointed to the inadequate and weak theoretical underpinnings of the principles. Dahl highlighted the cultural constraints that tend to limit the universal applicability of the principles.

One of the unintended consequences in this regard is Simon's attempt to differentiate between fact and value. The fact-value dichotomy resulted in exchange of articles[13] between public administration establishment represented by Waldo and Simon who later decided to leave the field altogether. However, the debate is very much alive today. This was illustrated by the Simon-Argyris debate in 1973.[14] And the continuing debate on the fact-value dichotomy is an unintended consequence itself.

Culture-Bound Character of APA

Robert Dahl's cryptic comment in 1947 to the effect that public administration is to be understood in more than domestic terms if a science of the subject is to be developed[15] remains valid today. "The comparative aspects of public administration have largely been ignored." He was basically indicting the culture-bound character of APA. Volumes of literature on administrative systems of different countries, especially non-European countries, have accumulated after World War II, but two limitations among American scholars are noticeable. The, 'right' attitude and, 'proper' orientation are lacking. They tend to generalize about a country's political-administrative system without a prior understanding of the cultural patterns and value systems of the people. Their only source of information are the local elites. Unfortunately, APA has made little use of whatever knowledge available in Comparative Public Administration (CPA). The unintended consequence is the limited and waning interest of American scholars about the field (CPA). Recently, efforts by American Society of Public Administration (ASPA) to revive and activate CPA is seen in the establishment of Society for International and Comparative Administration (SICA)[16] and a drive for a cosmopolitan membership. The unintended consequence of this development remains to be seen.

Impact of Behaviouralism

Behaviouralism, which originated in political science, instead of enhancing, hurt APA's chances to develop as a professional discipline. First, it depreciated the study of governmental and political institutions and proposed to substitute it with the study of individuals. Second, it discounted as irrelevant of much of what was already known in political science and emphasized mastering of knowledge in such fields as psychology, sociology, and anthropology. Third, it demanded undue rigour in designing of theories and models with strict attention to logical rules, explicitness in definition and assumptions, operationalism in the statement of hypotheses, empirical testing of hypotheses, and the primacy of quantitative methods. Fourth, consistently with its emphasis on science, behaviouralism proscribed prescription. Fifth, despite the claimed focus on individual behaviour, behaviouralist's emphasis on quantitative methods led to the study of single individuals as whole persons.[17]

Behavioural approach to public administration can be found in Simon, et al., *Public Administration.*[18] It was followed by a few others.[19] The unintended consequences of this approach are two-fold. It not only undermined the philosophical background of APA, but at the same time discouraged practitioners and scholars with 'wrong' (non-quantitative) background to contribute and thereby hampering the growth of the field.

Lack of Synthesis of Existing Ideas and Knowledge

A serious student in public administration will discover that no systematic effort has been undertaken to synthesize the ideas and knowledge that flow freely in the discipline. Several reasons for this phenomenon are plausible. First, APA's origin is in political science. Second, it has a low status in the mother discipline. Third, is its indiscriminate and sometimes unwarranted borrowing from other disciplines without proper understanding of the core of those disciplines, and this resulted in 'mismatch' of ideas and some cognitive dissonance in the field. Fourth, more enthusiasm is noticed to say something 'new' rather than compiling systematically the existing ideas and concepts. Lastly, attempts are initiated to formulate theories for grand purposes without realizing that the base for this sort of enterprise is rather shaky.

The unintended consequences that resulted from these deficiencies in APA are quite a few. These are, (i) basic issues as to how public administration should be approached (i.e., apolitical, amoral, and ahistorical remain unanswered); (ii) changes in 'vocabularies' usually give the mistaken impression of progress when none has been made; and (iii) public administration is still trying unsuccessfully to acquire some 'new insight' from other social science discipline and the field of management. The sole exception from this trend in APA is Dwight Waldo[20] who has written numerous books, articles and monographs most of which attempt to synthesize ideas in the field as well as indicate the directions toward which public administration is heading. But, unfortunately, his contributions have not had the impact that they deserve.

Conclusion

There is a distinct feeling now in the field (APA) that there is little understanding among some scholars as to what is happening in the real world. This is manifested in two forms. First, some younger scholars give the impression that a revolution is taking place out 'there', when in reality very few things have radically changed. Second, some established scholars are so much immersed in their 'work' that they generally either do not have the time or the inclination to know what is happening outside the academia. This incongruence between theory and practice has several unintended consequences. The gap between theory and practice has widened. This can be illustrated by the extensive usage of the "discarded" principles in real organizations. Additionally, one often bears the complaints from professionals that they have little use for non-operational concepts and ideas from scholars who paint a distorted or concocted picture of reality. Recent efforts to bridge the gap have not achieved much success, partially because of the euphoric attitude of some scholars to romanticize the world and its inhabitants-the people.

Notes

1. Woodrow Wilson, "The Study of Administration", *Political Science Quarterly* II (June, 1887), pp. 197-222.
2. Ibid. Wilson opined that administration (governmental) should be removed from the strife of politics and should concern itself with the detailed execution of plans laid down in law. To properly and efficiently execute the tasks set for administration, a large measure of discretion is necessary for the civil servant, who should not be hampered in his work. At the same time, Wilson insisted, administrators must be responsive to public opinion. Keith M. Henderson, *Emerging Synthesis in American Public Administration* (Bombay: Asia Publishing House, 1966), p. 7.
3. Frank J. Goodnow, *Politics and Administration* (New York: Macmillan, 1900). In *Politics and Administration*, Goodnow contended that there were "two distinct functions of government". Politics, said Goodnow, "has to do with policies or expressions of the state will", while administration "has to do with the execution of these policies". Separation of powers provided the basis for the distinction, the legislative branch, expressed the will of the state and formed policy, which the executive branch administered those policies impartially and apolitically. Nicholas Henry, *Public Administration and Public Affairs* (Englewood Cliffs, New Jersey: Prentice Hall, 1975), p. 6. Like Wilson before him, Goodnow recommended the strengthening of the executive over internal administration and the reduction of legislative control and interference. Gerald E. Caiden, *The Dynamics of Public Administration* (New York: Holt, Rinehart and Winston, Inc, 1971) p. 34.

4. Leonard D. White, *Introduction to the Study of Public Administration* (New York: Macmillan Company, 1926). This book among other things stressed that politics should not intrude on administration. But interestingly in a later work White questioned the separation of politics from administration. See Leonard D. White, *The City Manager* (Chicago: University of Chicago Press, 1927).
5. William F. Willoughby, *Principles of Public Administration* (Washington, D.C.: Brookings Institution, 1927). Willoughby's concern in this book was in developing a science of administration centred around a separation of politics from administration.
6. See F.M. Marx, ed., *Elements of Public Administration* (Englewood Cliffs, New Jersey: Prentice-Hall, 1946); J.D. Kingsley, *Representative Bureaucracy* (Yellow Springs, Ohio: Antioch Press, 1944), Paul H. Appleby, *Big Democracy* (Alfred A. Inops, 1945); and Appleby, *Policy and Administration* (University of Alabama Press, 1949). All these works (text books, case study) argued with some justification the political nature of public administration and the political role of administrators.
7. Willoughby op. cit. was clearly enthusiastic about discovering and applying scientific principles to administration so that administrators become more efficient in carrying out their responsibilities. Also see Frederick W. Taylor's *Principles of Scientific Management* (New York: Harper and Row, 1911) and Henri Fayol, *General and Industrial Management* (London: Pitman, 1930).

   Taylor and Fayol, from their experience in industries in USA and France, formulated certain scientific and universal principles which they believed could be used in formal organizations to enhance their productivity. The writings of both Taylor and Fayol influenced and continue to influence public officials and scholars.
8. Luther Gullick and Lyndall Urwick, eds., *Papers on the Science of Administration* (New York.. Institute of Public Administration, 1937).
9. James D. Mooney and Alan C. Reiley, *The Principles of Organization* (New York: Harper and Row, 1939).
10. Herbert A. Simon, "The Proverbs of Administration", *Public Administration Review*, VI (Winter, 1946), 53-67; Simon, "A Comment on the Science of Public Administration", *Public Administration Review*, VII (Summer, 1947), pp. 200-203; Simon, *Administrative Behaviour*, (New York: The Free Press, 1947).

11. Dwight Waldo, *The Administrative State* (New York: Ronald Press, 1948).
12. Robert A. Dahl, "The Science of Public Administration: Three Problems", *Public Administration Review*, VII (Winter, 1947), pp. 1 -11.
13. See for example, Dwight Waldo, "Development of Theory of Democratic Administration" together with spirited comment by Herbert A. Simon and reply by Waldo, *American Political Science Review*, XLVI (March, 1952), pp. 81-103, and *American Political Science Review*, XLVI (June, 1952), pp. 494-503.
14. Chris Argyris "Some Limits of Rational Man Organization Theory", *Public Administration Review*, XXXIII (May-June, 1973), pp. 253-266; Herbert A. Simon, "Organization Man: Rational or Self-Actualizing?", *Public Administration Review*, XXXIII (July-August, 1973), pp. 346-353; Chris Argyris, "Organization Man: Rational and Self-Actualizing", XXXIII *Public Administration Review* (July-August, 1973.), pp. 354-357.
15. Dahl emphasized the need to take into account "the relationship between public administration and its social setting", for as long as the study of public administration is not comparative, claims for "a science of public administration sound rather hollow". Dahl anticipated then the emerge of Comparative Public Administration as a field of study within American Public Administration. See Dahl, "The Science of Public Administration", op. cit.
16. In 1976, American Society for Public Administration under the auspices of some scholars interested in Comparative Public Administration, formed Society for International and Comparative Administration to broaden the purview of erstwhile CPA. By the end of 1976, SICA brought out some occasional papers.
17. For an excellent analysis of the impact of behaviouralism on public administration, see James W. Fesler, "Public Administration and the Social Science: 1946 to 1960" in Frederick C. Mosher, ed., *American Public Administration: Past, Present, Future* (Alabama: University of Alabama Press, 1975) especially pp. 113-116.
18. Herbert A. Simon, D.W. Smithburg, and V.A. Thompson, *Public Administration* (New York: Knopf, 1950).
19. John M. Pfiffner and Robert Presthus, *Public Administration* (New York: Ronald Press, 1967). The book was first published in 1953.
20. It is difficult to cite all of Waldo's works as some of these were never published and mostly read in conferences. The published pieces are

not only too many but published in many different places (i.e., in journals, edited books, his own books etc). So, I have chosen only a few of his works to illustrate my point. Waldo, *Administrative State*, op. cit. Waldo, "Development of Theory of Democratic Administration," op. cit. Waldo, "Theory of Organization: Status and Problems" in Waldo, et al., *The Study of Organizational Behaviour: Status, Problems and Trends* (Washington, D.C.: American Society for Public Administration, 1966); Waldo, "Public Administration", *International Encyclopedia of the Social Science* (New York: Crowell, Coller and Macmillan, Inc, 1968); Waldo "Scope of the Theory of Public Administration" in James C. Charlesworth, ed., *Theory and Practice of Public Administration: Scope, Objectives and Method* (Philadelphia: The American Academy of Political and Social Sciences, 1968); Waldo, *The Study of Public Administration*, (New York: Random House, 1955); Waldo, "Public Administration," *Journal of Politics*, (May, 1968) pp. 33-38; Waldo, "Developments in Public Administration", *The Annals*, 404 (November, 1972) pp. 217-254.

4 The Classical vs Modern Organization Theories in Developing Countries

Amer Al-Koubaisy

There is no doubt that the major causes of both development and decline in the administrative systems are strongly rooted in the ecological factors surrounding them and that administrative systems in all nations are inequitably affected more deeply by the external development of their political social and economic systems than by their internal subsystems or their laws and regulations. Some writers have gone further when they stated "that the dominant managerial philosophy in a given country is in large part the product of the external environment".[1]

But this is not to deny that the administrative systems can experience significant changes both qualitatively and quantitatively if a meaningful development in the structural and human variables can be introduced from within the administrative system.

In this article, however, we will argue that the more such internal change in the administrative system can be balanced and adapted with the external environment, the more valuable and significant its contribution to administrative development becomes.

How to Improve an Administrative System from Within

Is organization simply a structure, or does it also include the people within the structure? To many theorists and classical writers "organization is not people". They argue that "people have about the same relationship to the organization as the driver and passengers in an automobile have to the automobile itself".[2] If we want to improve the effectiveness of the automobile in reaching its objectives, that is, improve it as a means of rapid, safe and comfortable transportation, we can do this in a factory, far away from the people who will ride in it. To these theorists:

> Just as it would be unwise to design an automobile exactly to fit the dimensions, personality and tastes of one individual, because it would then be unlikely to fit the needs of anybody else, in the same way the organization should not be tailored to fit individual personalities.[3]

But research findings at Harvard University, the University of Michigan and other institutions demonstrate that the organizational structure itself can either facilitate or handicap the motivational and social development of the people. These conclusions show that to the extent that the organizational structure facilitates participation, communication and delegation, it also motivates the people to highest productivity. In other words, the design of the automobile, according to this group of theorists, must always be predicated upon the characteristics of the people who will use it and the environment in which it is to be used. In the following pages we will discuss these two schools of thought in some detail before examining the relevance of either one to the improvement of administrative systems in new nations.

The Bureaucratic Approach

In the literature of this field one can easily find a large number of principles and propositions which were widely accepted and practiced by public and private organizations during the first half of this century. It has been argued that most of these principles foster maximum efficiency and economy, make the organization relatively easy to control, and achieve coordination reasonably well. Among these principles are usually the following:

1. Lines of authority in the organization must be clear.
2. No one in the organization should report to more than one supervisor.
3. The responsibility and authority of each supervisor should be understood by everyone concerned.
4. The number of people reporting to one supervisor should be no more than the number whose efforts he can effectively direct and coordinate.
5. Authority to act should be delegated as much as possible to the units or individuals nearest the point where action must be taken.
6. Every function needed to accomplish the organization's purpose should be assigned to a unit of the organization.
7. The organization should be flexible, but ordinary changes in it should be made gradually except under highly special conditions.
8. Administrative efficiency is increased by grouping the workers, for better control, according to (a) purpose, (b) process, (c) clientele, or (d) place.

The works of Taylor, Fayol, Mooney, Urwick, Gulick, White, Gaus, Stene[4] and many others stress the significance as well as the necessity of these principles for any effective organization. Max Weber is perhaps the most well-known theorist who argues the technical superiority of the bureaucratic form of organization, which is largely characterized by the above principles. To Weber, the bureaucratic organization is the one most capable of attaining the highest degree of efficiency and the most rational form of administration. Weber says:

> Precision, speed, unambiguity, knowledge of the files, continuity, discretion, unity, strict subordination, reduction of friction and of material and personal costs – these are raised to the optimum point in the strictly bureaucratic administration, and especially in its monocratic form.[5]

Today, the bureaucratic approach to organizational development is still favoured by many writers in both developed and new nations. Dimock, for example, says:

> The things they admire about it are its exactness and its reliability, its logical symmetry, its elimination of chance and individuality, its reliance upon 'the one best method', the fact that it treats everyone the same and hence avoids playing favourites.[6]

Many administrators in new nations still strongly feel that it is the bureaucratic model which can fight the battle against personal subjugation, nepotism, and subjective judgements, which are common features in most of these societies.

To the behavioural scientists, however, efficiency and rationality are not the right criteria for measuring the development and the success of administrative systems. They have argued that efficiency and rationality, with which the traditionalists are mainly concerned, can only be achieved by making the employees fully dependent and submissive and requiring them to utilize only a few of their less important abilities. Argyris, in this regard, says:

> The formal organizational principle makes demands of relatively healthy individuals that are incongruent with their needs. Frustration, conflict, failure and short-term perspective are predicated as resultants of this basic incongruency.[7]

Criticizing the bureaucratic type of organization, Bennis says:

> This form of organization is becoming less and less effective, in that it is hopelessly out of joint with contemporary realities and with managerial practices in general. So within the next

> twenty-five to fifty years, we should all be witness to, and participate in, the end of bureaucracy and the rise of new social systems better able to cope with twentieth-century demands.[8]

The Behavioural Approach

During the last three decades, behavioural scientists have been studying the factors that motivate people within the administrative systems. One of the most systematic efforts in this direction was Maslow's hierarchy of needs.[9] According to his theory, the needs of human beings are organized on five levels. Once the lower-level needs are met, the higher levels become increasingly important as motivators of behaviour. Maslow's theory has been the basis on which most modern theories of organization depend.

Theory X vs Theory Y

During the fifties McGregor developed what he calls theory X and theory Y.[10] The former is his expression of the traditional point of view toward managing human beings within organizations. According to this theory, all materials, equipment and people must be used efficiently to produce goods or services if the organization is to be successful. And in order to get people to work well and hard, to what the organization wants, management has to direct, persuade, reward, punish and control them. McGregor argues that theory X, by emphasizing efficiency through direction and control is failing in our present-day society. Along with Maslow's theory he points out that theory X does not provide for the effective motivation of people whose physical and safety needs are satisfied and whose social and egoistic needs are therefore dominant.

Stressing the need for a better understanding of human nature than is required by theory X, McGregor presents theory Y as the alternative. He feels that its assumptions are generally supported by the findings of many behavioural scientists in recent years. Theory Y holds, first, that people do not like or dislike work inherently, but rather develop an attitude toward it based on their experiences with it. Second, while authoritarian methods can get things done, through direction, control, threat, and punishment, they are not the only methods for doing so. There is nothing inevitable about them, and their undesirable side-effects need not be tolerated. Third, people select goals for themselves if they see the possibility of some kind of reward, be it material or purely psychic, and once they have selected a goal they will, in pursuing it, work at least as vigorously as they would have under pressure from supervisors. And finally, imagination, ingenuity and creativity are characteristics of most human beings, but it is only under the right conditions that the average man will seek to display such characteristics and fulfil his responsibilities toward them.[11]

Now, ten years after McGregor developed theory Y, he has still not found it necessary to change its major assumptions. What he finds instead is that theories X and Y cannot be compared on the same scale, because they are qualitatively different. In a more recent book, he says:

> The belief that man is essentially like a machine that is set into action by the application of external forces differs in more than degree from the belief that man is an organic system whose behaviour is affected not only by external forces but by intrinsic ones. Theory X and theory Y therefore are not polar opposites. They do not lie at extremes of a scale. They are simply different cosmologies.[12]

The Authoritative vs The Participative Theory

Since 1947 the Institute for Social Research at the University of Michigan has been studying the human problems involved in administrative and management practices. In 1961, Rensis Likert, its Director, published a summary of findings and a new administrative theory based on empirical research.[13] A few years later he added to his original theory and supplied additional proof of its usefulness.[14]

Likert, in his work, differentiates between authoritative and participative systems of organizations. The authoritative systems have been conceptualized as exploitative, benevolent and consultative. The three types of systems are placed on a continuum representing different degrees of control. The exploitative-authoritarian has more unilateral control than the benevolent and consultative. Likert's ideas on how management ought to deal with people have been evolving into what he calls a 'modified theory' or the participative system of organization. The participative system stands in greatest contrast to the exploitative system. It resembles, in fact, the style of management which McGregor developed in theory Y. Under Likert's participative system, people at every level feel a real responsibility to the organization's goals, and they work hard to reach them. Managers have complete confidence and trust in their people. The employees have complete freedom to express ideas about the work.

Moreover, Likert has been able to relate productivity to his systems. He has shown, for example, that the nearer the management system is to the participative system, the more productive the organization is. It results also in lower costs, higher earnings, better employee attitudes and higher morale.

The Mechanical vs Organic Theory

Shepard, Burns and Stalker[15] have all agreed that it is no longer adequate to perceive organization as a kind of machine, in the way Max Weber did.[16] They have attempted to replace such a mechanical idea of bureaucracy with what they feel is its natural alternative: an 'organic' system. This organic organization can adapt spontaneously to the needs of the internal and external systems, rather than operating through programmed codes of behaviour which are contained in the formal role specifications of the mechanical structure. To Shepard, the organic organization is based on the following principles:

1. Good management is understood to be the emergent product of adequate working relationships among the organization's members.
2. The cement of the system is mutual confidence.
3. The structure of the organization must correspond to the network of interdependence among members required by the organizational tasks.
4. The principle of multigroup membership is substituted for the mechanical concept of supervision.
5. The wide sharing of control and responsibility created by the foregoing leads to the principle that "conflict of interests must be resolved by the use of problem solving".[17]

In the literature of organization theory, one can also find many other attempts by scholars, in discussing effective versus ineffective organization, to set up two 'ideal types' or organizations. To mention only a few, Gouldner differentiates between what he calls the 'rational' and the 'natural' models. He points out that if we focus primarily on the natural model we will miss or under-emphasize several important aspects of the rational model.[18]

Among the rest are Litwak,[19] who differentiates between the 'bureaucratic' and 'human relation' models; Bennis,[20] who speaks in terms of 'habit' and 'problem solving' models; Barnes,[21] who stresses the differences between 'closed' and, 'open' systems, and White,[22] who develops the 'dialectical' model as an alternative to the bureaucratic type of organization.

Argyis has examined most of the above models and contrasted them to each other. He has found from his analysis that there are only slight variations amongst them. He finds that all these men have agreed that the organization which is variously called 'Y' by McGregor 'participative' by Likert, 'organic' by Shepard and others, 'natural' by Gouldner, 'human relations-oriented' by Litwak, 'open system' by Barnes, 'problem-solving' by Bennis (and – I will add to them dialectic – by White), "tends to develop greater organizational flexibility, commitment, responsibility and effectiveness in problem-solving and adapting to the environment".[23]

The question we are very concerned with here is: how relevant are these theories and an ideal type of effective organization to our discussion of new developing nations? Or, to put the question in a different way, what type of organization theory would be more relevant to the balanced administrative system which these nations need?

The Relevance of The Classical Theory to New Nations

To the classical students as well as to many practitioners and career-oriented administrators, the bureaucratic type of organization, or what is now commonly called the theory X type of organization, seems more appropriate to new nations than all other alternatives. This viewpoint, however, has been justified by different hypotheses and propositions. There are, first, those who argue that the trend toward bureaucratization is generally related to the tendencies of these nations to grow larger in total population, to become more complex in specialization, more urbanized and wealthier per capita as time passes. The proposition they present is that the more complex these societies become, the more conflicts are generated, and the larger the governmental organization must become. All this in turn will increase the probability that all jobs will meet the criteria for bureaucratization as Weber described them.[24]

John Dollard says in this regard:

> The large organization is necessarily, it seems, run by a bureaucracy which is specialized as to job, organized in hierarchies of power, distributed in status according to rank rather than individual talent, governed by a few at the top who recruit their successors, and rationalized so as to see the individual as a mere instrument.[25]

The bureaucratic type of organization is also more relevant to these nations because of the limited financial and material resources they have. Here, therefore, efficiency and economy must be emphasized more than responsiveness and representation. In a recent article, Wurzburg says:

> The ordering of man's life is essential to prevent the chaos arising out of an uninhibited grasp for unlimited resources. The means to do so are organizational. The most efficient form of organization is bureaucracy. Hence the politics of scarcity produces the bureaucratic method of control.[26]

This argument has been supported by Braibanti, who says:

> The demands of economic development can be met only by an oligarchic bureaucracy.[27]

The classical theorists have often argued that despite the varying goals and environments of different organizations, it is possible to identify basic similarities in structure and process which can be conceptually analysed and made explicit.

> Mooney, who is very authoritative among these writers, said once Our study of governmental organization back to remotest ages reveals one fact of deepest import: in this sphere there is nothing new under the sun. This fact confirms our thesis that the principles of organization are universal and hence must appear in the governmental forms of every age.[28]

On the empirical level, Harbison and Meyers, in their study of administrative practices in twenty-three countries, made a number of generalizations concerning many bureaucratic principles which did not differ fundamentally from country to country.[29]

Last, but not least, the advocates of the classical theories in new nations think that the environment there is not quite favourable to the application of modern theories simply because they require a democratic style of administration.

In these new nations, says one author, there are definite limitations on the use of democracy in management. Quite obviously it can yield little in areas in which technical knowledge and competence are demanded. Democracy connotes deliberation, and deliberation takes time which is not then available. If democratic practices are carried to extreme limits, they can, in effect, so diffuse responsibility that responsibility cannot be located.[30]

The Relevance of Modern Theory To New Nations

G. Sjoberg, in his occasional paper *Ideology and Social Organization in Rapidly Developing Countries*, says:

> My thesis is that the kind of 'bureaucracy' that characterizes the pre-industrial civilized society and the Weberian type of bureaucracy in the advanced industrial order both serve to sustain the status quo and are not easily amenable to demands for resocialization within rapidly industrializing societies. Both types of organization stress hierarchical relationships, order and control.[31]

What these nations need, according to Sjoberg, is an ideal-typical model which is committed to a revolutionary type of ideology and which permits change in the values and beliefs of clients.

From the point of view of most students of the "new public administration movement", administrative development in changing societies can hardly be achieved without attempting to cope with demands for change by engaging in a dialectic involving both old and new.[32] Theory Y, for example, is considered as a means for introducing the new elements required for such change. At the same time, writers who have little faith in the ecological approach and take little notice of the environmental impact on management have also realized the significance of modern theory to new nations. To these students, "emerging bureaucracies in underdeveloped states are less intricately imbedded in the matrix of culture, since the bureaucracy is often more secular-minded and Western-oriented than the public mass".[33]

Modern theories are also advocated by those who try to change organizations by first changing the behaviour of the organization's members. By changing human behaviour, it is argued, one can cause the creative invention of new tools, or one can cause modifications in power structure. In surveying the people approach, Leavitt says: "one is immediately struck by the fact that the recent literature dealing directly with organizational change is heavily people-oriented".[34] Students of administrative development in many new nations now are convinced that people within the organization must be changed first before a structural and institutional change is introduced. An Indian author, for example, says:

> Unless the man is made to look different or asked to think differently or motivated to function more purposively, no amount of investment in structural sophistication or modernization in machine-procedure will be in a position to hit the jackpot by way of raising the level of development or productivity. The critical ingredient, the bureaucrat himself, must, therefore, be freed from the existing conceptual orthodoxies, age old affiliations and narrow mental grooves so as to be the fitting torchbearer of a new and bright development order.[35]

A few overseas writers, attracted by Western and European thoughts and ways of life, encourage the application of most modern organization theories developed in these advanced countries. These writers, however, emphasize the need for these theories more than their relevance to new nations. Charles Malik, for example, says:

> No country in Asia or Africa can possibly live today apart from the more advanced countries of the world. On the one hand, it desperately needs them; on the other, they will not allow it to live by itself. They speak of independence, but independence is a most relative term, and in the intellectual and spiritual matters, there is no independence. In virtually all cases independence is a myth.[36]

From the above assumption, Malik makes this conclusion: "if the new countries of Asia and Africa are to survive and develop, they must enter into the living European world of thought and organization."[37]

Critique of Modern Organization Theory

In contrast to those, who argued the question of which classical or modern theories are more relevant to administrative development in new nations, this author, like many other writers, feels that neither of them is relevant. First, I do not believe that any single, general organizational theory – at least not X or Y – can combine all the advantages and avoid all the shortcomings of other theories, since no one theory can cover everything involved in administrative development. For example, choosing either X or Y would imply, for one thing, that the one chosen contains a better rationale for dealing with superior-subordinate relationships. Actually, though, the supervision style under either theory has its own advantages as well as disadvantages, and one method is not necessarily more effective than the other under all circumstances. On the one hand, under theory X, the supervisor sees himself as a management representative. He is the authoritarian, task oriented supervisor, who puts the management's goals first and the employees' needs second. The employees would, therefore, be expected to turn aside from their formal supervisors and follow their own informal leaders. Conversely, the supervisor under theory Y identifies himself strongly with the employees. His first loyalty is to them, and in his communication with management he will tend to play up employees' demands. Thus, he may get employees' acceptance, but at the same time he is likely to alienate management and cause his supervisors to mistrust him, weakening his influence with them. What we need then is not to shift from one style of supervision to another, but to combine them both and arrive at a balanced style of supervision which considers the interests and needs of employees as well as of the administration.

In regard to productivity and economy, neither theory X nor theory Y is wholly satisfactory. Writers like Katz, Maccoby and Morse note that the close supervision and higher degree of centralization, required by theory X are inversely related to the productivity and efficiency criteria.[38] On the other hand, if we use theory Y, the material cost of designing administrative organization specifically to fit the dimensions, personality and tastes of all individuals cannot be provided by these nations at this stage of their development. Therefore, it is not enough in these countries to design all organizations to provide greater opportunity for psychological success and self-esteem. The participants must also be capable of meeting the challenges and accepting the responsibilities involved.

From the ecologists' point of view, it is also true that neither the classical nor the modern theories can be accepted as a universal or cross-cultural theory. To these writers, human motivation and behaviour in any productive or public enterprise is a function of various complex environmental factors. Many of these factors are naturally beyond the control of the people in charge of its administration. The ecologists, Farmer and Richman, have found through their empirical and cross-cultural studies that:

> Direction and leadership techniques which prove effective in the American firm may prove inadequate, or even disastrous, when applied to firms in Saudi Arabia, Japan, or India.[39]

Gonzalez and McMillan, after serving as consultants on business administration training in Brazil, concluded that management philosophy is highly culture-bound.[40] Oberg says:

> My own experience in international management leads me to believe that cultural differences from one country to another are more significant than many writers now appear to recognize.[41]

To the ecologists, managerial effectiveness cannot be achieved by shifting from the traditional theory to the modern theory. Such a shift can be effective only if it is necessitated by or is relevant to the cultural and environmental factors in the society.

Megginson has pointed out that the cultural elements that have the greatest influence on managerial effectiveness are the spiritual values and the educational system. The spiritual values are implied in the managerial philosophies and form the assumptions upon which managers make their decisions. The educational system determines the knowledge and analytical processes used by the executives in the decision-making process. Megginson also adds that "spiritual values largely influence personal objectives, which are the ends desired, while education determines the means of achieving these goals".[42]

Other writers have denied the relevance to new nations of the McGregor, Likert, Shepard and other modern theories of organization, by criticizing the Maslow hierarchy of needs, which is considered the major theoretical framework of these theories and models. Bryan Davies, for example, says:

> This model (Maslow's hierarchy of needs) has the advantage of coherence, and also of intuitive plausibility with respect to Western individual cultures, though it would seem difficult of validation even there. The antnropological evidence of Mead, Malinwovsky and Gluckman, etc., suggests that the model would certainly not survive transfer to all cultures. (A general hierarchy of needs model, might do so, but the specific physical-social-egoistic ordering proposed by Maslow would not).[43]

Keith Davies is another writer who has argued the need of new nations for different theories of management on the grounds of the different needs and motivations the employees have in these nations. He says:

> In underdeveloped countries, most employees are still seeking basic physiological and security needs. Hence, some of the more sophisticated and elaborate motivational devices of modern industrial management may not be appropriate in these countries. The needs of their workers may be more simply

> reached by direct motivation Therefore, they require management to show them simple, direct evidence that if they work more effectively they will receive more. In other words, work must be interpreted in terms of their immediate needs, rather than waiting for indirect results through a complex economic system. Accordingly, action which would be inappropriate in an advanced country may sometimes be workable in the underdeveloped country.[44]

Finally it is true that modern organization theories have some serious drawbacks in terms of their orientation and applicability to different types of cultural and economic needs. The various theories of organization which are largely developed in the United States, for example, focus primarily on the person in a given organization, in a given environment, trying to determine how the organization might function better. Because of this, Whyte wants new nations, who try to set up their institutions and organizations on these models, to be careful. In Whyte's words:

> Imitation of institutional models from industrialized nations is dysfunctional for the developing nations. The imported model often does not fit the needs of the host culture. Furthermore, the model is a product of particular historical circumstances in the exporting country. Members of that institution would not recreate it in its present form if they were to build anew.[45]

Conclusion

From the above analysis one would conclude that a balanced model and culture-bound theories are required, not only to bring the administrative, political and economic subsystems into a balanced situation, but also to build up an internal balance within the administrative system itself. The former, in fact, can hardly be achieved without the latter.

The modern theories of organization discussed above require a choice between complete centralization or extreme decentralization in structuring the organization. These theories have assumed that centralization and decentralization are distinct types of organizations and that elements of both cannot be found within the same organization. Such a distinction, says Allen, is specious:

> It would be as meaningful to attempt to classify pneumonia found in men as male pneumonia' and that found in women as female pneumonia.[46]

These theories have also failed to consider the need of rapidly changing societies and organizations for a balanced model of centralization and decentralization, a model which is needed for pragmatic and purely administrative reasons as well as for the ecological reasons already discussed. Selznick, in this regard, once said:

> The increasing complexity of organizational tasks makes decentralization and the delegation of responsibility to intermediaries inevitable. But such a measure brings forth the organizational paradox of goal displacement, bifurcation of interests between the central system and its decentralized sub-units. There is a tendency for the latter to neglect the main organizational goals in favour of their limited sub-goals. In this way sub-goals, from simple means, become ends in themselves. This situation makes the needs for centralized control stronger and the circle may start all over.[47]

Ignoring such factors, modern organization theories are mainly directed toward the development of either overpowering manipulative organizations, or organizations that will keep people happy. Happiness and manipulation, however, can be fine guides to the administrative development only if they are combined and balanced with each other in a pragmatic rather than oriented idealistic way. A balanced organization, on the other hand, cannot be achieved if all administrators are either task-oriented or personalities. A balanced organization requires, first of all, a balanced administration and leadership. In describing what a balanced administrator is, Dimock says:

> The top executive is balanced when he comes to possess a personality that qualifies him for a position of leadership, for inspiring confidence in others because he is interested in them and does not treat them merely as pawns in his own selfish designs. He is balanced when his sense of fairness imparts to his employees the assurance that their fortunes, both individual and collective, are safe in his hands, and that he will not make decisions on the basis of prejudice, favouritism or arbitrariness. He is balanced when he is not overly specialized, so that he does not become lopsided or merely a technician. He is balanced when be is sufficiently broad to be a good co-ordinator, because no executive is worthy of the name unless he can plan, integrate and combine all components of his enterprise into a unified and smoothly working whole.[48]

In my opinion, an effective administrative organization must maintain a balance between its internal elements as well as between them and the external subsystems in the society. Experience has shown that no ideal theory can be applied in new nations if it does not consider such needs. What will serve these nations best is a pragmatic and realistic model which is internally developed and comprehended. Harvey Sherman says:

> The only plea I would make is that the degree of centralization or decentralization for a particular enterprise or function be determined pragmatically in terms of such factors as public convenience, economy, quality of service, availability of skilled personnel, need for control, and general effectiveness.[49]

Modern organization theories such as that developed by McGregor, Likert and Shepard might cause confusion for administrators of developing countries who try to choose between their two conflicting styles. This is mainly because the bureaucratic theory of organization which McGregor calls theory X is expected to work well in some situations, while theory Y might work better in the others. What will happen then if an administrator prefers to apply theory Y in an area where theory X is expected to function effectively? Theory Y also should not be embraced everywhere on the ground that it is strongly oriented toward the development of man. Man from our point of view, is distinguished from other elements of administration, in that his development is not something that is done to him or for him. His development instead is growth, and growth can only come from within, and not from without.

Notes

1. R.N. Farmer and B.M. Richman, *Comparative Management and Economic Progress*, Richard D. Irwin, Inc. (Homewood, Illinois, 1965), p. 119.
2. Louis A. Allen, *Management and Organization*, McGraw Hill Book Company, Inc., (N.Y., 1958), p. 58.
3. Ibid.
4. F. Taylor, *Scientific Management*, Harper, (N.Y., 1947); H. Fayol, *General and Industrial Management*, Pitman, (N.Y., 1947); J.D. Mooney, *The Principles of Organization*, Harper. (N.Y., 1947); L. Urwick, *The Elements of Administration*. Harper, (N.Y., 1944); L. Gulick and L. Urwick, *Papers on the Science of Administration*; (N.Y., Institute of Public Administration, 1927); L.D. White, *Introduction to the Study of Public Administration*, (N.Y., 1939); J. Gauss and others (eds.), *The Frontiers of Public Administration*, Univ. of Chicago Press. (Chicago, 1936); and E.D. Stene, "An Approach to Science of Administration", *American Pol. Science Review*, Vol. 34 (Dec., 1940), p. 1125-1137.
5. H. Gerth and C. Wright Mills (eds.), *From Max Weber: Essays in Sociology*, Oxford Univ. Press, (N.Y., 1953), p. 214.
6. M. Dimock, *The Philosophy of Administration*, p. 161.
7. Chris Argyris, *Personality and Organization*, Harper (N.Y., 1957), p. 74.
8. W.G. Bennis, *Changing Organizations*, McGraw Hill Book Company,(N.Y., 1966), p. 59. A.H. Maslow, *Motivation and Personality*, Harper and Row (N.Y., 1966), p. 5.

9. A.H. Maslow, *Motivation and Personality*, Harper and Row (N.Y. 1966), p. 50
10. Douglas McGregor "The Human Side of Enterprise" in *Proceedings: Fifth Anniversary Convocation of the School of Industrial Management* (Cambridge, 1957). Also under the same title, in book form McGraw Hill Book Company (N.Y., 1960).
11. William R. Van Dersal, *The Successful Supervisor in Government and Business*, Revised, Harper and Row (N.Y. and Evanston, 1968), p. 90.
12. Douglas McGregor, *The Professional Manager*, McGraw Hill Book Co., (N.Y., 1967), p. 79-80.
13. Rensis Likert, *New Patterns of Management*, McGraw Hill Book Co., (N.Y., 1961).
14. Rensis Likert, *The Human Organization: Its Management and Value*, McGraw Hill Book Co. (N.Y., 1967).
15. H.A. Shepard, "Changing Interpersonal and Intergroup Relationship in Organization", in James March (ed.), *Handbook of Organization*, Rand McNally, (N.Y.) and R. Burns and G.M. Stalker, The Management of Innovation, Tavistock Pub. (London, 1961).
16. Max Weber once said: "Bureaucracy is like a modern judge who is a vending machine into which the pleadings are inserted together with the fee and which then disgorges the judgement together with its reasons mechanically derived from the Code". See R. Bendix, *Max Weber, An Intellectual Portrait*, Doubleday and Co., Inc. (N.Y., 1960), quoted in Bennis, op. cit., p. 46.
17. H.A. Shepard and Robert Blake, "Changing Behaviour through Cognitive Change", (mimeo) presented at the annual meeting of the Society for Applied Anthropology (May, 1961), Part I from which the above is quoted was written by Shepard, quoted in C. Argyris, *Integrating the Individual and the Organization*, John Wiley and Sons, Inc. (N.Y., 1964), p. 184.
18. Alvin, W., Gouldner, "Organizational Analysis" in Robert K. Merton, Leonard Broom and Leonard Cottrell (eds.), *Sociology Today*, Basic Books (N.Y., 1959), p. 400-401.
19. Eugene Litwak, "Models of Bureaucracy which Permit Conflict", *American Journal of Sociology*, Vol. LXVII (Sept. 1962), p. 177-184,
20. Warren Bennis, "Leadership Theory and Administrative Behaviour", *Administrative Science Quarterly*, Vol. 4, No. 3 (Dec. 1959). p. 259-301.

21. Louis B. Barnes, *Organization Systems and Engineering Groups.* Graduate School of Business, Harvard University, (1960), Ch. VIII.
22. Orion F. White, "The Dialectical Organization: An Alternative to Bureaucracy", in *Public Administration Review*, Vol. XXIX, No. 1.
23. C. Argyris, *Integrating the Individual and the Organization,* p. 185.
24. Anthony Downs, *Inside Bureaucracy,* Little Brown and Company (Boston, 1967), p. 255-256.
25. John Dollard, Review of Robert Presthus's "The Organizational Society" in *The New York Times Book Review* (Oct. 1962).
26. Frederic Wurzburg, "Bureaucratic Decay" in *Journal of Comparative Administration*, Vol. 1, No. 4 (Feb. 1970), p. 388.
27. R. Braibanti, "The Relevance of Political Science to the Study of Underdeveloped Areas" R. Braibanti and Spengler (eds.), *Tradition, Values and Socio-economic Development*, p. 143.
28. J.D. Mooney, *The Principles of Organization*, op. cit., p. 57.
29. See Winston Oberg, "Cross-Cultural Perspective on Management Principles" in *Academy of Management Journal*, Vol. 6, No. 2 (June, 1963), p. 129-130.
30. C.T. Hardwick and B.F. Lanjuyt, *Administrative Strategy*, Simons-Boardman Public Corporation (N.Y., 1961). p. 324.
31. Gideon Sjoberg, *Ideology and Social Organization in Rapidly Developing Countries*, CAG occasional papers, (Bloomington, Indiana, Dec. 1966), p.16.
32. Wesley E. Bjur, "What is the New Public Administration" in *Public Administration Review*, Vol. XXX, No. 2, Mar./Apr. 1970).
33. R. Braibanti, "The Relevance of Political Science to the study of Underdeveloped Areas", p. 179.
34. Harold J. Leavitt, "Applied Organizational Change in Industry: Structural, Technological and Humanistic Approach", in J. March (ed.) *Handbook of Organization*, p. 1151.
35. B.K. Day, "Bureaucracy and Development-Some Reflections", *Indian Journal of Public Administration*, Vol. XV, No. 2, Apr./June, 1979), p. 247-248.
36. Charles H. Malik, "Ideals for Export", in Maneck S. Wadia, *Management and the Behavioural Sciences*, Alien and Bacou, Inc., (Boston, 1968), p. 533.
37. Ibid.

38. Daniel Katz, Nathan Maccoby, and Nacy C. Morse, *Productivity, Supervision and Morale in an Office Situation*, Ann Arbor Michigan Survey Research Center, Institute for Social Research (1950).
39. R.N. Farmer and B. B. Richman, *Comparative Management and Economic Progress*, p. 8.
40. R.F. Gonzalez and C. McMillan Jr. "The Universality of American Management Philosophy", *Journal of the Academy of Management*, Vol. 4, No. 1 (April, 1961), p. 33-41.
41. Winston Oberg, "Cross-Cultural Perspective on Management Principles", *Journal of the Academy of Management,* Vol. 6, No. 2 (June, 1963), p. 129-130.
42. Leon C. Megginson, "The Inter-relationship and Interaction Between the Cultural Environment and Managerial Effectiveness" in *Management International Review*, Vol. 7 (1967), p. 69.
43. Bryan Device, "Some Thoughts on Organizational Democracy", *The Journal of Management Studies*, Vol. 4, No. 3 (Oct. 1, 1967), p. 270.
44. Keith Davies, "Managing Productivity in Developing Countries" in S. Benjamin Prasad (ed.), *Management in International Perspective*, Appleton-Century-Crofts, (1967), p. 158-159.
45. William Foote Whyte, "Imitation or Innovation: Reflections on the Institutional Development of Peru", *Administrative Science Quarterly*, Vol. 13, No. 3 (Dec. 1968), p. 370.
46. Louis Alien, *Management and Organization*, p. 157.
47. P. Selznick, "An Approach to the Theory of Bureaucracy", *American Sociological Review*, Vol. 8 (1943), p. 47.
48. M. Dimock, *Philosophy of Administration*, p. 34.
49. Harvey Sherman, *It All Depends: A Pragmatic Approach to Organization*, p. 82.

5 Systems Approach to the Study of Administrative Organization

Sangeeta Sharma

In the context of the development of 'scientific methods' we might note what philosopher of science Stephen Toulmin remarked: "The heart of all major discoveries in the physical sciences is the discovery of novel methods of representation and so of fresh techniques by which inferences can be drawn and drawn in the ways which fit the phenomenon under investigation".

'Systems concept', one of the most logical and scientific methods being successfully transplanted in social field of study has revolutionalized the social thinking processes. This approach is helpful in analysing the social phenomenon scientifically and logically, but its application in the field of organizational analysis is bit different from the natural sciences where the object under investigation can be subjected to experimentation in various possible ways with the help of instruments and scientific technologies, while in social field, basic unit of analysis is human being and his behaviour who himself is the most interesting phenomenon of the society. Conversely, the applicability of systems approach in the world

of natural sciences is well established where one is facilitated by laboratory devices to create a controlled environment and to develop other supportive and complementary structure necessary for the system synthesis.

Some methodological principles of systems had been devised by Ludwig Von Bertalanfy who was the originator of General Systems Theory. He developed his theory with the sole object of providing a uniform framework for investigating various scientific and social phenomena occurring during the process of time. According to Bertalanfy, the notion of systems is defined as "any arrangement of system as of parts or elements in a whole applies to a cell, a human being, a society as well as to an atom, planet or galaxy".

Using Bertanlanfy's work as the base, Kenneth Boulding formulated the theory of 'systems hierarchy'. Major idea behind this theory was that a given system is a part of much larger system which, in fact, is part of other bigger system, thus creating a hierarchy of super-systems, systems, and subsystems. For instance, if we are studying a particular department in the government organization, then particular department is a 'subsystem' in relation to the government organization which is a system; the nation makes the super-system. One must be clear about the fact that this hierarchical representation is relative one, e.g., even that particular department under study is a full system in relation to its own sections and wings.

Norbert Weiner's theory of informations and his model of cybernetic scan also be considered a landmark in the development of systems theory. Besides, Talcott Persons' conceptual scheme for the analysis of the social system, needs special mention. He utilized the theory of 'open system' to maximum extent for studying different social structures. Similar studies were made by David Easton in political science. His model of 'demand' and 'support' operating in the system is quite well known by now. Easton asserts that there are two kinds of stresses to which the political systems may be subjected. These stresses can be coped with various kinds of responses at both the cultural and the 'structural' levels. Further, Easton says that all systems are characterized by a 'critical range' beyond which if any stress is made the system will result into disintegration.

As far as application of system approach is concerned, public administration is still in a phase of infancy. Efforts of prominent scholars such as Fred Riggs and Ira Sharkansy have opened up new possibilities for research in this area.

Major Characteristics of Systems

Systems Defined

A major difficulty which one comes across while defining systems concept involves the use of this concept in most diverse scientific and practical activity with obviously different meanings.

Despite this difficulty we can define it as: A system is a logical and systematic grouping of distinct yet interdependent components assembled for the purpose of achieving a predetermined objective. This system operates in an environment with which it continually interacts.

Components of Systems

Components basically constitute the skeletal body of system. We can categorize components into different types as: (i) physical components. (ii) individuals as components; (iii) formal components; (iv) informal components; (v) 'role' components; and (vi) organizational 'norms and values' as components.

1. *Physical Components:* Physical equipments are necessary for the functioning of the administrative or organizational systems. These include official building, sitting arrangement in the office or department, availability of other facilities as electricity, air-conditioning, etc.
2. *Individual Components:* These are basic requirements for the composition of a social system. Functioning of individual actors as biological organisms and as

personalities in an organization engaged in achieving predetermined goals is a prerequisite to the operation of the system. From here emerges individual behaviour.

3. *Formal Components:* These include material for cementing the formal structure, the pattern of hierarchy, supervision and controlling procedures, unity of command, etc.
4. *Informal Components:* Coexisting with formal components, the informal components play a decisive role. Informal groups are always linked with the systems processings which are formed due to the clustering of people possessing similar interest and sharing a common ideology. These groups assume certain role and develop 'group dynamism', which is the result of interaction between different groups. Further group dynamics can be viewed as the internal nature of group, and tells about how the groups should be organized.

Linking Mechanisms in Systems

All subsystems or parts of the systems are interlinked by the linking mechanisms. There are the mechanism devised for tying up different parts in a common organization matrix. Mechanism which are generally identified are: (1) communication systems; (2) roles; and (3) decision-making.

1. *Communication:* Johnson, Kast and Rosenwig comment on the interrelationship between structure and communication as follow:

> Organization structure is definitely tied to communication system. The relationship is apparent when formal structures, channels and media are involved; for informal alignment and irregular information flow, the relationship is not as evident.

Communication basically outlines the information system and cybernetic model. Media for communication are through psychological processes like perception, learning and motivation, language, coding signals, etc.

2. *Roles:* Secondly in a system, everybody is bound by 'roles' which he acquires from the system itself.
3. *Decision-Making:* Process of decision-making is another binding force to keep these parts interconnected.

Systems Boundaries

Systems theorists define the systems under study by stating its boundaries. The use of boundary concept enables to define any ongoing process as system. It also helps in setting up the framework and in establishing 'relationship' among various sub-parts building up a system.

A statement of boundaries will, by determining the contents of the 'systems' place limits on the subsystems to be studied. Interestingly, a social system is bounded by pseuds boundaries – boundaries which are not distinct enough to demarcate different systems and subsystems. While doing so one provides arbitrarily limits to the 'social system'.

This semi-permeable membrane permits certain admissible elements into the system from its supporting environment and vice-versa. Thus, a process of 'importation' and 'exportation' of energy and the process of 'input-output' exchange goes on through these systems boundaries. This is the place from where inputs are injected with the system and outputs are liberated in the environment outside the system. But these places are not well defined in social system.

Systems Environment

Environment is a source of supplying 'inputs' to the system as a result of which outputs get transmitted to the environment. It is a medium through which information travels and sends necessary signals to different sub systems. Besides it is a medium through which, feedback mechanism operates. We can study different types of environment such as organic physical environment, cultural environment and psychological environment.

1. *Organic Physical Environment*: All relationships between the social system and physical environment are mediated through behaviour of the organism. Social community is related to physical environment through economy which is primarily social; and technological systems.
2. *Cultural Environment*: Culture is not something which is inherited but it is 'learned' by 'humans'. In a given system cultural pattern are institutionalized as suggested by Talcott Parsons. Behaviour of an individual actor gets affected by these cultural institutions of the system.
3. *Psychological Environment*: Freud's famous principle of 'reality' is the principle of ego adaptation in the social environment. Psychological environment facilitates the psychological process which comprises perception, learning and motivation. All 'behavioural systems' operate in this environment which describes individual behaviour, group behaviour and organizational behaviour.

Parameters of Systems

1. *Inputs:* Types of inputs fed to any system determine the nature of the system, e.g., money, land and labour, drawing up of monetary and fiscal policy are the inputs, if the system is economic. Similarly rules enforcement. selection of personnel, determination of hierarchical pattern are the administrative inputs necessary for the administrative system.
2. *Throughputs:* It is the process of conversion of 'inputs' into 'outputs'. Several reactions are taking place within the 'black box' to complete this transformation, e.g., training of personnel, functioning of motivational systems, degree of influential exercises, etc.
3. *Outputs:* Outputs are the final products of whole of the process ready for release into the outside environment.

Feedback Mechanism

Feedback is an output redelivered as 'input' introduced with the process from where 'output' was delivered.

Multisystemic feedback mechanism can also be seen in a systems process when output of subsystem 'A' becomes input for subsystem 'B' and so on. The ultimate output of the whole system gets reinjected at various points of subsystems functioning.

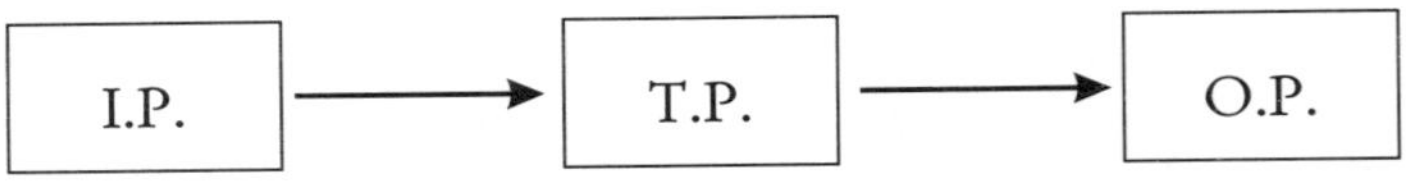

Systems Equilibrium

Every system has a tendency to stabilize itself. While doing so it establishes certain constant ratio between inputs and outputs. Thus, they try to occupy a position of equilibrium. Principle here is of Lechataliei who mentioned that any 'internal' or 'external' factor making for disruption of the system is countered by forces which restore the system as close by as possible of its previous state. Lewin's concept of quasi-stationary equilibrium also explains this process in a system. He observed that an adjustment in one direction is countered by a movement in the opposite direction; these movements are approximate but not precise.

Thus, in social systems, inputs and outputs are in dynamic change of state.

Systems Goals

Any system first of all fixes the targets on the basis of which a system is built. Collective effort of its constituents makes it possible to achieve them.

Systems process is the process by which society rationally calculate and control them through collective action.

Utility of Systems Approach and its Limitations

The contribution of systems approach in deriving certain universally stated logical principles to study various systems varying from physical systems, chemical systems to social system is remarkable, specially in social disciplines where it has helped a lot in understanding and adopting scientific methodologies. It has modernized our viewpoints by attacking on old established theories. It is now generally held that not a single discipline can grow unless and until it develops and utilizes research techniques to acquire research knowledge; in developing these technique, systems approach plays a very important role. It gives scientific and logical solution of any problem, thus provides a proper insight to the theoretical or practical problems of the system. It does not concentrate on one aspect of the problem but takes into account other related factors too – like social, economic, psychological, cultural, etc. Further, it has bridged the gaps between different fields of study.

Moreover, it suggests many possibilities for science philosophies to shake hands with social philosophies. In addition, it improves the motivational systems so as to motivate individual working in the system.

Limitations

Human and his behaviour is the major part of emphasis in social studies. In a society or in a system or in an organization he is not merely acting as living organism but at the same time is an individual personality, an economic man, a social man and an organizational man. As a matter of fact individuals assume different 'roles' in different identities. This factor restricts the application of pure scientific principles to this field of study.

'Social events' or 'happenings' cannot be reconstructed in exactly similar manner, while in natural sciences, 'events' not only can be reconstituted but can be preserved for a long time. Besides, 'instruments' for measuring 'social behaviours' are yet to be devised. Generally we measure 'human behaviour' through psychological tests; results of which are approximate, not precise. Further, in a social process of individual is acting as a 'media of exchange', he can be physically identified but if these exchanges are in terms of 'behavioural segments' it is difficult to provide system boundaries. Sometimes 'man' in a social system tries to personalize the relationships which causes failure of this approach. In addition, some methodological and logical problems arise in systems analysis such as selection and analysis of specific methods in systems research, the methods evolving theoretical conceptualization. In research techniques which we adopt are non-systems instruments, thus we often substitute non-systems analysis for systems analysis of object under investigation. And importantly, we do not have a criteria to define outside environment and its essential features.

Thus, systematic construction of a methodology and logic of systems research requires specific language to evaluate the correctness of the systems statements and their significance.

Application of Systems Approach in an Administrative Organization

Administrative systems are not the exception to this universally accepted utility of systems approach. This approach can successfully be applied to study different administrative behaviour and to analyse administrative phenomena occurring in the administrative organizations. Briefly,

- It has developed many administrative techniques like in decision-making, new techniques have been introduced for choosing the best among alternatives.
- Introduction of computer systems in administrative analysis is another major contribution of systems approach.
- It develops 'administrative managerial skills' to cope with the changing environment of science and technology, like application of statistical and mathematical techniques in administration for its precise evaluation.
- It formulates administrative policies systematically.

- Controlled systems can be applied to check administrative plans.
- It reforms the administrative climate necessary for the growth of administrative system.
- This approach helps the government system to take requisite steps to reorient and reorganize the government administration in accordance with the socio-political processes of democratization.

It is necessary therefore to further strengthen the conceptual as well as empirical bases of systems analysis in administrative sciences.

6 New Public Management: Emerging Concerns

Ramesh K. Arora

Ever since the discipline of public administration was given an identity more than hundred years ago, there has been a constant confluence of management science and public administration. The impact of F.W. Taylor was evident in the writings of L.D. White and W.F. Willoughby; French scholar Henri Fayol built bridges between management and public administration; Chester Barnard was the prime motivator of Herbert Simon; the contemporary management super-guru, Peter Drucker has perspicaciously analysed government bureaucracies from a managerial angle; the fusion theory of Chris Argyris has been tested in the context of American federal government; and today the burgeoning world of management science has its penetrating effect on the intellectual development of public administration. This convergence appears as a natural consequence of the integrated development of the discipline since the core of public administration has always been its external political context as well as its internal organizational (read managerial) dynamics What is internal to a public administrative system is its process of management and what is external to it is its political (hinging also on socio-economic) environment in which it functions. It is universally accepted that most maxims, principles, guidelines and dictums of efficiency, economy and effectiveness have emanated from the writings of management thinkers and that they have been adopted and adapted by the scholars of public administration in their distinctive intellectual ambience. Both management and public administration are applied sciences. Hence leaving aside their individual contexts of control and accountability, there is no drastic differentiation between the two as far as their cardinal goals and roles are concerned.

Current Paradigm

Currently, if there is one 'paradigm' in the discipline of public administration, it is perhaps 'New Public Management' (NPM).[1] This paradigm of NPM emerged on the heels of the movements of re-inventing government (1992) and good governance (1992). The sub-title of the book *Re-inventing Government* is *How the Entrepreneurial Spirit is Transforming the Public Sector*. If we closely examine this sub-title of book by David Osborne and Ted Gaebler, it would be evident that both these scholars were 'describing' what was already evident on the administrative scene. Hence, they were not essentially prescriptive but primarily descriptive while highlighting the presence of entrepreneurial governments. Truly, the movement of managerializing the government had started even before this monumental volume was published. Writings of these and other scholars had already appeared in 1980s (and even earlier) which highlighted the need for adopting, in an effective manner, sound management practices in government systems. One is reminded of what was happening about nine decades ago when Taft Committee was appointed to transplant Taylorism into the government system. Little wonder, certain scholars have branded NPM as neo-Taylorism. Even if we avoid a debate on a neologism like 'neo-Taylorism', it must be contended that public administrative organizations have liberally borrowed, models and modes from its more vibrant sister discipline – management.

A historical perspective would reveal that bureaucracies throughout the world have rarely responded effectively to environmental challenges on their own. They have generally lagged behind the times. In 1968 itself, when Dwight Waldo was organizing the first Minnowbrook Conference, Peter Drucker had come out with his perceptive volume, *The Age of Discontinuity* which made a prescient analysis of the incompetence of bureaucratic government. One can even see this exasperation with strait jacketed bureaucratic system in the writings of Harold Laski, Warren Bennis, Robert Reich, Tom Peters and Alvin Toffler and others.

And it is ironical that remedies to bureaucratic ailments have been offered more by scholars of management than by the wise men of public administration. But, what goes to the credit of public administration scholars is their alacrity and competence to imbibe and incorporate the pertinent and the precious from any other discipline and mould it as per their own intrinsic agenda and ambience. NPM is only one such manifestation of this resilience of public administration.

Essential Premises

The Organization for Economic Cooperation and Development (OECD) believes that through NPM, public sector is being made more managerial. The introduction of a more contractual, participative and discretionary style of relationship between levels of hierarchy, between control agency and operating units, and between producing unit, be they public or private. Further, the OECD avers that most countries are following two broad avenues to improve production and delivery of goods in services in public organizations. These two avenues are:

1. Raise the production performance of public organizations (to) improve the management of human resources including staff, development, recruitment of qualified

talent and pay-for-performance; involve staff more in decision-making and management; relax administrative controls while imposing strict performance targets; use information technology; improve feedback from clients and stress service quality; bring supply and demand decisions together (e.g., through charging users).[2]

2. Make greater use of the private sector (to) promote a dependable, efficient, competitive and open public procurement system for contracting out production of publicly provided goods and services and contracting in intermediate goods and services; and, end monopoly or other protection for suppliers.[3]

In sum, the OECD view on NPM involves the following aspects of administrative management:

- Improving human resource including performance pay.
- Participation of staff in the various stages of decision-making, relaxing control and regulations, yet prescribing and ensuring the achievement of performance targets.
- Using information technology to an optimum level in order to make Management Information System (MIS) more effective and enrich policy and decisional systems.
- Providing efficient services to clients and treating them as customers and even as members of the organization.
- Prescribing user charges for services in order to make the customers as more integral part of the public sector management.
- Contracting out services as a part of the privatization plan.
- Deregulation of monopolies and deconcentration of economic power among various organizations.

There has been a plethora of literature of NPM and one finds in the myriad writings certain common concerns and foci. Briefly, the most common attributes of NPM are:

- Focus on outputs, with greater stress on results rather than procedures.

- Strengthening professional management.
- Ensuring high standards and measures of performance.
- Greater emphasis on output controls.
- Increasing decentralization of business decisional power.
- Greater accent in the public sector on adoption of private sector style of management practices, discipline and parsimony.
- Ensuring accountability, progressive leadership and greater understanding between political leadership and the public.
- Added responsibility of managers for results.
- Gradual decrease in the size of government.

Over the years, there has been one important shift in the thinking of NPM. In the early stage of entrepreneurial government, there was stress on de-governmentalization and privatization which was sometimes called downsizing or rightsizing. The government was expected to be lean and mean but now once again, it has been recognized that the imperatives and inevitability of government's role and responsibility as a crucial facet of national life cannot be undermined. For developing countries particularly, the role of government in engineering socio-economic change and bringing about goal-directed progressive multidimensional development is likely to remain supreme. Therefore, the contemporary emphasis is not on less government but on *better* government. This is where the value of sound managerial practices has permeated the field of public administration.

Continuity of a Tradition

A question arises as to why the scholars of public administration have not resisted the 'onslaught' of a NPM on their discipline. Perhaps it is primarily because of the fact that howsoever new-fangled NPM might appear to be, it has its organic linkages with 'old' public administration. Accordingly, one can surmise that traditional administrative and managerial theories which emphasized efficiency, effectiveness and economy have assumed a new form as integral components of NPM. The difference, of course, lies in the goals of the administrative systems in two divergent settings, but then NPM is not so much concerned with the goals of public administration, as with the strategies to achieve them. In this context, it ought to be appreciated that while the foremost concerns of New Public Administration (NPA) has been with the goals, values and the spirit of public administration, NPM, on the other hand, is principally interested in the structure and style of public administration. There are certain elements of NPM that are perceivable in NPA and vice versa. Essentially, both are complementary to each other.

As we move towards the future we are likely to witness two parallel administrative realities. The first, anchored in NPM, would be more germane to the milieu in developed nations where the government is emerging as a facilitator and moderator of goal-directed change. The other reality will be more reflective of the enterprise of change in developing nations where the government's responsibility and role in tackling poverty and backwardness will remain prominent and legitimate for many more years to come. In a country like India, the traditional public administration focusing on organizational restructuring and managerial efficiency will continue to be ensconced on a pedestal of time-tested authenticity. And, besides, the principal values and concerns of NPA as well as NPM would also continue to perennially re-energize the discipline as well as the profession of public administration. Thus, in the foreseeable future, public administration is destined to flourish in a poly-paradigmatic environment facilitating its multifaceted growth.[4]

Notes

1. See for a perceptive analysis of the theme, Hughes, *Public Management and Administration*; and Halachami and Bouckaert (eds.), *The Enduring Challenges in Public Management*. For a compar-

ative perspective, see Christopher Pollitt and Geert Bouckaert, *Public Management Reform: A Comparative Analysis* (New York: Oxford, 2000). Also see, L.K. Kaboolian, "The New Public Management: Challenging the Boundaries of Management vs. Administration Debate", *Public, Administrative Review*, Vol. 58, No. 3 (1998), pp. 189-193; and D.G. Mathiasen, "The New Public Management and its Critics", *International Public Management Journal*, Vol. 2, No. 1 (1999), pp. 90-111.

2. Hughes, *Public Management and Administration*, p. 67.
3. Ibid., p. 68.
4. For a glimpse of the multifaceted character of public administration, see Bidyut Chakrabarty and Mohit Bhattacharya (eds), *Public Administration: A Reader* (New Delhi: Oxford, 2003). Also see Ramesh K. Arora. (ed.), *Public Administration: Fresh Perspectives* (Jaipur: Aalekh, 2004).

Section II

THINKERS AND THEIR THOUGHTS

7 Utility of Max Weber's Concept of Ideal-type Bureaucracy in Public Administration

T.K. Jain

There are certain common qualities which are shared by a set of objects, events, and ideas, and, while on the other hand, they differ in other characteristics. A concept consists of a structure of these common qualities which are related to each other. Therefore, concepts may differ in respect to a particular aspect because concepts "belong to particular persons".[1] Broadly speaking, there are three kinds of concepts. There are concepts which are abstract and are not directly observable in the real world. There are concepts which are directly observable in the real world. Graham calls the former as analytic concepts and the latter as synthetic concepts.[2] Somewhere between the analytic concepts and the synthetic concepts lie the 'ideal-type' concepts.

The purpose of constructing ideal-type concepts is to make one's analytical framework as clear as possible. The ideal-type concepts involve the selection of those possible variables which are directly observable in the real world as well as those which could be utilized to assess a particular problem. The very term of 'ideal-type' is an indication of the fact that an abstraction as well as real process have been applied.

Weber's Concept of 'Ideal-type' Bureaucracy

Weber's ideal type bureaucracy is a concept which has certain empirical elements and into which is weaved a precise and consistent logical form. This logical form, in its purity, may not be found in concrete reality.

In his ideal type constructs, weber classified authority on the basis of its legitimacy. He envisaged three types of authorities which exist in different organizations. They are:

Traditional Authority: The subjects in traditional authority accept the authority of the superiors as justified on the grounds that this is the way in which the organization is always run.

Charismatic Authority: Charismatic authority is usually related to individual leadership. The relationship takes the form of a leader and disciple where disciples are expected to accept his authority because they are 'awed' by it.

Legal-rational Authority: Legal-rational authority is based on valid rules that is where rules are applied in accordance with ascertainable principles for all members of the corporate group.

Weber termed the administrative staff needed for implementing valid rules and which is appropriate for legal rational authority as bureaucracy. On the one hand, bureaucracy contains empirical elements which were formulated in an inductive way; i.e., by observing certain characteristics of concrete organizations, while on the other hand, bureaucracy contains assumptions which were derived from the alleged ideal meaning of such structures, for example, the rational basis of decision-making in an organization.

Weber assigned certain interrelated characteristics to the concept of bureaucracy. According to Weber, bureaucracy defines a relation between legally selected or nominated authorities and their subordinate officials. This relationship is characterized by certain defined rights and duties which are prescribed by written regulations. According to Weber, the prescribed written regulation also state the authority relations between positions which are appointed or legally ordered. The appointments and promotions are made on contractual basis and are regulated accordingly. Monetary salaries are paid for the services rendered. In Weber's opinion, a strict separation of office and incumbent must be observed in the sense that the official does not own the means of administration and cannot appropriate the position, A government administration so defined must be understood as part of legal order that is sustained by common belief in its legitimacy. The legal order is reflected in written regulations, such as enacted laws, administrative laws, court precedents, etc., which govern the employment of officials and guide their administrative behaviour.

From the above discussion, three elements of Weber's concept of bureaucracy may be observed.

1. Weber's emphasis was on the belief in legitimacy on the foundation of administrative conduct which already precludes an interpretation of organizational behaviour in terms of specific ends.
2. Weber's emphasis was on orientation toward abstract norms as an integral part of rule of law as a fundamental characteristic of bureaucracy. Weber hypothesized that organizational analysis can be related to the study of bureaucracy if it recognizes not only informal relations in a hierarchical organization but also continues to offset their effects on the organization or to subject these relations to norms developed for this purpose.
3. The defining characteristics of bureaucracy, as suggested by Weber, have one aspect in common, namely the attempt to safeguard the officials from all effects of the society that might infringe on the possibility of effective and efficient implementation of policies.

Thus it can be stated that Weber saw bureaucracy as a concept where an organization is engaged continuously in pursuing the organizational goals, objectives through coordinated effort within the defined and explicit boundaries.

Utility of Weber's Concept of Ideal-type Bureaucracy

Weber has been severely criticized for his concept of ideal-type bureaucracy, However, most of these criticisms are irrelevant either because the critics assume that the ideal-type has the same logical status as of a simple classificatory type, or simply as an empirical model.

Weber's concept of bureaucracy is of great utility in the study of organizations, more so of public organizations than in business organizations, because this concept identified the characteristics that are shared by most of the bureaucracies. Much of the misunderstanding stems out from the failure to relate the type of administrative staff and organization to the appropriate form of authority. Weber was not of the view that the kind of administrative staff one might expect to find in a given political system would vary with the form of legitimate authority claimed and accepted in that society. It may be pointed out that he was of the view that the kind of legitimacy which is claimed, the type of obedience expected from the subordinates, the kind of administrative staff developed to guarantee it and the mode of existing authority, will differ fundamentally from one organization to another. Thus, Weber's concept of bureaucracy can be termed as a 'Universal Concept'. Despite the fact that Weber emphasized the inductive character,[3] the general character of a class or group are clearly visible in the concept of bureaucracy.

For the purpose of testing the utility of a concept in social sciences, the following two conditions may be enquired into:

1. The first condition for testing the utility of a concept is to see whether or not the concept has and includes a careful referent to specific empiricism. This requirement indicates that the concept must relate itself to something in the real world which has been specified by defining characteristics. Definitions are not made in vacuum, on the contrary, they are constructed and reconstructed in the light of established knowledge and perspective theory.

This condition is adequately fulfilled in Weber's concept of ideal-type bureaucracy, as Weber tried to identify the administrative characteristics of a certain kind of organization. Thus, he was not obliged to use all or even the most important organizational aspects in so far as these aspects existed in other types of organizations as well.

2. The second condition requires that the concept has theoretical significance, that is, each definition of a concept can be used in meaningful statements about the real worlds.

Weber has carefully explained the use of pure ideal type authorities both on empirical and analytical grounds. Though the absence of real counterparts did not invalidate their use for purposes of analysis, it led Weber to construct the various forms of authority and administrative staff in such a way that they contained elements of several ideal types.

Weber claimed that in the three claimed grounds of legitimacy, the legal-rational was inherently much weaker than either the charismatic authority or traditional authority. Thus, Weberian concept of ideal-type bureaucracy has a definite empirical aspect which helps in identifying, classifying, and understanding existing organizations. Consequently, Weberian concept of bureaucracy has proved highly useful in empirical analysis of organizations and has a well recognized influence on contemporary organization theory.

The Weberian concept of ideal-type bureaucracy has significant relevance and importance in the field of public administration. According to Weber, public administration is expected to maintain legitimacy of the state as the social system with the monopoly on the claim to the legitimate exercise of physical force.[4] This conceptualization of public administration is much richer than a politics-administration dichotomy or the idea of public administration as another political process or simply the indentification of public administration with government administration.

Given this field of public administration, i.e., to maintain legitimacy of the state as the social system, with the monopoly on the claim to the legitimate exercise of physical force, the question arises as to what kind or kinds of bureaucracy(ies) would be appropriate to implement the policy. It seems that Weberian concept of ideal-type bureaucracy is the answer. At the time Weber wrote, one of the most important measures of personal responsibility was how long one had worked for an organization: movement from one organization to another was considered as a mark of irresponsibility. Though this pattern has changed, the change has primarily been in the Western world, particularly in the USA, where as in the countries of Asia, Africa, Latin America and in various European countries like the UK and France, the Weberian measure of personal responsibility not only exists but is considered very important.

The second factor, which is persistent in Western countries, is the increased degree of mobility. Under the circumstances, an individual in an organization has to deal with persons of different cultural backgrounds and different values. In the earlier part of the twentieth century, an individual began his career in an area, raised his family, established his personal relationship and community image, and died in the same town. The Weberian concept of bureaucracy assumes that an individual enters the organization for the rest of his career and reaches the highest position of authority in due course of time. Though this value system has substantially changed, the Weberian concept has not lost its validity even if mobility of certain class of men, in a certain part of the world, has increased. There are organizations where people have the outlook as envisaged by Weberian concept of bureaucracy.

Conclusion

Thus, it may be said that Max Weber developed his concepts in terms of the meaning that individuals attribute to their actions. The ideal-type concepts bring together certain relationships and events into a complex which is conceived as an internally consistent system. Though this construct in itself is Utopian, it has been arrived at by analytical accentuation of certain elements or reality. One of the major purposes of constructing the ideal-type concept of bureaucracy was to challenge the assertion that human affairs and behaviour could be studied only historically and that each genetic was unique by showing that generalized theoretical categories are essential to prove casual relationships in the human and cultural field as they are in natural service.

It must be understood clearly that Weber's ideal-type concepts should not be treated as labels to be applied to social-phenomena, but as concepts on which to base programmes of research. Weber conceived two parts and purposes of his ideal types: (1) construction of ideal-type on the basis of the subject under comparative, historical evidence; and (2) analysis of the subject under investigation in terms of its derivation from or approximate of these concepts. Martindale observes that Weber does not so much compare ideal-type to real phenomena, in order to establish and investigate their discrepancy rather he uses the ideal-type as a tool for the historical comparison of two or more real situations.[5]

Thus, it can be stated that Weber's concept of ideal-type bureaucracy has immense utility for the field of public administration and more so for comparative public administration.

Notes

1. Abraham Kaplan, *The Conduct of Inquiry* (Scranton: Chandler Publishing House, 1964) p. 49.
2. George J. Graham, *Methodological Foundations of Political Analysis* (Toronto: Xerox College Publishing, 1971), pp. 49-50.
3. Kaplan, op. cit., p. 83.
4. Larry Kirkhart, "Towards Theory of Public Administration," in *Toward a New Public Administration: The Minnowbrook Perspective,* by Frank Marine (ed.) (Scranton: Chandler Publishing House, 1971), pp. 155-156.
5. D. Martindale, "Sociological Theory and the Ideal Type," in *Symposium on Sociological Theory*, by L. Gross (ed.), 1959, p. 88.

8 Administration: Thoughts of Urwick and Gullick

R.M. Khandelwal and Pushplata Khandelwal

In the 19th century, due to the industrial revolution, many attempts were made by number of scholars to develop certain principles of industrial organization to meet the requirements of modern industry. Among such attempts mention may be made of the works of Tylor, Max Weber, Henery Fayol, Gullick and Urwick.[1] They developed their theories keeping in view the organizational efficiency.

At the time of industrial revolution there was a need to find out certain principles in order to get more and more efficiency in Industrial organization, therefore most of the scholars paid their attention in this direction.

Urwick and Gullick have been influenced by the machine model of man developed by Tylor. The idea of Henery Fayol and his studies in industrial management also influenced the thinking of these two authors to a great extent.

Deriving inspiration mainly from the works of Tylor and Fayol, the two thinkers have developed the classical theory of organization which is also known as the administrative management theory. They believed it to be possible to develop a science of administration based on principles.

Urwick: Background, Orientation and Writings

Lyndall F. Urwick was born in Britain in 1891 and had his education at the Oxford University. He served as Professor in the University of New South Wales. Urwick, a Lt. Col., during the First World War in the British Army, was associated with a number of International Management Associations, such as the International Management Institute, Geneva, the International Committee of Scientific Management, the Committee on Education for Management, and the American Management Association. He was considered to be an outstanding consultant on industrial management.

Urwick has authored, co-authored and edited a number of significant books and papers. Following are his major publications:

Books

1. *Papers on the Science of Administration.*
2. *The Elements of Administration.*
3. *The Making of Scientific Management.*
4. *A Short Survey of Industrial Management.*
5. *A Golden Book on Management.*

Papers

1. "Principles of Direction and Control" in John Lee's *Dictionary of Industrial Management* (1927).
2. "Scientific Principles and Organization" in *American Management Association* (1938).
3. "Notes on the Theory of Organization" in *American Management Association* (1952).

Gullick: Background, Orientation and Writings

Luther H. Gullick was born in Osaka, Japan in the year 1892. He obtained Ph.D. in 1920 from Columbia University. He served on the National Defence Council during the First World War. From 1920, for about 40 years, he had been associated with the City Research Institute at New York. He also served as the administrator of New York City during 1954-56 and President of the Institute of Public Administration, New York during 1960-62. Gullick not only served as a Professor in several universities but also a consultant in administration in several countries. He was also a member of the President's Committee on Administrative Management.

He has several books and research articles to his credit. Important among them are:

1. *Administrative Reflections on World War II.*
2. *Metropolitan Problems and American Ideas.*
3. *Modern Management for the City of New York.*

Both Urwick and Gullick had rich experience in the working of not only the civil services but also military organizations and industrial undertakings. It is because of this, we find, continued references to discipline and efficiency in their writings. Though they borrowed certain concepts like line and staff from the military organization.

Contribution of Urwick

Recognizing that the gap between the physical and the social sciences caused the science of management to remain imprecise, Urwick undertook in his books to demonstrate that the body of knowledge about management is sufficiently large to make it a more scientific, more unified field than was commonly supposed. To do this he chose the works of several leading proponents of management such as Fayol, Tylor, Follet and Mooney and systematically analysed their thoughts, concepts and principles.

Various early authors who followed similar lines of inquiry and developed principles, were alike in many respects. Their principles and concepts were developed from different cultures, different countries and different professions. Urwick reasoned that a highly useful and reliable body of knowledge already existed and needed co-relation. This was his major contribution. He pointed out the existence of these similarities and how to corelate them. In the process of doing so, Urwick aided and interpreted the ideas of many of these writers, placing them in proper perspective, while at the same time imparting some of his own personal concepts.

Principles of Management

Urwick has discussed the broad range of principles of management. He propounded six principles of management which are as under:

1. Principles of Investigation.
2. Principles of Objective.
3. Principles of Organization.
4. Principles of Direction.
5. Principles of Experiment.
6. Principles of Control.[2]

Classical Principles of Organization

Urwick's also contributed in the field of organization. He listed 29 principles of management. These are also known as classical principles of organization. He used the terms 'management' and 'organization' interchangeably. Urwick's principles of organization are as follows:

1. Investigation
2. Forecasting
3. Planning
4. Appropriateness
5. Organization
6. Coordination
7. Order
8. Command
9. Control
10. The Coordinative Principle

11. Authority
12. Scalar Process
13. Assignment of Functions
14. Leadership
15. Delegation
16. Functional Definition
17. Determination
18. Applicative
19. Interpretative
20. General Interest
21. Centralization
22. Staffing
23. Spirit
24. Selection and Placement
25. Reward and Sanctions
26. Initiative
27. Enquiry
28. Discipline
29. Stability[3]

Urwick emphasized delegation-principle. In his opinion, authority and responsibility must be co-terminous, co-equal and well-defined. His principle of specialization suggests that so far as possible each individual should perform only one function. This gives rise to three kinds of formal relations: line, functional and staff. The functional relation suggests a department which is responsible for a specialized function. He suggested the use of staff subordinates in the work of coordination.

He has also expressed his views on committees, conflict, leadership, planning and selection of personnel. According to his views in committees, there is no responsibility or accountability for the individual. Committees are used as a shield against mistakes and to avoid personal responsibility and accountability because a divided responsibility is no man's responsibility. Urwick wrote that a committee is like a corporation wherein "neither a soul to be damned nor a body to be kicked".

He has also expressed his view on leadership. According to him, a leader should have four functions to his role:[4]

1. he embodies and represents the organization he serves;
2. he initiates thought and action;
3. he administers routine; and
4. he interprets to others the purpose and meaning of what is done.

Gullick's POSDCORB Formula

As a framework for his neutral principles, Gullick used Fayol's five elements of administration: planning, organization, command, coordination and control. In doing so, however, he separates forecasting from planning in order to give it special emphasis.

Gullick goes much farther in expanding Fayol's categories. What is the work of the Chief Executive? He asks.

His answer is POSDCORB, a verbal artifact made up of the initial letters of seven types of administrative activities:[5]

1. *Planning*, that is working out in broad outline the things that need to be done and the methods for doing them to accomplish the purpose set for the enterprise.
2. *Organizing*, that is the establishment of the formal structure of authority through which work subdivisions are arranged, defined and coordinated for the defined objectives.
3. *Staffing*, that is the whole personal function of bringing in and training the staff and maintaining favourable conditions of work.
4. *Directing*, that is the continuous task of making decisions and embodying them in specific and general orders and instructions and serving as the leader of the enterprise.
5. *Coordinating*, that is the all important duty of interrelating the various parts of the work.

6. *Reporting*, that is keeping those to whom the executive is responsible informed as to what is going on, which thus includes keeping himself and his subordinates informed through records, research and inspection.
7. *Budgeting*, with all that goes with budgeting in the form of fiscal planning, accounting and control.

In this list of seven activities, planning, organizing, and coordinating are taken over from Fayol. Fayol's command appears under the heading of direction. His control is covered in part by budgeting and reporting.

Gullick's Principles of Organization

Gullick enumerates ten principles of organization. In working out of these principles Gullick was very much influenced by Fayol's fourteen basic elements of administration. The principles are:[6]

1. Division of Work or Specialization
2. Bases of Departmental Organizations
3. Coordination through Hierarchy
4. Deliberate Coordination
5. Coordination through Committee
6. Decentralization
7. Unity of Command
8. Staff Line
9. Delegation
10. Span of Control

Among the ten principles of organization, Gullick lays special emphasis on division of work.

Combined Contribution of Gullick and Urwick

Despite their interest in dealing with administration as a whole, most of the Gullick-Urwick principles deal with the structure of formal organization.

There are following eight most widely popularized principles:

Fitting People to Structure

Urwick defined organization in his book *Elements of Administration* as "determining what activities are necessary to any purpose or plan and arranging them in groups which may be assigned to individuals". Whatever he says in this principle is that every effort must be made to find or fit people to the structure.

One Top Executive

Urwick warns against the use of committees for purpose of administration. He expresses his views in the Report of the U. S. President's Committee on Administrative Management.

Unity of Command

Gullick viewed that a man cannot serve two masters. Confusion, inefficiency and irresponsibility may arise from the violation of this principle.[7]

Staff: Special and General

Gullick and Urwick formulated this principle during the period when it became clear that higher executives needed the help of larger number of experts and specialists. This raised a problem of relation between the specialists and line officials.

Though this concept was taken from military organization but Gullick dealt with this problem relating to staff and line:

> Gullick insists, the task of staff expert is to devote their time exclusively to the knowing, thinking and playing functions. They must not be given administrative authority and responsibility. Second problem was relating to executive difficulty in supervising a large number of subordinates including special staff experts.

Their answer to this problem is to provide help through 'general staff' as distinguished from 'special staff'.

The Basis of Subdivisions

According to Urwick and Gullick, in assigning functions to groups of people, the first principle is homogeneity. In the simplest of all cases this homogeneity may be based on the identity or similarity of four factors

(i) the purposes they serve
(ii) the processes they use
(iii) the person or things they deal with
(iv) the place where they work

Delegation

Urwick maintains that lack of the courage to delegate properly and of knowledge how to do it is one of the most general causes of failure in organization.

Matching Responsibility with Authority

While Fayol emphasized the need to promote a sense of responsibility, Urwick deals with both sides of the authority – responsibility and relationship under this principle. It is not enough to hold people accountable for certain activities. It is also essential to delegate to them the necessary authority to discharge that responsibility.

Span on Control

According to Urwick "no supervisor can supervise directly the work of more than five, or at the most, six subordinates whose work interlocks". This is the administrative counterpart of psychological conception of 'Span of Attention'.

Gullick identified various factors that may influence the optimum span, particularly the capacity of an individual executive, the nature of work performed, the stability of an organization and the geographical factors.

Limitations of Ideas

1. Herbert Simon criticized and pointed out some limitations of the classical principles of organization and management including the ideas of Urwick and Gullick. He said that these are the proverbs of administration. Almost every principle is acceptable – contradictory principle.[8]

According to Simon, if unity of command, in Gullick's sense is observed, the decisions of a person at any point in the administrative hierarchy are subject to influence through only one channel of authority, and if his decisions are of a kind that require expertise in more than one field of knowledge then advisory and informational services must be relied upon to supply those premises which lie in a field not recognized by the mode of specialization in the organization. For example, if an accountant in a school department is subordinate to an educator, and if unity of command is observed then the finance department cannot issue direct instruction to him regarding the technical, accounting aspects of his work. His conclusion is that unity of command in the Gullick's sense, has never existed in any administrative organization.

Simon suggests that in case of two authoritative command conflicts, there should be a single determinate person whom the subordinate is expected to obey.[9]

So far as principle of the basis of subdivisions of Urwick and Gullick is concerned, he criticized that there are fundamental ambiguities in the meaning of the key terms – 'purpose', 'process', 'clientele' and 'place'.

He further expresses his view that this ambiguity is easily illustrated for the case of an administrative organization. A health department conceived as a unit whose task is to care for the health of the community is a purpose organization; the same department works as a unit which makes use of the medical arts to carry on its works is a process organization.

Another contradictory situation relates to the principle of span of control. One principle asserts that administrative efficiency is increased by keeping the levels of organization to the minimum. But when levels are reduced the span of control increases resulting in the violation of another important principle.

2. Another limitation in the writing of these classical thinkers is the importance they attached to the structure of administration while almost neglecting the role of men in the organization. As Urwick remarks that "it is impossible for humanity to advance its knowledge of organization unless the factor on structure is isolated from other consideration".
3. Principles of Gulick and Urwick were also criticized by L. D. White.[10] He says that the terms of line, staff and auxiliary agencies, hierarchy, authority, centralization, etc., are useful terms for describing or classifying administrative situations, they are no more, they provide no guidance as to whether a given system more or less should be highly centralized, nor as to whether auxiliary agencies should be given more or a few duties. These are not rules, they suggest only working rules of conduct.
4. Some authors like Claude S. George[11] feel that Urwick is not an innovator in the field of management in the sense that Fayol and others were. He has made a contribution, however, by his timely consolidation of the managerial principles developed by others. It sometimes happens that men who express the right theory at the right time make a greater contribution than the pioneer whose ideas were disregarded because they were decades ahead of their time. This is how Urwick has served the management.
5. Gullick and Urwick showed concern only for the formal organization to the total neglect of the informal organizational processes. It is a matter of common knowledge that organizations do not conform to the formal model all the time.

6. Simon and March pointed out important limitations to the classical administrative science (including the ideas of Gullick and Urwick). These are as follow:[12]

   First, relates to the improper assumptions.

   Secondly, phenomenon of programme evaluation receives little attention.

   Lastly, there is little appreciation of the role of intra-organizational conflict of interests in defining limits or organizational behaviour.

7. Lastly, as pointed out by V. Subramaniam[13] that classical theorists only deal with the problems of management in the organization and not the other operational problems that involves the other levels of management.

Relevances of Thoughts

1. Though POSDCORB formula has become out of date or some authors feel that it is an incomplete formula but POSDCORB served as a convenient starting point for innumerable writers interested in dealing with different aspects of administration or to use a term which soon came into wide use, with different administrative processes. Many writers on public or business administration took this list and through additions, subtractions and amendments, adopted it to meet their needs.
2. In spite of criticism from various quarters the classical administrative theory stands out prominently in the literature on administration even today. No textbook on administration is without a discussion of the principles of organization and the ideas of Gullick and Urwick.
3. There are common elements between the classical theorist and the works of several contemporary writers on administration. The commonness of approach relate to an interest in the structure, administrative economy, and efficiency, settlement of conflict, delegation of authority and decentralization.

Notes

1. For details see, Gullick, "Organizational Behaviour".
2. Lyndall F. Urwick, "Principles of Direction and Control".
3. Lyndall F. Urwick, *The Elements of Administration.*
4. Ibid.
5. Luther Gullick and Lyndal Urwick, eds., *Papers on the Science of Administration* (New York, 1937).
6. Ibid.
7. Luther Gullick, "Notes on the Theory of Organization".
8. Herbert Simon, *Administrative Behaviour.*
9. Ibid.
10. L.D. White, *An Introduction to the Study of Administration.*
11. Claude S. George, *The History of Management Thought.*
12. Simon and March, "Classical Organization Theory and its Criticism", *Public Administration Review*, 966.
13. V. Subramaniam, "The Classical Organization Theory and its Critics", *Public Administration Review*, 966.

9 Administrative Thought of Chester Barnard

Purushottam Nagar

Chester Barnard, who was probably the greatest synthesizer of the structural and the human relations' schools of administration, will always be remembered as one of those administrative theorists who changed the course of modern administrative thought. Barnard's profound understanding of the nuances of administrative behaviour and his empirical observations of the organizational dynamics vested in him a unique ability to interpret the patterns of human behaviour in administration. His monumental work, *The Functions of the Executive* (1938) still remains one of the major classics on administration. Although Barnard published another work of considerable significance, *Organization and Management* in 1948, it is the former study which brought its author to the forefront of scholarship in the fields of public as well as business administration. Barnard's major thrust in the book was to set forth a theory of cooperation and organization and to present an analysis of the executive process.

Barnard underlined the importance of cooperation in the organizational systems and highlighted the fact that a formal organization is a system of cooperation which is conscious, deliberate and purposeful. He observed that an organization is an open natural system and its effective functioning depends upon the cooperative relationship among its various parts. In fact Barnard defined efficiency in terms of provision of satisfaction which is sufficient to, ensure that cooperative efforts are forthcoming.

A cooperative system has certain inherent characteristics which also function as the requisite of the system. These elements are: a common impersonal organizational purpose, satisfaction of the motives of the individual working in the organization, and an effective process of communication.

It may be noted that in Barnard's view, a formal organization should involve a synthesis of three elements: these relate to a common objective, a communication network and a willingness on the part of individuals working in the organization to cooperate with each other for achieving the larger common objective. Thus, Barnard's organizational model was a goal-oriented model which underscored a commonality of purpose which, in turn, could act as a uniting force for the members of the organization. Barnard held that an important dimension of goal legitimacy is the acceptance of that goal by the people involved. This would create a favourable climate for an organization to operate. Certainly, he recognized the importance of personal objectives and goals and envisaged the impact of these objectives on the organizational-goal structure.

It is clear from Barnard's analysis that he advocated the surrender of narrow personal objectives for the sake of broader organizational goals. However, he realized that in order to get maximum cooperation from individuals in an organization, a system of incentives must be prevalent in the organization. Only through a rational system of incentives would the individuals be willing to continue in the organization, as also to contribute to the growth of the organization.

An important mechanism through which various individuals working in the organization can form a cooperative network is a sound communication network with a system of adequate feedback. The information about the goals, objectives, policies and programmes of organization should reach all those who are part of the organizational system, and those who have linkage with the system and its clientele. In a small organization, communication is direct and face-to-face while in a large organization it is complex and indirect.

Barnard underscored the fact that the channels of communication must be clearly defined, must be known to all, be direct and short, and be as complete as possible. He also observed that the managers working in the communication system should have adequate competence and that every communication should have behind it necessary sanction of the competent authority.

Barnard defined authority in terms of its acceptance by the receiver of a command. The propensity of greater acceptability of a command is likely to increase in case a command is communicated in a language that is intelligible and the command is consistent with the objectives of the organization and the individual values of the receivers of the command, and is feasible in its application. Thus, Barnard entrusted great responsibility on the shoulders of the givers of the command, who before issuing any order should take into account the possible reaction that it would evoke with the receivers of the command.

Barnard's concept of responsibility was also based on a unique interpretation. He defined responsibility as the power of a particular code of morals to control the conduct of the individual in the presence of strong, contrary desires or impulses. Certainly he was aware of the legal, technical, professional and other codes that impinge upon the responsibility of an executive, but in his view, the most important role is played by the moral codes of an individual. These codes interact with the set of legal, technical and professional codes and this interaction results into a new set of composite codes which determine the nature of the organization.

Barnard laid great stress on the significance of balancing the positive and negative motivations of the individuals working in the organization. He defined positive motivations in terms of inducements provided by the organization in the form of wages and other incentives. On the other hand, negative motivation refer to the contributions made by the participants in the organization. Barnard observed that a member of an organization would generally remain in the organization only if the inducements that he receives are greater than the contributions that he makes to the organization. This balance between what is given and what is taken will have to be interpreted in terms of an individual's own preferences, attitudes and outlook. Thus, a manager in an organization should try to bring about greater effectiveness in the organizational functioning by satisfying to the greatest possible extent the motivations of the members of the organization.

It is interesting to note that even before Herbert Simon had come out with his classical work, *Administrative Behaviour*, Barnard had underlined the importance of the mechanism of decision-making in the total organizational set-up. Essentially, an organization is a system of decision-making. Barnard opined that organizational decision-making is much more logical and rational than what is found in decisions made by individuals. In fact, major decisions relate to synthesizing means with ends in a manner wherein with minimum possible means, the stated objectives are accomplished and the ends are met. A decision-maker should analyse the organizational situation and try to identify those factors which are relatively more strategic and relevant to the organization. A systematic controlling of these factors can help in creating situations of rational decision-making.

Barnard, himself being a prominent business executive for a long time, concentrated upon the analysis of the functions of the executive, Briefly, he outlined three major functions of the executive, viz., maintaining the communication system, obtaining essential services from subordinates and formulating purposes and objectives of the organization at all levels. An executive can increase the effectiveness of organizational system by maintaining an informal climate in the organization so that there is absence of tension and interpersonal distrust in the system. An open system of communication can help in creating greater sense of participation among members in the total organizational dynamics. Further, Barnard observed that obtaining essential services from subordinates can be facilitated by a correct selection of staff and providing necessary inducements incentives, training and supervision to the staff as also by creating a climate of high morale in the organization.

An important dimension of Barnard's analysis relates to formal and informal organizations. He recognized that along with the formal organization, an informal organization also operates. This coexistence of the two levels of organization is an essential feature of almost all organizations in the present-day complex world. An informal organization deals with the relationships and communications that the formal structure is unable to handle effectively. Essentially, informal organization is the result of the interaction between the structure and the psychological forces and it establishes certain attitudes, customs, habits and institutions which have a significant bearing on the total organizational culture.

It is interesting to note that according to Barnard, formal and informal organizations are the cause and effect of each other and that both are considerably interdependent. An informal organization, according to Barnard, generally plays a positive role in the organization by creating favourable climate for interpersonal relationships.

Chester Barnard is still rated as among the most important pioneer of contemporary administrative thought. His contribution in the areas of decision-making, informal organizations, communication systems, motivations, authority, responsibility and administrative leadership has been immense. Being a top business executive, he himself could obtain empirical knowledge of the actual functioning of administration. But he was not content with that. He assiduously studied the theories of administration and management and tried to create a blend of the organizational principles and their applications. Rightly, therefore, he became a forerunner of behavioural revolution in administrative thought. His analysis is full of academic brilliance and managerial acumen. Barnard's place is reserved forever in the annals of administrative thought.

Abstracts From the 'Conclusion' of *The Functions of the Executive* by Chester Barnard

In closing this study I shall first state what at the present time seem to me to be the more important general conclusions which may be drawn from it; and then offer certain more personal observations on its significance as a whole. The conclusions to which I would especially invite attention follow:

1. Physical and biological factors are basic in cooperation; if these factors permit, then social factors are essential to secure it. Cooperation, thus, may be called the process of synthesizing in action three quite different orders of factors.
2. From the point of view of organization, which is the chief instrument in economic development, all capital, whether of improvements, or machines, tools and edifices, is always a part of the physical environment. The direct significance of capital is that it reduces the limitations imposed by the natural environment on cooperation.
3. All complex formal organizations grow from and consist of unit organizations, the inherent properties of which are the determining factors in the character of the complex.
4. The properties of unit formal organizations are determined by physical, biological, and social factors. The understanding of those factors and of the processes essential to conformation to them is the central method of the study of formal organization.

5. The major structure of any society of substantial size is its complex of formal organizations, rather than its institutions, customs, etc., which are abstractions chiefly constructed on observed uniformities in the concrete acts, including the verbalizations, of such organizations as well as of individuals.
6. Informal organizations are found within all formal organizations, the latter being essential to order and consistency, the former to vitality. These are mutually received phases of cooperation, and they are mutually dependent.
7. Disturbances of the equilibrium of cooperative systems have come from false ideologies, particularly on the part of those who are leaders or executives in formal organizations. The effect of these false notions is to vitiate the sense of experience when consciously dealing with problems of the theory of organization, and to reinforce personal predilection, prejudices, and interests, as destructive factors, in the guidance of organization practice.
8. In this way arise four principal errors: an oversimplification of the economy of organization life; a disregard of the fact and of the necessity of informal organization; an inversion of emphasis upon the objective and the subjective aspects of authority; and a confusion of morality with responsibility.
9. The essential process of adaptation in organizations is decisions, whereby the physical, biological, personal and social factors of the situation are selected for specific combination by violational action.
10. Error of decision must be large because of the unbalance due to the difference in the precision of perception as respects the physical, the biological, and the social environments. This is a general factor limiting successful cooperation.
11. Since any cooperative system contains physical, personal, and social factors, at least three secondary abstract systems of utilities, related to these factors respectively, are pertinent. To these must be added a primary system of utilities related to the whole organization. Each of these secondary systems comprises of the phenomena or factors

of the respective classes, together with the utilities attached to them by the organization.

12. All scientific knowledge is expressed in languages and symbolic systems. These are socially developed with meanings that are socially determined and all, 'finally' accepted observations of phenomena are cooperatively arrived at. Therefore, all sciences in the widest sense comprehend both social factors and others of different orders, depending upon their subject matter. Disregarding the social factors of science in the sense just stated, we find two kinds of abstract systems of knowledge other than those stated under 11, next above, as follows: (a) systems which relate exclusively, or substantially so, to one or the other order of factors (physical, biological, social), and (b) those which 'cut across' or comprehend two or more orders of factors.
13. An increasing degree of cooperation implies an increasing moral complexity. It is impossible for men to endure a high degree of moral complexity without commensurate technological proficiency.
14. The strategic factor in cooperation generally is leadership, which is the name for relatively high personal capacity for both technological attainments and moral complexity, combined with propensity for consistency in conformance to moral factors of the individual.
15. The strategic factor in the dynamic expression of leadership is moral creativeness, which precedes, but is in turn dependent upon, technological proficiency and the development of techniques in relation to it.
16. The strategic factor in social integration is the development and selection of leaders. The process is usually unbalanced by excessive emphasis either upon technological proficiency or upon moral status. In some ages moralities may have been cultivated in excess of the technological capacity to support them. In the present age the emphasis is upon technological proficiency which is not adequately guided by the necessities of the cooperative system as a whole.

10 Peter Drucker: The Father of Modern Management

Rakhi Pardasani

Recognized as the 'Father of Modern Management', Peter Drucker explains through his writings how the discipline of management has emerged and how it has changed through times and what its shape is going to be in the future. He states that thinkers came to know about the existence of management during World War I as at that time a large number of unskilled workers had to be made productive in practically no time and this was done by applying the principles of scientific management of Taylor. Since then, a good many principles of management were propounded and applied to various fields. With the allies winning the World War II, the field of management got prominence as their victory was attributed to effective management with the basic assumptions changing and giving rise to another set of assumptions. For example:

1. Previously, management was thought as business management only, but now it has become a distinguishing organ of all organizations, be they non-profit organizations or public enterprises or private units.

2. It was believed that there can be 'one right organization' based on strict hierarchical lines but time has taught us that organizations should be structured on the basis of tasks. Some high risk tasks require strict hierarchy, while others may require deliberation or team work.
3. Other assumption being there is "one right way to manage people". This assumption has undergone change with the emergence of a new class of workers called 'knowledge workers' as now our main concerns have shifted from how to manage the people to how to lead this new emerging force is they are masters in their fields and it is the job of management to make productive the specific strengths and knowledge of each individual and make the most out of them, which is a biggest challenge for it today.
4. It was considered that technologies and end uses are fixed and given, but today technologies criss-cross as any technological development may not be confined to that industry only and has tremendous impact on other industries as well. End uses cannot be taken as fixed as these can be multiple; for example, beer was previously packed in glass bottles only but now other options are also available such as plastic or metal cans.
5. It was assumed that the scope of management is legally and politically defined which does not hold true, as it is today decided operationally and economically.
6. The assumption that only the inside of organization is the domain of management has also gone obsolete as no organization can survive if it does not concentrate on results, i.e., what it is delivering to customers and for that the management should pay attention to the outside environment, i.e., the changing market conditions and the overall economy and should continuously innovate in order to withstand the competition.

Keeping in view the above changes, we will now elaborate on some of the basic ideas of Drucker.

What is Management?

Management, according to Drucker, is a 'liberal art'. Liberal, because it deals with the fundamentals of knowledge, self-knowledge, wisdom and leadership, and art, because it is concerned with the practice and application of this knowledge in achieving the desired results effectively. Management can be best understood by the tasks it has to perform. These are:

1. Establishing the specific purpose and mission of the institution, whether public or private. This being a very important task as institutions exist to fulfil a particular mission and so it should be well defined and clear. It differs for public and business enterprises and for non-profit organizations as business enterprises' main concern is to base their performance on economic basis or on profitability whereas non-profit organizations' main concern is to deliver best services to the customers. Drucker wants business enterprises to learn from non-profit organizations and base their mission on delivering better goods and services rather than concentrating on profits.
2. The other important task of management is to make worker effective and work productive. This task of management, according to Drucker, is unlikely to change with time and it should continuously work for making human strengths effective and human weaknesses irrelevant.
3. Every organization is part of the society and so management should look for the social impact the organization is having on the environment and fulfil its social responsibilities.

Purpose of Business

The basic purpose of business, according to Drucker, is to create the customer and for this it has to perform two main functions, viz., marketing and innovation.

Marketing is what customers want to buy? It is not based on what company wants to manufacture or sell but on the values of customer. It sells what customer values, Drucker defines innovation as the task of endowing human and material resources with new and greater wealth producing capacity. A business enterprise can exist only in an expanding economy and so business enterprises should innovate. Innovation can result in an improved or a new product, which may be costly but can help in making economy more productive. It differs from invention or research and development, in that it is not always technological but can be social, economic, political as well and takes into its ambit all activities and parts of business whether finance, marketing, manufacturing, etc.

The following things must be kept in mind while defining the purpose of business:

1. Objectives must be derived from
   (a) What the business is, i.e., considering who is the customer? where it is? and what it buys?
   (b) What our business will be? Say in few years when there will be new trends and other changes, e.g., changes in population.
   (c) What it should be? As with the changing times the present products will become obsolete and so the organizations should continuously innovate and straightforward the replacement of the present product with the new product.
2. Objectives must be operational so that the performance can be measured according to them.
3. There should be multiple objectives, say marketing objective, innovative objective, profitability objective, productivity objective, etc.
4. After framing objectives, the organizations should concentrate their resources on these objectives.

Management by Objectives

A strong proponent of management by objectives, Drucker does not consider management by drives a good option to put in the resources of organization. As, according to him, the changes brought about by these drives are temporary and these may also lead to unnecessary concentration on one phase or part of job leaving aside the important ones.

The objectives, according to Drucker, should be set by the managers themselves and they should continuously measure their performance against these. He suggests the use of 'manager's letters' for setting the objectives, which are filled by the managers and contain the list of the objectives they have set for themselves. What they think is expected of them? What are the objectives of their boss? What they expect their boss to be?

Every person working for the organization should have a detailed knowledge of its mission with the objectives they have to perform. Drucker has noticed an improvement in the overall performance of the workers if they know the purpose of the organization and how they are going to help the organization in achieving this with their contribution.

Drucker also believes in self-control rather than external control and warns the organizations against excessive use of reports and procedures; a lot of time is wasted in filling forms and making reports.

Management and Entrepreneurship

'Management' and 'entrepreneurship', according to Drucker, cannot be seen separately and are necessary for the success of organization as "not to know how to innovate is the single largest reason of failure of existing organization and not to know how to manage is the single largest reason of failure of new venture".

Drucker observes: "Entrepreneurship is neither a science nor an art. It is a practice. It has a knowledge base. Knowledge in entrepreneurship is a means to end. Indeed, what constitutes knowledge in practice is largely defined by the ends, that is, by practice".

Drucker has also suggested some entrepreneurship strategies to be adopted by the organizations. These are:

1. *Being Firstest with the Mostest:* It is all about creating something new and different and once it begins to produce results, the innovation has to be ready to mobilize resources massively or it will be just like creating a market for the competitor.
2. *Creative Imitation:* It exploits the success of others. The new product innovated lacks something. Creative imitation is just to imitate it and remove those lackings which can be providing additional features, segmentation of product or service or its proper positioning.
3. *Entrepreneur Judo:* It is all about cashing on what the big business enterprises fail to do. They may reject the invention altogether which they have not themselves introduced, they may concentrate on high profit market leaving the smaller customers, they may die for quality which may not be of value to all the customers, they try to maximize rather than optimize. Taking advantage of these bad habits small entrepreneurs can enter into their domain and can even dethrone them.
4. *Ecology Niche Strategy:* It aims at being so inconspicuous that no one is likely to compete. It makes practitioners immune to competition. This includes:
   (a) *Tollgate strategy:* The product should be so essential to process that risk of not using it be greater than the cost of product.
   (b) *Speciality-skill strategy:* It is all about developing a high skill at a very early stage. It should be both unique and different and one should constantly work for its improvement; indeed, it has to make itself obsolete.
   (c) *Speciality market strategy:* It aims at systematic analysis of a new trend, industry or market, developing a

specific innovation, contributing accordingly and continual work to improve the product or the service so that improvement once obtained will be contained.

Concept of Knowledge Worker

Management has made possible for the organizations to employ large number of knowledgeable people having specialization in their respective fields, and to get their services. This new class of workers is termed as 'knowledge workers' and so there are both manual and knowledge workers in the organization. In order to improve the overall performance of these knowledge workers, it is important for management to work for increasing the productivity of these knowledge workers as has been done in the past for manual workers. This, he suggests, can be done by:

1. asking "what is the task" in order to concentrate on that task only;
2. continuous innovation;
3. concentrating on quality rather than quantity as in case of manual workers quantity of product matters more and we put restraints on quality, i.e., the minimum quality standards we want but we cannot do the same in case of knowledge workers and they should increasingly work for improving their quality; and
4. treating them as assets and providing opportunities for their growth.

Besides knowledge workers, he talks of one more class, i.e., the technological class, which constitutes the knowledge workers doing the manual work as well, e.g., the surgeons.

Japanese Strategies

Greatly fascinated by the way Japanese have established themselves in the international market, Drucker cites various examples of their success in his writings. The factors, which have attributed to their success, are:

1. Japanese institutions are mission-driven. They start with a mission rather than with their own rewards and with what they have to make happen outside themselves, in the market place, to deserve a reward.
2. They are opportunistic, they continuously plan for every conceivable contingency so that they, can move with lightning speed wherever an opportunity exists.
3. Japanese companies are decentralized into powerful, autonomous company-wide functions, such as engineering, manufacturing and marketing. This makes easier to form company-wise teams to work on designs outside the existing product scope.
4. They adopt the strategy of organized abandonment. They do this by starting with a deadline for abandoning today's new product with three new products the day it was first sold. For this, they work on three parallel tracks:
   (a) First track is called 'Kaizen' which is organized work on improvement of the product with specific goals and deadlines, e.g., a 10 per cent reduction in cost within 15 months or 10 per cent improvement in reliability or 15 per cent increase in performance.
   (b) Second track being 'Leaping', i.e., developing a new and different product out of the old.
   (c) Third is 'Innovation'. Thus, they bring three replacements in practically no time.
5. Japanese are moving from Total Quality Management (TQM) to Zero Defects Approach. TQM is impossible to achieve and any lacking will result in overall product degradation. Zero Defects is the right approach, which can be achieved by the operators rather than the engineers as in case of TQM through the use of computer simulation.
6. 'Keiretsu' is a Japanese management concept in which the suppliers to an enterprise are tied together, by entering into contracts with their main customers for planning, product development, cost control and so on. Previously, the strategy was to gain control of all the suppliers, which

was not considered a better option and this led to increase use of 'keiretsu' by the big enterprises. Though, nowadays, this is also replaced by 'genuine partnerships'.

These are few Japanese strategies and the important ones which according to Drucker had lead to their success and which the western countries also should learn from them.

Leadership

Drucker rejects the traits or charismatic theories of leadership and is of the view that leadership is performance based. Leaders, according to him, should know what needs to be done, i.e., what is right for the organization?

The purpose and mission of the organization should be clear in their mind. They must set their objectives accordingly and they should also communicate those objectives to their subordinates as well, in order to gain their trust. They should take the responsibility of their decisions.

Leaders should know when to stop pouring resources into things that have achieved their purpose. They should know what they cannot do and should not try to do it, rather they should take the services of those who can do that job better than them. They should try to create human energies and human vision.

Drucker calls on the need to pay attention on character development now with help of churches and synagogues than on executive development which according to him is much talked of.

Commenting on how the organizations in future will look like, Drucker says: "In the coming future the organizations will face the crisis of retaining the employees (knowledge workers) in the organizations. As the promotion opportunities are less and everyone cannot be promoted, they should work on making their jobs challenging which can give them satisfaction and can help in retaining them".

Drucker sees more and more organizations going for joint ventures and alliances as they have now understood that to face the competition in market, they should associate with the best organizations in the industry as any one organization cannot gain excellence in all the fields. organizations will become inter-dependent, more market and customer driven in near future.

He suggests that in order to respond to the rapidly changing market, they must anticipate changes and then make assumptions. To be correct in their assumptions, they should also suppose that what will happen if the opposite were true.

Drucker continued to explore and interpret the social as well as managerial realities throughout his life. His profundity of ideas and vision will shape future generations of management technology and behaviour.

Section III

COMPARATIVE AND DEVELOPMENT DIMENSIONS

11 Development: A Contradictory Discipline in Social Sciences

S.L. Meena

There is no dearth of attempt on the part of scholars from different disciplines at defining 'development'[1] Consequently, development has to be defined variously. It has almost meant the figure of an elephant being defined by a blind man. Disciplinary bias has blinded the scholars and there is no wonder if 'development' is viewed as 'economic growth', 'modernization', 'nation building', 'social change' or 'simply a state of mind'. Almost every scholar before making an attempt to define development admits that there is an utter confusion prevailing about the meaning of 'development'. Yet, every scholar's attempt at defining 'development' in a new way only adds to the mist of confusion. Still, the content analysis of the various definitions does enable scholars to offer a commonly agreed view of development as an "action-oriented and goal-oriented system".[2] But this is too broad a view to have any semblance of reality. It almost makes development a mirage.

In this article, no fresh attempt is made at defining 'development', but an effort is being made at clearing some confusion by way of sifting the existing literature on the much used concept.

Confusion or mystery created by the word 'development', as said earlier, is echoed by many. To cite a few examples: To Fred W. Riggs, "development looks increasingly perplexing as it has become fashionable".[3] Ferrel Heady finds that the term raises "serious question about what is meant and what is intended and excluded... The meaning of development often is not precisely defined, and the very term itself has invidious implications".[4]

In taking stock of definitions on 'development', let us begin from the narrow and go towards the broader view of it, say from concept of 'development' to its macro dimensions. Since economists were the first to grapple with the task of defining 'development' and possibly the only social scientists who were able to agree on what, 'development' means in economics, the first narrow view of development can be taken as 'economic growth' or 'economic development'. One more reason for 'development' being treated in economic terms is that compared to social and political changes, economic changes are definitely more tangible, that changes in society that can be measured in quantifiable terms triumphed over the change that can only be felt or at best seen. But to blame economists alone for taking a very narrow view of 'development' will be unjust.

Political scientists in their attempt to define the concept of development have also suffered from the same fallacy. To take one example to drive the point home, Joseph LaPalombra considers development "as the capacity of political system to handle or manage changes in demands that confirm in over time".[5] Although he concedes the importance of other factors such as economic and social when he obscures that "there are, of course, other kinds of development that are of particular interests to economists, sociologists and the like",[6] his according primacy to the political dimension is revealed amply and clearly when he states:

> I assure that changes in the economic, social and psychological sectors may and probably do affect political change, but I do not

> consider that these phenomena are absolutely interdependent and much less than what emerges in the political sphere as abjectly dependent on what happens in other sectors of society. Indeed I assume that political development is in part a discreet or independent phenomenon which can and often has and does influence changes in other sectors.[7]

Probably LaPalombara is being sentimental. It is difficult to accept the premise of object or total dependence of political change on other changes. Moreover, to say that there is not any implicit dependence of political change on other changes is like taking an ostrich-like view of the problem. Through such narrow definitions, development is being crucified at the altar of fake differentiation of disciplines.

Let alone define, even to understand 'development', social scientists will have to acquire first and later see through the concept of social science; unfortunately, social science has come to mean a convenient category under which to place some sciences in order to distinguish them conveniently from other sciences like the physical and the natural sciences. Social science never acquired identifiable conceptual meaning and it brought some disciplines together only to fall apart within. We are all, to use the structural functional analogy, social scientists structurally but functionally only economists, sociologists, political scientists, public administrationists and the like.[8] Political and other changes in society may or may not be interdependent, but they certainly are interlinked or interlocked and therefore it is hard to tell most of the time which change is effect and which the cause.

There are also definitions of development which try to compound all types of changes into one. Saul M. Katz, for instance, observes:

> Development is a major social change from one state of national being to another more valued state. It involves a complex of mutually related economic, social and political changes. Economic changes sometimes seem more evident and generally

> lead themselves more readily to quantification, but they are only one aspect of a total process. Changes are the result of both previous history and current experience of the country and in turn, provide the basis for future changes.[9]

From Katz's definition, it is clear that development is not an exclusive change in one aspect of society, it is a change for better, and in effecting such changes continuity with the past stage is never broken. Development, thus, is an all-round, positive, gradual, and never ending change, The distinction that development, should not be treated merely as economic growth is also made by Cohn and Geiger when they advocate in most clear-cut terms not to treat the development as synonym of growth.

> The term 'development' is not used synonymously with growth. In the underdeveloped countries of Asia, Africa and Latin America, development requires social and cultural change as well as economic growth, that is, qualitative transformations must occur, concurrently with quantitative increases. There is in fact a reciprocal relation between the two, and neither process is likely to continue for long or go very far without the other. Hence development means change plus growth.[10]

Although by growth, Cohn and Geiger mean economic growth, they nevertheless help us locate one more characteristic of development, that is, development is a change of both qualitative and quantitative type and that the quantitative type of change is not the preserve of economics only. To explain this, let us take an example from Indian situation. If the non-observance of untouchability by caste Hindus is taken as an indicator of social change, this has to be measured both in terms of number (growth) and type (quality), that is, how many caste Hindus do not observe untouchability will tell us about development in terms of quantitative change and how far or to what extent untouchability is not observed, having pariahs as neighbours, dining with them, marrying with them, etc., will indicate the qualitative change. Thus, development in every sphere should mean not only quantitative changes but qualitative changes also.

Some do not agree with this proposition, for to them development and growth are distinct and quite separate phenomena. For instance, Fred W. Riggs does not consider quantitative changes as 'development'. He observes that "by development we refer to changes in the basic structural arrangements of society and economy not the degree to which these structures are productive or non-productive. The term 'growth' can be used for a different variable from development".[11] This is not convincing to put it simply, development can be a quantitative change, a qualitative change, and a combination of both qualitative and quantitative changes. Quantitative changes cannot be brushed aside because beneath, they are qualitative. After all, quantitative changes are nothing but qualitative changes which are given the dressing of gradation or numbers.

Placing of emphasis upon qualitative aspect of change, perhaps originated as the reaction to the early emphasis laid on quantifying development, as is evident from Milton Esman's definition of development:

> Development denotes a major social transformation, a change in system states, along with continuum from peasant and pastoral in industrial organization with assimilation and institutionalization of modern physical and social technology are crucial ingredients. These qualitative changes affect values, behaviour, social structure, economic organization and political process.[12]

Returning to Cohn and Geiger, what is objectionable in their definition is their presenting the need for social and cultural changes to underdeveloped countries. No doubt, the underdeveloped countries need more development and this is more so, in the economic sphere, as in the social and cultural terms, the developed countries have their own problems mainly created through unprecedented and unbalanced economic development and they surely require as much social and cultural development as developing countries need, if not more. If there are countries in the world which are paying heavy price for identifying 'development' purely in economic terms, they are the developed ones.

As 'development' is misconstrued to be chiefly economic or political or as it is presented as a panacea for all the ills of underdeveloped countries, it is also surrounded by yet another controversy, that is some consider development to be 'modernization', which in turn is considered as a synonym for 'westernization'. Ferrel Heady finds no distinction between development and modernization. He points out that 'development' and 'modernization' (or modernity) are related concepts that are widely but variously used to refer to major social transformation involving a complex of social, economic and political changes.[13] On the contrary, Bendix offers a clear-cut distinction between development and modernization and to him development means, to put it in formular form, industrialization + modernization. By industrialization, Bendix refers to economic changes brought about by a technology based on in – animated sources of power as well as on the continuous development of applied scientific research.[14] Modernization, as Bendix refers relates to all those social and political changes that accompanied industrialization. Among these are: urbanization, changes in occupational structure, social mobility, development of education as well as political changes from absolutist institutions to responsible and representative governments and from a laissez-faire to a modern welfare state. Thus, according to Bendix,[15] the term 'development' may be used when reference is made to related changes in both of these spheres'.[16] Development, therefore, is a combination of both techno-economic and the socio-political changes. Bendix's definition can be explained in the following form:

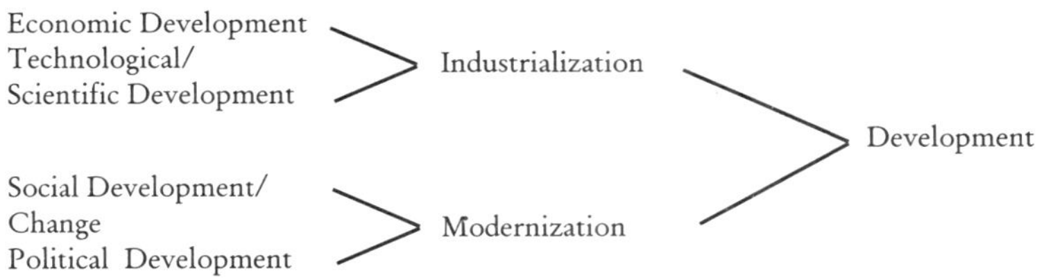

Of course, these changes are not taking place in isolation. There is a good deal of interchange and inter-effect. What then becomes a matter of prime importance is to treat development as an indicator to judge whether it is proper or improper, balanced or imbalanced development. If there is more industrialization but less modernization, it is low development. In the same way, the reverse will also indicate low development. The question is, do such imbalances order? Unfortunately, the history of 'development' is full of such imbalances and developed countries are not free from it. Alfred Diamante has shown the way of ranking countries on certain economic and political indicator that there are about 66 countries which are politically in 'developmental' stage but are economically either underdeveloped or very underdeveloped.[17] There are only 19 countries which are developed both politically and economically. One wonders whether even these countries will remain under the category of 'developed', if some indicators of social change are added to the list. This only goes to show that there are countries which are highly industrialized or highly modernized, but their status as 'developed' remains a doubtful question. Bendix helps us understand that, 'development' is not 'modernization' or 'industrialization' but an outcome of a balance between the two. It is the child of 'modernization' and 'industrialization'.

For distinguishing 'development' from 'westernization' we will turn to Bendix once again. He has very lucidly pointed out that whereas westernization can serve as a basis for 'development', every development need not be a prototype of 'westernization'. Bendix says:

> There is nothing inherently wrong about using the history of western societies as the basis of what we propose to mean by development as long as purely nominal character of this definition is understood. The history of industrial societies must certainly be one basis for our definitions in this field. Trouble arises only when it is assumed that these are 'real' definitions that development can mean only what it has come to mean in some western societies. Development is not necessarily, the adoption of western institutions.[18]

If we understand 'development' so far, it has come to mean:

(i) a change for better,
(ii) never ending change,
(iii) gradual change,
(iv) a combination of qualitative and quantitative change,
(v) change in all spheres – political, social, economic and administrative, and
(vi) not necessarily a copy of western countries.

Out of these, whereas item (i) to (iv) and item (vi) help clear many doubts about development, item (v) makes our understanding of 'development' more complex. If by 'development' we mean a combination of social, political and economic developments then we cannot be sure what development really is, unless we are clear about what economic, social and political mean.

A perusal of the current status of economic, social and political developments is offered below to indicate that so far except economic development, other developments are yet to acquire a clear-cut, unanimous, commonly agreed upon meanings.

Meaning of 'Development' in Social Science Disciplines

Disciplines	*Current status of development*	*What development generally means*[19]
Economics	No dispute over the meaning of development. Disagreement lies over the means of achieving it.	Economic productivity.
Political Science	No agreement over the concept of political development. Instead of achieving any consensus there is a tendency to desist from using the concept.[20]	Democratization, political capacity, or expanded governments.
Public Administration	The term 'administrative development' is recently coined by the famous term inventor, F.W. Riggs; it is yet to gain full currency and has so far met with indifference.	Bureaucratization, optimum efficiency, performance or capability to assume all burdens.
Sociology	The term social development' is almost discarded. Sociologists prefer the use of term 'social change' and view development more as natural process rather than as planned action.	Social change or social differentiation.

Viewing 'development' in terms of its social, economic and political dimensions, has not helped us understand it any better. However, it is useful to view development, in terms of the society as an entity.[21] Thus item (v) provisionally can be simplified to mean 'development' as a social change.

Setting aside the controversy of defining development as social change or in segmented fashion as political, economic and social change, some scholars have tried to offer a very general definition of development. Spengler, for instance, considers that development in general takes place, "when an index of that which is deemed desirable and relatively preferable increases in magnitude".[22] F.W. Riggs feels that the very essence of development in "the increasing ability of a social system to shape or reshape its environment, and hence its ability to make decisions".[23] Edward W. Weinder takes every psychological view of 'development' when he thinks, "development is a state of mind, a tendency, a direction".[24] All these definitions have one thing in common – they point toward the need for change from the present state to a better state of living on the part of human beings. Although these definitions do offer a new dimension to the meaning of 'development' – ability of individuals to take decisions, preparing oneself mentally for change – they do not fully free 'development' from its different aspects such as political, social and economic. What is that common thread running between these different changes? Can we discern it?

Looking for a common variable in economic, social, political and administrative development, one finds only one ingredient which is ubiquitous, namely degree of diffraction. The more productive economics always require a high degree of specialization of labour or differentiation of roles, that is diffraction. Specificity of function is also a characteristic of the most efficient administrative systems. We have seen that differentiation of political from administrative roles is another manifestation of diffraction. It may be more difficult to define social development but one element is certainly increasing complexity of social organization, as evidenced by a shift from primary to secondary organization. In all these spheres, development clearly involves increasing specificity.[25]

Thus to Riggs 'diffraction' is 'development' and this development can be both positive and negative. In fact, according to Riggs, "the central variable in development is increasing differentiation of structures rather than any particular consequence of that differentiation, whether it be productivity capital formulation, income distribution, personal security or some associated political social or administrative variable".[26] The prospects of negative development are at least as great as those of positive development, but once we recognize the possibility of 'negative development', we can always gear our efforts at achieving 'positive development' and constantly try to keep the 'negative development' at bay. Riggs' ideas of equating diffraction with development can be accepted with certain amendments. However 'development' may be defined, the underlying idea of it embracing, "the entire living organism in aspect and time to further the cause of material and social progress of mankind"[27] cannot be ignored. Hence if diffraction is development, it should not be anything but positive because development is not a 'natural process'. It is planned throughout fully and carried out programmatically. So any diffraction is not development. Moreover, there is limit to diffraction. We may stop diffracting the moment we find that diffraction no longer offers us the positive results and yet 'development' will continue. The Hawthrone experiment, which Riggs himself quotes provides the answer. Diffraction can be taken at best as a possible aid to development, it can be one of the indicators.

This brings us to the question whether development is 'natural' or a 'planned action'. John D. Montgomery considers development to be, "usually conceived as an aspect of change that is desirable, broadly predicted or planned, and administered or at least influenced by government action".[28] Milton J. Esman is more emphatic about development being a planned action. He says:

> Development is not 'natural' process which need only be let free to evolve not, a series of bottlenecks which enlightened policy makers, like production expediters can break successively to permit restrained energies to flow freely. It is a series of human task for which the physical, social, psychological and institutional resources are seldom available in sufficient quantity or in the proper combinations, the obstacles to achievement are often over powering and time is a relentless enemy to those who hope to realise results in decades rather than centuries.[29]

Even Riggs himself believes that for development to take place, there is a need for "the institutionalization of sanctions capable of compelling the elite to accept constitutional restraints on their own ability to exercise power in arbitrary fashion".[30]

Thus, development is not only planned but induced change. There is a need for somebody externally injecting it, and here, the government as the biggest of all the institutional forms, comes to play a very pivotal role in effecting planned changes either directly or indirectly through various institutions in society. Still, planned change can be only, although major, one aspect of development. There are various forces in the society which are not and cannot be fully controlled by the machinery of any government and such forces can contribute to or hamper the process of development. To the extent they contribute these can be unplanned development. But development is chiefly that change which is positive, all-round balanced, qualitative and contributes towards making the like of human being happier. The following diagram can explain the subtle distinction between change land development:

CHANGE
POSITIVE→PROGRESS→PLANNED
NEGATIVE→REGRESS→UNPLANNED
DEVELOPMENT

Although unplanned positive change can and does contribute to development, it is desirable to achieve 'development' in a planned way as this only prevents waste of scarce resources but allows to achieve a more balanced change, for development is "a systemic endeavour to meet the challenge which has been thrown by lightening advancement of science and technology and integrate the forces thus generated in a way that social system does not suffer from major jerks of dislocation".[31] On the basis of these various characteristics, one can have a feel of development' but one cannot still operationalize 'development' as its meaning in the form of social and political development is not available in operationable term, though this is not the case of economic development. So long these are not available, development can be merely an academic exercise and no doubt, students and scholars of development will be subjected to the criticism that there is gap between the academic interests in development and its practice in many developing countries. Schaffer cannot be unjust when he raps members of the 'comparative groups' by opening that "in practice the members of the group saw well enough that something or other consistently prevented them from being sufficiently 'action-oriented' To put it in another and harsher way, they had their conferences and wrote their papers, but the practitioners did not seem to take much notice, and changes in developing countries did not seem to be directly affected".[32] Members of the comparative groups are failed by social scientists in general and political scientists and sociologists in particular. Having realized that development is 'something more' than mere, 'economic development' they did not have the instruments to measure that 'something more'. In order that development as a concept is operationalized, there is a need for urgently evolving a concept of 'social sciences' without which the aimless academic kite-flying will go on.

Notes

1. For different meaning of development, see:
   a. D.E. Apter, *The Politics of Modernization*, Chicago University of Chicago Press, 1965.
   b. M.J. Esman, "The Politics of Development Administration" in John D. Montgomery and E.J. Siffin (ed.), *Approaches to Development: Politic, Administration and Change*, New York: McGraw Hill, 1966.
   c. J. Lapalombara (ed.), *Bureaucracy and Political Development*, Princeton: Princeton University Press, 1963.
   d. L.W. Pye, *Aspects of Political Development*, Boyton Little Brown & Co., 1966.
2. E.W. Wiender, *Development Administration: A New Focus for Research*.

3. "Administrative Development: An Elusive Concept", in Montgomery and Siffin, op. cit., p. 225.
4. *Public Administration: A Comparative Perspective*. Englewood Cliff N.: Prentice Hall, 1966, p. 10.
5. LaPalombara, "Alternative Strategies for Developing Administration Capabilities in Emerging Nations", in Riggs (ed.), *Frontiers of Development Administration,* Durham, N.C.: Duke University Press, 1970, p. 175.
6. Ibid.
7. Ibid.
8. F.W. Ridley, *The Study of Government*, London: George Allen & Unwin, 1975, p. 156.
9. "Exploring Systems Approach to Development Administration", in Riggs (ed.), *Frontiers of Development Administration*, op. cit,' p. 110.
10. Cohn Gerhard and Geiger Theodore, *Country Programme in the Emerging Countries: An Agenda for Research*. Washington Brooking Institution, 1962, p. 47.
11. *Administration in Developing Countries*, Boston: Houghton. Mifflin, 1964, p. 420.
12. Esman, op. cit., p. 59.
13. Esman, op. cit., p. 30.
14. Reinhard Bendix, *Nation-Building and Citizenship*, New Delhi Wiley Eastern, 1969, p. 5.
15. Ibid.
16. Ibid.
17. "Bureaucracy in Development Movement Regimes", op. cit., p, 497.
18. "Bureaucracy in Development Movement Regimes", op. cit., p. 5-6.
19. See Heady, op. cit., p. 31.
20. See Gerald E. Caiden, *Dynamics of Public Administration: Guidelines to Current Transformations in Theory and Practice*, New York: Rinehart and Winston, 1971, p. 267.
21. Heady, op. cit., p. 31.
22. Joseph J. Spengler in Braibanti and Spengler (ed.), *Tradition, Values and Socio-Economic Development*, Durham, N.C. Duke University Press, 1963.
23. *Frontiers of Development Administration*, op. cit, p. 26.
24. op. cit., p. 9
25. *Administration in Developing Countries*, p. 419-20.

26. Ibid, p. 421-22.
27. Shaukat Ali and Garth H. Jones, *Planning, Development and Change: An Annotated Bibliography* on, *Development Administration*. Lahore: Punjab University Press, p. 12.
28. Approach to Development, p. 259.
29. op. cit., p. 71.
30. "Administrative Development: An Elusive Concept", p. 253.
31. Shaukat Ali and Garth IT Jones, op. cit., p. 12.
32. Bernard B. Schaffer, "Comparisons, Administration and Development", *Political Studies*, XIX, 1971. p. 330.

12 Development Administration: Some Conceptual Issues

Ramesh K. Arora

It is paradoxical that 'development administration' despite being one of the most overused concepts of policy sciences, has remained relatively under-theorized. Whatever attempts of conceptualization have been made in this area suffer from a lack of specificity and operationalization. In this short paper, an attempt is being made to explore the diversity of 'Meanings' attached to the major foci associated with it.

Two Interrelated Themes

In the literature, the term 'development administration' has been used in two interrelated senses. First, it "refers to the administration of development programmes, to the methods used by large-scale organizations, notably governments to implement policies and plans designed to meet their development objectives".[1] Second, development administration, "by implication, rather than directly, involves the strengthening of administrative capabilities".[2] These two aspects of development administration, i.e., the administration of development and the development of administration are intertwined in most definitions of the term.

Edward Weidner, a pioneer in the field of development administration, has defined it as "the process of guiding an organization toward the achievement of development objectives".[3] These objectives, Weidner explains elsewhere, are "progressive political, economic, and social objectives that are authoritatively determined in one manner or another".[4] Weidner's definition, thus highlights the following elements of the process of development administration:

1. increasing the capacity of an administrative system to achieve certain specified objectives;
2. these objectives are multifaceted, and are political, economic, and social in character;
3. the objectives are determined 'authoritatively', i.e., by 'Government' and other authoritative bodies, if any.

It is evident that while the first element of the definition concerns the increase of 'capacity' of the administrative system, the second and the third refer to the goals for the achievement of which such capacity has to be utilized. Students of development administration have recognized that the 'administration of development' and 'development of administration' are functionally interrelated to each other. This orientation is reflected in the analysis of scholars such as Jose Abueva, Inayatullah, B.S. Khanna and Hahn Been Lee.[5] Amplifying the interrelatedness of these two variables, Riggs has argued:

> The reciprocal relatedness of these two sides [of development administration] involves a chicken and egg type of causation. Administration cannot normally be improved very much without changes in the environmental constraints (the infrastructure) that hampers its effectiveness; and the environment itself cannot be changed unless the administration of development programmes is strengthened.[6]

Administrative System as an Independent Variable

It is pertinent to note that most of the research on development administration has considered the administrative system and the changes within it as independent variable, while the developmental goals are treated as dependent variables. Weidner, for example, has suggested that the programmes or innovations introduced in a country could be classified as among the principal independent variables, the output or goal accomplishment the ultimate dependent variables, and environmental or cultural factors intervening or intermediate dependent variables.[7] This view is also subscribed to, among others, by Fred Riggs, Joseph La Palombara, and Martin Landau. Interestingly, a similar orientation prevails in the discipline of comparative politics where political development theorists such as Samuel Huntington, Karl Deutsch, Samuel Eisenstadt, Robert Holt, and John Turner have considered the political system as independent and/or intervening variables in the study of the processes of political development.

Planning as an Instrument of Development

Increasing the administrative capability to achieve developmental goals in an 'efficient' manner is associated with the concept of planned development, which is based on the desire to achieve particular results within a given period of time and with minimum of cost. It is noteworthy that the concept of planning had an important place even in traditional public administration, particularly in the works of Henri Fayol and Luther Gulick. And today, development administration is considered to be concerned with the formulation and implementation of the four p's – plans, policies, programmes, and projects.[8] Associated developmental models have an underlying assumption that "there are noticeable different time series; that the succession of these states implies the system is heading somewhere; and that there are orderly processes which explain how the system gets from its present state ... (to wherever) it is goings".[9] Such directional change has been emphasized by several students as the main thrust of development administration. A scholar has identified development administration as an "administration of planned change".[10] However, not all planning may be developmental, and not all development administration may be planned. Likewise, planned directional growth and 'system change' may or may not move together.[11] Finally, it has been recognized that planning, like any other rational action, may have unintended as well as intended consequences.

Complexities of the Goal Model

The conceptualization of development administration involves the problems associated with the construction of any goal oriented model. As Samuel Katz has observed, it is difficult to define goals for development action. It may be that existing goals are not being met or are not expected to be met in the future. Or, more often, these may be just anticipated objectives based upon observations of conditions somewhere else, e.g., when a developing nation attempts to emulate developed nations.[12] Goal identification is "never simple, and in complex developmental change situations it can be very elusive and difficult. Formal and informal, stated and unstated, intended and unintended, planned and not planned – and goals of whom – these are a few of the dimensions that need to be taken into account".[13] Not much research in comparative public administration has yet tackled these problems. Lack of clarity on important aspects of goal-orientation sometimes causes confusion about the true nature of 'development' administration.

Developmental-Non-Developmental Dichotomy

Since all organizations have at least some kinds of goals, they could, by virtue of having a goal-orientation, claim to fall under the rubric of development administration. This eventually would pose the problem of distinguishing between the developmental and the non-developmental public organizations. It has been recognized that development administration is generally similar to the 'traditional' (apparently non-developmental) public administration insofar as it is concerned with how rules, policies, and norms are implemented by government organizations. On the other hand, it is contended that a developmental administrative system differs from a non-developmental one in its objectives, scope, complexity, and degree of innovation in its operation.[14] In attempting to explain such differences, Irving Swerdlow has used examples of an urban renewal programme (apparently developmental) and the running of a city water department (apparently non-developmental). Swerdlow has remarked:

> Perhaps the difference lies in the degree of difficulty encountered in executing these functions, the amount of 'pioneering' required, and the difficulties of finding adequate procedures for moving people who are unwilling to move, for reconciling conflicting interests in redesigning a section of the city, for establishing new relationships which involve major changes in how people and governmental agencies customarily do business.[15]

In reference to Swerdlow's comment above, Wood has argued that in a developing country, operating an urban renewal programme and running a city water department might present the same degrees of difficulty in meeting the requirements of innovation, resources, public support, and inter-organizational support.[16] In fact, running a city water department in an 'emerging' nation might encounter greater problems than an urban renewal programme does in a developed country. Both types of programmes would be called 'developmental' in a developing country. Using Swerdlow's general definition of developmental administration, one may thus recognize that differing mixes of administrative departments will be seen as developmental in different ecological settings.

Colonial vs Non-Colonial Bureaucracy

A popular contention in developing nations appears to be that the developmental processes start only after political freedom has been achieved. Thus, distinctions are generally made between a colonial and a non-colonial bureaucracy.[17] Such distinctions generally overlook the fact that even in the colonial period a country may have had developmental programmes and plans, such as India had in the early 1940s, and that it is equally plausible that a country with self-government may be unable to initiate programmes which could truly be called 'developmental'. Thus, it would be an over-generalization to claim that a colonial administration is a 'law and order' administration, while public administration under self-rule is a developmental administration. It has been well recognized that maintaining social order takes top priority in most emergent nations, while the development efforts generally suffer due to various reasons.

Developmental Structures

Often within an administrative system, some organizations are termed or treated as developmental, while others are not. Indeed, there could be certain structures, such as developmental planning units and development banks, which seem by definition to relate particularly to development programmes. However, this does not imply that there exist any purely non-developmental agencies. When rigid distinction is made between developmental and non-developmental activities and some particular officials are designated as 'development officials', there is a danger that the morale of other (non-developmental) officials could go down. Moreover, in allowing such a dichotomy to result in an emphasis on 'new' institutions for development, planners may neglect the real adaptation of 'existing' institutions to changing environmental conditions.[18] It is worth recognizing, for example, that the success of taxation and law and order institutions is fundamental to the success of developmental organizations and activities.

Administration of Developing Countries

Another factor contributing to an apparent developmental-non-developmental dichotomy is a conception or impression that development administration is concerned solely with the administration of developing countries. Such assumption can only reduce the utility of the concept of development administration in its application to the comparative analysis of 'developed' and 'developing' countries. In fact, it is almost impossible to find totally developmental or single-purpose oriented bureaucracies in empirical situations, although some scholars have held that all programmes in developing countries have acquired a developmental thrust. Indeed, in the literature of the contemporary comparative public administration movement, there has been a heavy emphasis on the study of bureaucracies in 'developing' nations, and relatively little attention has been given to bureaucracies in 'developed' countries except as this has been considered helpful in understanding the 'developing' countries.[19]

A dominant emphasis on the administrative system of 'developing' countries is in consonance with the primary objectives of the Comparative Administration Group, but such an emphasis should not be viewed as prescribing any limitation on the future research in the field. With the social systems of 'developed' countries passing through a period of turbulence, it is imperative that students of public administration study issues relevant to the need to enhance the capabilities of the administrative systems to withstand and direct social change. In the contemporary Western nations. continuing socio-economic and political development has thrown up new administrative problems. Consequently, an emerging focus on the developmental aspects of public administration is already discernible, in American administrative theory.[20] It is clear, then, that there could be no rigid dichotomy between the nature of administration in 'developing' and 'developed' societies, although it is fairly well recognized that the emerging nations have to face greater challenges of rapid societal change.

Innovative Administration

Some scholars have identified development administration with a high degree of innovation in administrative system, which in turn is expected to encourage innovations in non-administrative areas. Weidner has stressed that:

> ...the problem of how to maximize the effectiveness of a bureaucracy so that it contributes to growth in the direction of modernity or nation-building and socio-economic progress is a problem of how to strengthen innovation forces in the bureaucracy.[21]

It has been stressed that development administration, by its very nature, is innovative. For example, Victor Thompson has observed that development administration implies organizational ability to innovate.[22] However, this should not imply that there are some administrative systems which lack innovation absolutely and, therefore, are entirely non-developmental. What this means essentially is that an administrative unit devoted to the attainment of developmental goals is likely to need greater innovation and creativity than the one engaged primarily in 'routine' administrative activities. But again, what is 'routine' in one environmental context may be developmental in another.

Conclusion

It should be clear, then, that neat distinctions between developmental and non-developmental administrations cannot be made. Too often a dichotomy which makes sense in ideal-type terms is assumed to be parallelled by absolute differences which are associated with specific concrete organizations. Like the politics-administration dichotomy, the error in making. such distinctions lies in the attempt to dichotomize concretely where differences lie only in degree of emphasis as with 'warm' and 'cold' in that what is 'developmental' in one setting might not be so regarded in another. Nothing is either fully developmental or non-development "except as thinking makes it so". 'Nevertheless, as the term 'development administration' is used in the literature, it refers to those administrative systems or organizations which are centrally concerned with the achievement of progressive socio-economic and political goals, and which are innovational in attitudes and operation. Furthermore, in general terms, administrative systems of all 'developing' nations are considered to be engaged in the dynamics of development administration.

Notes

1. Fred W. Riggs, "Introduction", in Riggs (ed.), *Frontiers of Development Administration* (Durham, N.G: Duke University Press, 1970), hereafter cited as *Frontiers*, p. 6.
2. Ibid.
3. *Technical Assistance in Public Administration Overseas: The Case of Development Administration* (Chicago: Public Administration Service, 1965), p. 200.
4. Weidner, "Development Administration: A New Focus, for Research", in Ferrel Heady and Sybil Stokes (eds.), *Papers on Comparative Public Administration* (Ann Arbor: Institute of Public Administration, University of Michigan, 1962), p. 104.
5. For views of these authors, see their articles in Weidner (ed.), *Development Administration in Asia* (Durham, N.C.: Duke University Press, 1970). For a classification of various definitions of administrative development, see, Rakesh Hooja, "Administrative Development: The Concept Re-explored", *Administrative Change I* (1973), pp. 78-91.
6. "The Idea of Development Administration", in Weidner (ed.), *Development Administration in Asia*, hereafter referred to as *Asia*, pp. 32-33. Riggs, "The Context of Development Administration" in Riggs (ed.), *Frontiers*, p. 75.
7. "The Elements of Development Administration" in Weidner (ed.) *Asia*, p. 24.

8. Donald C. Stone in the Introduction to *Education for Development Administration* (Brussels: International Institute of Administrative Sciences, 1966), cited in W. Wood, "Development Administration: An Objection", *Indian Journal of Public Administration*, XIII (1967), p. 702. One major focus of the Comparative Administration Group, as identified by Milton Esman, has been the process of development planning. See Esman, "CAG and the Study of Public Administration" in Riggs (ed.), *Frontiers*, pp. 52-58.
9. Robert Chin, "Utility of System Models and Development Models for Practitioner" in Warren Bennis, et al. *The Planning of Change* (New York: Hort, Rinehart and Winston, 1961). p. 208.
10. V.A. Pai Panadiker, "Development Administration: An Approach", *Indian Journal of Public Administration*, X (1969), p. 35.
11. For a discussion on this point, see Weidner, "The Elements of Devel· opment Administration", p. 24.
12. Katz, "A System Approach to Development Administration", in Riggs (ed.), *Frontiers*, p. 134.
13. Weidner, "The Idea of Development Administration", p. 24.
14. Katz, op. cit., p. 120.
15. "Introduction", in Swerdlow (ed.) *Development Administration: Concepts and Problems* (Syracuse, N.Y.: Syracuse University Press, 1963).
16. Wood, op, cit., p. 714.
17. See, for example, S.C. Dube, "Bureaucracy and Nation Building in Transitional Societies", *International Social Science Journal*, XVI (1968), pp. 229-236.
18. Wood, op. cit., pp. 702-713.
19. Ferrel Heady, "Bureaucracies in Developing Countries" in Riggs (ed.), *Frontiers*, p. 459.
20. See, among others, Frank Marini, (ed.), *Toward a New Public Administration* (Scranton: Chandler Publishing Co., 1971); Dwight Waldo (ed.) *Public Administration in a Time of Turbulence* (Scranton Chandler Publishing Co, 1971).
21. Weidner, "Development and Innovational Roles" in his (ed.), *Asia*, p. 421.
22. Thompson, "Bureaucracy and Innovation", *Administrative Science Quarterly*, IX (1965), 1-20.

13 Riggs's Concept of Formalism

B.S. Bhargava

During the last three decades or so, a number of states have come into existence in Asia, Africa and Latin America. These newly born politically emancipated states have started their journey on the road to modernization and industrialization. These states which from political and economic angles are called 'developing states' are, sociologically speaking, 'transitional societies'. It is unmistakably implied in the existing literature that these states are in a transitional phase; they are neither traditional (fused) societies nor modern (diffracted) societies, but are of somewhere between the two. If one follows the models of Riggs, then the 'prismatic model' covers these transitional societies.

Developing countries have to face multidimensional problems. These problems are: political (legitimacy, political structure and infrastructures, law and order, etc.) and economic (eradication of poverty, disease, hunger, etc.).

What is a choice before a newly-born State which tries to establish political, social and economic institutions suited to overall national development? Developing states, quite often, try to adopt foreign models. For example in the field of political institutions, many states have adopted either parliamentary system of Great Britain or the presidential system of USA or a mixture of the two. So is the practice in the field of economy, where many developing states have adopted 'economic plans' as a tools for systematic economic development. In developing states one or the other foreign model is followed with the assumption that since a particular developed country has achieved positive results as result of following a specific model, the model can also be helpful in other situations. Obviously, the developing societies aspiring for rapid modernization and development, seem to have very 'limited choice'. Evolving own institutions through a process of trial and error may take very long time, which developing societies cannot afford.

It has been observed that developing countries, consciously or unconsciously, adopt foreign models. If for this phenomenon, developing countries are to be held responsible, then the colonial powers should be held equally responsible for this state of affairs. During the time of colonial rule, the thinking appeared to be prevalent that what was best for the colonial power could be well transplanted or exported to a colony.

Attitude of Ruling Elites

The studies made on politics in developing areas reveal that in almost all the developing states, the ruling elites are development-oriented and to a greater extent, western-oriented. Most of them, having been trained in western education, somehow or the other, find solutions to their problems in foreign models, especially those of developed societies such as the USA and major European powers. The point needs no elaboration that just after their independence, many states of Asia, Africa and Latin America started with 'democratic systems' which was more or less based on the western model. But after some time, democracy toppled down in one after the other countries and its place was taken by militant dictatorship or by a modernizing oligarchies. Pakistan and Nigeria are two glaring examples of this type of change. Why did this happen? Besides other reasons, the most important reason was that efforts were made to implant democratic system in a soil that was not congenial for its growth. This has made many scholars of political science and public administration conclude that institutions cannot be imported unless ecological factors have a propensity to receive them. This is not only true with political systems but also with other subsystems like bureaucracy, local government, etc.

Furthermore, it seems to be an appropriate observation that when institutions of a diffracted society are imported by a transitional society, there are always apprehensions about their proper functioning. If somehow they go on operating, then transitional societies, because of several ecological factors, are not able to get the expected results.[1] Further, the citizens may not be able to understand 'innovations' (foreign institutions, ideas or values or norms). In this context, the concept of formalism propounded by Fred Riggs gains significance.

What is Formalism?

Riggs in his 'sala' model has used the term 'formalism' in a special sense which is quite an untraditional usage. But, there are scholars such as V. Subramaniam[2] who consider this term as an 'unhappy' one and prefer other terms or phrases such as 'lack of congruence' or 'divergence in theory and practice' to the Riggsian term.

While discussing the 'sala' model, Riggs has narrated certain characteristics of a prismatic society. Formalism is one of these characteristics, others being heterogeneity and overlapping. He writes:

> By formalism I refer to the degree of discrepancy or congruence between the formally prescribed and the effectively practised, between norms and realities. The greater the congruence, the more realistic the situation, the greater the discrepancy, the more formalistic it be comes.

At another place, he observes:

> By formalism I wish to distinguish the extent to which a discrepancy exists between the prescriptive and descriptive, between formal and effective power, between the impression given by constitution, laws and regulations, organizational charts and statistics, and actual practices and facts of government and society. The greater the discrepancy between the formal and effective, the more formalistic is a system.[3]

Obviously, the concept of 'formalism' is very wide in scope. This can be found in social system of a country, and in various other subsystems such as political, administrative and economic.

Other Significant Aspects

First, formalism, as explained above, should not be considered as an exclusive characteristic of a transitional or a prismatic society. The concept is a relative one, which can be used in terms of differences in degree of congruence between the 'formal' and the 'effective'. We can hypothesize that in developed countries there is 'less degree of formalism' and in transitional societies there is 'greater degree of formalism'. In fact, one can find examples of poorly enforced laws in every country. In USA which is a developed, industrialized and democratic society, one can find elements of formalism which are manifested in problems such as the state of Blacks. A country like the United Kingdom having the oldest democracy based on the ideas of equality of human beings, finds itself in the grip of intricate problems of colour discrimination. Are these not examples of the differences between values and practice?

Secondly, it would be unrealistic to say that formalism in a transitional society is rampant in all aspects of life (social, economic, political, administrative, etc.). There may be many institutions in a developing country which are working satisfactorily and no distinguishable difference is found between their prescription and description, yet in other aspects, quite a good degree of formalism is traceable or observed.

Thirdly, there may be different kinds of formalism prevalent in a system. Riggs mentions some possible kinds, such as 'constitutional formalism', 'administrative formalism', 'academic formalism', etc.

Fourthly, it is not possible to provide an exact measure of the degree of formalism in a society as a whole, but it may be possible to calculate some indices for specific activities. Riggs gives an example: "If a compulsory education law, for example, requires that all children between six and 11 must attend schools, but a survey reveals that only half of the children in this age group are attending, then we could use an index of 50 per cent as a measure of the degree of formalism".[4]

Fifthly, whatever may be the difficulties in measuring the degree of formalism, it (the concept) can be used as a tool which can be helpful in describing, in relative terms, as to which system/subsystem is more formalistic than the rest. Riggs, after analysing the 'constitutional formalism' of Thailand and the Philippines, arrived at the following relative judgement: "Despite these evidences of greater realism in the Philippines constitutional structure, as compared with the Thai, the degree of formalism is considerable".

Causes for the Existence of Formalism in Transitional Societies

The studies made by Riggs, especially of Thailand and the Philippines, clearly prove that formalism exists in these societies in many fields. It is discernible in constitutional structures, administrative organizations and in other structures of society. I think it is equally correct to say that in almost all the transitional societies, formalism exists to a considerable extent.

There may be a number of reasons for this characteristic of a transitional society. To list a few, we can say that the limited choice of models as discussed earlier, lack of differentiated structures, specificity of roles, cultural lag, rising expectations of the people, fashion for adopting foreign institutions with the idea that they have functioned well in other countries, ruling elites, craze for symbolic outputs (prestige projects, etc.), elements of ascription in recruitment of roles, technical assistance programmes which include prescription for foreign institutions, and lack of human and material resources are the important reasons. However, to say that in a particular case of formalism, a specific factor is responsible, appears to be a very difficult task. Nevertheless, keeping in view the totality of ecological factors of a given society, some rough conclusions can be drawn,

Some Examples of Formalism in Transitional Societies

In this section, certain examples from transitional societies have been given, which may help us to identify the existence of formalism in one field or the other.

Many a time, a law which is formalistic sets forth a policy or goal which is not administratively put into practice. A number of examples can be cited from Indian experience in this context. Dowry in marriage is a traditional feature of family system which is typically Indian in character. Following this custom, the parents of the bride give cash and domestic presents to the parents of the bridegroom. It is inherent in the psychology of people that 'to have a son is a matter of pride'. Preferences to the birth of a son than of a daughter, and praying to God for a son, explains the same feelings. The increasing awareness of the resultant vices of this custom, the Government of India passed a law prohibiting dowry, but what we find in practice is the ineffectiveness of the law. This is probably because of deep-rooted values attached to this institution by the people in general. Administrative measures, if at all any, for the execution of the law appear to be ineffective.

In developing countries, politicians appear to think that by making laws, the desired changes can be brought about. This may in fact lead to working of institutions which may not produce the desired results. Many developing countries, including India, adopted planning as a tool for economic development. India is known for nicely formulated bulky five-year plans (the emphasis on heavy industries in Indian planning seems to be largely inspired by similar predisposition in Russian planning). Original targets have rarely been achieved. That is why, quite often, we hear a remark that Indian plans are mere paper plans. Poverty, hunger and disease are dominant on the Indian scene. Most of this is a result of formalism in economic administration.

In many transitional societies, cultural norms and practices constitute 'cultural hurdles' in development administration. Agehananda Bharati opines:

> In India and in other regions (e.g. Ceylon and East Pakistan now Bangladesh) where predominant importance is given to the spiritual world, and religious radiation is the guiding reference for behaviour, people may be reluctant to cooperate when innovation seems to conflict with religious tradition. Most cultural hurdles in India derive from the strength of religious tradition. Mundane efforts are considered basically trivial – a powerful impediment to development administration on all levels.[5]

However, it should be noted that religious traditions by no means always pose hurdles to innovation; in many cases it can be of positive benefits to modernization. Hindu scripture speaks of 'niskama karma' (action without the desire for its fruits), and the second in the four stages of life in the Hindu religion, artha, is one of keen participation in any social activities which improve material and ideal living standards among fellow men.

'Administrative formalism' is manifested in many a developing nation. Whatever may be the efforts in adopting ultra-modern techniques of administrative reforms (organizational charts, methods, budgeting principles, administrative filing systems and procedures, etc.), they are not effective because of the bureaucratic norms and values in operation. If at all, there is any worth of these modern institutions and practices, the need for suitable attitudes of mind and habits of work are to be refined.

Consequences of Formalism

Formalism has certainly serious consequences, whether it is in administrative subsystem or in any other subsystem of society. Take, for an example, formalism in law enforcement. Riggs states:

> Changes in the degree of formalism in law enforcement can have important social consequences. They may also deeply affect, or reflect, the quality of administrative action. If, for example, a law is generally violated, opportunities arise for the corruption of administration. An inspector, knowing that a rule is being broken by a merchant is put in the position of being able to make trouble for him unless he receives some consideration. The shopkeeper knows that if he obeys the regulation, he will be put at a disadvantage in competition with his rivals. Hence, he has a keen incentive to resist enforcement, and if necessary, to offer the inspector something in the hopes of being left alone. The officer, for his part, may be badly underpaid. He knows that there is little realistic prospect for securing effective enforcement of the regulation, and so eases his conscience when he looks the other way.[6]

Does it not look like a snap of Indian scene taken with a foreign camera?

Is Formalism a Natural Feature of a Transitional Society?

Thus, it would not be wrong to say that formalism is an existential reality in almost all the transitional societies of Asia, Africa and Latin America. Is it a natural phase in the process of development through which every transitional society has to pass? What history speaks of about the developed societies in the context of their journey to modernization and industrialization? It appears that 'formalism' is only a dominant feature of a transitional society which may go on decreasing with the passage of development. Nevertheless, in practice, no society is free from formalism.

When the word, *natural* is added before 'formalism', it should not lead to the conclusion that it (formalism) is desirable or should be tolerated as a 'natural consequence' of the transitional phase in the process of development of a society. To minimize the degree is always a must. All this needs concerted and continuous efforts on the part of ruling elites, administrative personnel, and people in general, keeping in view the zeals of national integration and rapid social and economic development.

Notes

1. "Certainly we shall find in virtually every government of Asia, Africa and Latin America today formal agencies of administration which resemble those of Europe and the United States. Yet, somehow, closer inspection of these institutions convinces us that they do not work in the same way or that they perform unusual social and Political functions." Fred W. Riggs, *Administration in Developing Countries*, Boston: Houghton-Mifflin Co.. 1964, p. 12.
2. V. Subramaniam made this comment while delivering a lecture on Riggs's prismatic model to the participants of the MPA Group on 29 November, 1967 at the Institute of Social Studies, The Hague, The Netherlands.
3. Fred W. Riggs, *The Ecology of Public Administration*, Bombay: Asia, 1961, pp. 91-92.
4. Ibid. p. 101.
5. For details, see the paper, "Cultural Hurdles in Development Administration", in *Development Administration: Concepts and Problems,* by Irving Swerdlow. Editor, Syracuse, Syracuse University Press, 1963.
6. Fred W. Riggs, *The Ecology of Public Administration*, p. 101.

14 Development Management

Hans C. Blaise

It was a pleasure for me to find that the organizers of this seminar referred to development *management* rather than development *administration* when they suggested the topic of my talk at this seminar. I am constantly encouraging government executives to think of themselves as *public managers*. In my own mind – and, think that this view is shared by many people – administration connotes the more or less routine processing of activities according to established rules and regulations. Management, on the other hand, is a term that implies a more decisive and independent role in the design and control over an organization or programme in the pursuit of its objectives.

In traditional public administration a clear distinction was made between policy and administration. In this school of thought policy making was the prerogative of the legislators

---

This paper was presented at Seminar-Conference on the Comprehensive Fiscal Plan of the Government at Republic of the Philippines, Budget Commission, Manila on September 18, 1972.

and of the politically appointed executive leaders of the government, The role of the career civil servants was limited to the faithful execution of these policy in accordance with the legal and administrative rules and procedures regulating government operations. Experienced career executives in government are well aware of the fact that this clear separation between policy and administration is often a myth. The determination of economic, social, and political objectives and priorities is – and properly should be – the responsibility of elected and politically appointed leaders. Within that frame-work of objectives and priorities, however, there is ample opportunity for career government executives to formulate and manage programmes that would help to accomplish the established objectives. Indeed, without the dedicated and creative contribution of knowledgeable and experienced civil servants it would be difficult for the political leaders to give substance to their aspirations and goals.

In earlier times the role of government was largely restricted to maintaining law and order and to the provision of essential public facilities and services. During the last few decades, in almost all countries, government has begun to play a much more active part in the economic as well as in the social sphere. Even in non-socialist countries, government has taken significant initiatives in economic and social affairs and has become an important direct participant in the economic sphere. Not only is the scope of government activities expanding rapidly but also the tide of rising aspirations and expectations, combined with an unprecedented pace of technological change, necessitates constant innovation and adjustment in government management and operations. Unfortunately, the mechanisms and processes – and even the norms and attitudes – that as yet prevail in many government organizations are more suitable for regulatory and routine operations than for innovative, target oriented development programmes.

Let me suggest here some of the key characteristics of the structure and process of an organization that is primarily concerned with routine operations under more or less stable conditions, and compare those characteristics with those that would be desirable for an organization called upon to provide new goods and services in a constantly changing environment. The characteristics or desirable features of those respective types of organizations would be about as follows:

Organization for routine operations	*Organization for developmental activities*
1. a hierarchical structure of authority and control, with communication Primarily vertical, i.e., instructions and decisions are passed down the line from the top;	1. a network structure of control and authority, with maximum communication in all directions, based on each individual's ability to contribute to goal achievement;
2. a clear definition of the tasks and responsibilities of each officer;	2. a constant re-adjustment and re-definition of tasks and responsibilities in accordance with changing requirements;
3. the establishment of and adherence to a detailed system of rules, regulations and procedures;	3. a minimum and flexible set of rules, regulations and procedures;
4. an emphasis on reconciliation of differing views with a minimum of risk-taking and competition;	4. a stimulation of the expression of differing views, and an acceptance of risk-taking and competition;
5. an orderly system of individual recognition and promotion based largely on knowledge and experience;	5. a system that rewards initiative and performance at least as much as knowledge and experience;
6. limited interaction with other organizations, particularly with groups and organizations outside the government;	6. considerable interaction and consultation with other organizations, both in and out of government;
7. a long and flexible time horizon for programme formulation and execution.	7. a specific programme and project planning system with a defined time horizon.

The above I suggest, are some of the critical differences between the desirable characteristics of, on the one hand an organization that is primarily concerned with routine operations and on the other hand one that focuses on innovative programme achievement in a changing environment. The problem of many government organizations is that they attempt to be developmental while retaining the structure and processes that are more suitable for routine activities.

To change government organization to the point where they are better equipped to handle innovative, target and performance-oriented development programmes is not an easy task. There are constraints of the public services system as such, as well as deeply ingrained practices, habits and attitudes that need to be overcome to arrive at a more flexible and dynamic system of management and operations. In a way sidestepping the basic problems that are facing us, government have found a partial solution by creating a large number of semi-autonomous agencies that are less subject to the constraints of an outmoded pattern of organization and organizational behaviour. No matter how salutary such semi-autonomous agencies may be for progress in certain fields they clearly are not the ultimate solution. The very tendency to create agencies and organizations outside the normal framework is in itself an indication of a lack of flexibility within the system. Furthermore, the proliferation of semi-autonomous agencies reduces the possibility for management control of the top executives in government and results in serious problems of coordination.

Planning and Programming

Having presented some of my general views on the question of management in government, let me now be somewhat more specific. For the remainder of this session I would like to outline some approaches to management that will be directly relevant to the problems your respective departments, bureaux and agencies face in participating effectively in development planning and implementation. What I intend to present here does not require any far reaching changes in the structure and procedures of your organizations. All it requires is a systematic approach to the management of the programmes and projects for which you are responsible.

One of the serious shortcomings in the pursuit of economic and social progress is that the increasing competence and sophistication in macro planning at the national level is not accompanied by adequate emphasis on the detailed and systematic planning and implementation of programmes and projects. It is of little use for National Economic Councils and Budget Commissions to calculate the optimum allocation of available resources to the various economic and social sectors and sub-sectors if this is neither based on, nor followed through by the detailed and systematic process of programme and project planning and implementation. What I want to describe here is the management process, which is in fact the system of *planning, programming* and, *controlling* programmes and projects designed to reach given objectives. As a model for describing the management process I will borrow certain concepts and approaches from business management. This is perfectly feasible because there is no inherent difference between management in a private enterprise and in a government organization. First, let me list briefly the distinct steps that are involved in the management process:

1. setting objectives
2. identifying alternative means to reach the objectives
3. choice among the alternatives and establishing priorities
4. determining the plan of action to accomplish the objectives (including human and physical resource requirements)
5. establishing a time schedule
6. calculating the cost of the programme elements
7. setting standards for satisfactory performance
8. determining how performance is to be measured and reported
9. determining when and how to take corrective action.

Development management involves primarily the systematic translation of broad objectives and macro targets into specific programmes and projects. This needs to be done in sufficient detail to know *which steps* need to be taken *when* for *what purpose* at *what cost*. Only a detailed plan of action will lead to results and will allow for effective controls and for adjustments when necessary.

In Figure 1 the management process within an organization is presented in schematic form. it has been assumed here that the unit of our concern forms part of the larger entity, like a Bureau or a Division in a government Department. Following the boxes and steps in the graphic presentation, let me say a few things about each element in the management process.

Organization's roles, missions, and objectives

Assuming that we are dealing with an entity that is a functional unit in a larger organization (e.g., the Secondary Education Division within the Bureau of General Education), the smaller functional unit is bounded by the purposes, tasks, and objectives of the larger organization of which it is a part. It cannot carry out activities or pursue ends that are not within the specifications of the larger entity. Thorough familiarity of the unit's management with the objectives of the management of the larger organization helps to formulate objectives for the unit that will further those set by the organization, with greater likelihood that the unit's objectives will be meaningful and acceptable higher up.

Defining unit's roles and missions

A clear definition of the scope of work and of the capabilities of the unit, its sections and staff members is necessary to determine the range of work that the unit is prepared and competent to undertake. Are there areas of responsibility, experience and competence that are either not fully utilized or delimit the areas of action of the unit? Is there a clear understanding of the unit's responsibilities and capabilities both inside and outside the unit? Do the key staff members of the unit fully understand the nature and scope of the work of the

Figure 1
The Mangement Process

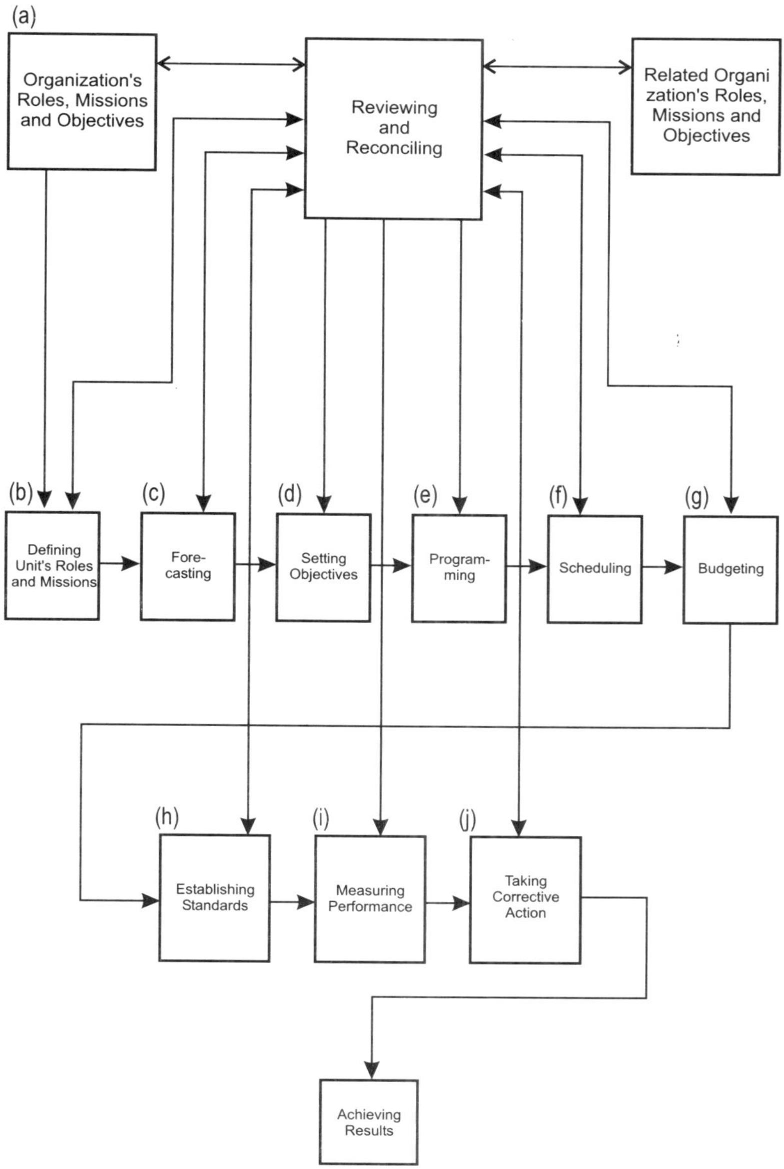

unit and recognize their role in the operation? These and related questions need to be asked in the context of an organization's work on programme planning and management.

Forecasting

Forecasting is a term more commonly used in business than in government. It is readily understandable that a business enterprise in the planning of its future production must estimate future economic trends, must anticipate the demand for its products, etc. Government units, however, must also estimate the demands for their services over a given period of time. The managers of those units must systematically collect information, and data, on developments inside and outside of government that may have implications for their operations. They must make estimates of the service requirements and opportunities that are likely to present themselves to determine the quantity, quality, cost and time schedule of services to be provided, The organization or unit that limits itself exclusively to the planning of specific projects that have been assigned to it or to planning only for the next fiscal year will not be able to respond effectively to future needs and opportunities. Unfortunately, in many government agencies public managers have too short a time horizon and the scope of their concerns tends to be too narrowly limited to the internal operations of their organization.

Setting objectives

At this point we become more directly concerned with development management as it relates to the planning and implementation of national development programmes. I want to stress, however, that an organization or unit is not in a good position to set objectives if it has not gone through the previous steps. The objectives of a unit may either be targets and projects that are being assigned to it by a higher level unit or they may be objectives that are formulated within the unit. In the latter case it may be necessary to convince some higher level executive or group outside the unit of the validity or the objectives and to obtain the required support, authority and funding for the programme of activities.

Regardless of the manner in which objectives are set, it is essential that they are specific and that their accomplishment is measurable. Reducing the primary school drop-out rate is not a viable objective, whereas, reducing the primary school dropout rate by 10 per cent over a three-year period has the necessary specificity. As suggested earlier, national development plans frequently specify objectives and targets that are much too broad to serve as guides for action to implementing organizations. Similarly, the objectives of a Government Department frequently need to be broken down into sub-objectives for Bureaux, Divisions and Sections. What may be a small element in the statement of objectives of the overall organization may become the major objective of one of the organization's units. Furthermore, even though the statement of the major objective may have sufficient precision for the determination of action by the organization as whole, this statement by itself is seldom an adequate guide for action for the units that perform the subsidiary roles and tasks required for the accomplishment of the organization's overall objectives. For each level of management the objectives of the unit must be a stated in such terms and with such specificity that a set of actions can be determined that will lead to their accomplishment and so that the process of implementation and the achievement of the objectives can be measured. In terms of management, objectives are not general statements of aspirations but concrete guides for action.

Programming

Programming is a critical step in the management process. It could be called 'planning at the action level'. Only too frequently is there an incomplete break down of the actions or steps required to carry out a programme or project in order to reach specified objectives. All major and distinct actions and resource requirements need to be identified and methods for the actions need to be identified.

Actually, programming is not - or should not be - one single process. More often than not, there are several possible paths to the achievement of objectives. Thus, going back to the earlier example of reducing the primary school drop-out rate, improvements in the quality of the teaching personnel, improved communication with the parents and the improved location of schools are among the actions that separately or in some combination conceivably contribute to the achievement of the objective (note that I am violating here my rule for specificity in objectives and means). As a sub-process in programming, we have to identify the possible actions leading to the attainment of the objectives. This needs to be done in sufficient detail to allow us to chose the most promising programme of action, which is a second sub-process.

Only after alternatives have been identified and a choice has been made can we work out in more detail the action involved in programme implementation and determine the resources required. Programming is a time-consuming exercise that involves all levels of the organization or unit. It does not only mean the analysis of the necessary personnel, materials and facilities, but also can be concerned with the analysis of the relevant laws and policies, the determination of the most suitable organizational structure, etc. In short, programming means the specification of all inputs and processes required to produce the desired results. This is best done by identifying in sequential form of major steps or activities and the respective requirements of each of those steps.

Although detailed and systematic programming is a difficult task, it should be recognized that without adequate programming there is no guidance for action no possible control over performance and not even the possibility to determine whether a programme is feasible.

Scheduling

Scheduling is closely related to programming but is best viewed as a separate step in the management process. It means charting activities over time to determine the time required for each activity and sequence of activities Thus scheduling is done on the basis of sequential ordering of related activities. By the charting of sets of activities over time we can determine when given sets are to be initiated and when resources for the respective activities need to be available. Techniques like PERT/CPM are extremely useful to ensure an adequate flow of action and resources.

Budgeting

With proper programming and scheduling the costing of a programme or project is not a major problem. In programming we have determined which activities are to be carried out in the pursuit of established objectives and what the human and physical requirements are. Through the scheduling exercise we have refined that further by stipulating when the resource requirements will arise. Budgeting, then, is little more than the expression of the required human efforts, materials and facilities in monetary terms.

Establishing standards

Also with regard to standards, the determination of what constitutes acceptable performance is not a major problem once we have broken down the programme of action into units of work and determined staffing, time and cost requirements. Reasonable expectations of resources and time requirements – especially when arrived at after proper consultation with those responsible for the work leads to the establishment of reasonable performance standards. Standards are yardsticks specifying the quality and the quantity of the work carried out. Standards not only serve to measure the effectiveness and efficiency of but also to help identify when and where corrective actions are indicated.

Measuring performance

Every action system needs monitoring devices to keep track of the extent and manner in which specified activities are carried out and goals are achieved. The measurement of performance is a management tool to control the operation, to be alerted to shortcomings and to make it possible to take corrective action when necessary. To allow for the measurement of performance decision need to be made regarding information to be recorded, reports that must be submitted and concerning the format and channelling of this information and the reports. Two caveats are in order with respect to data collection and reporting. One is that data should never be collected unless they are actually analysed and used as a basis for subsequent decision-making and action. A second and often ignored caveat is that data recorded and reports submitted should result in a feed-back to those who have collected that data and submitted them. Too frequently people at the operating level are required to collect and submit data without their understanding the significance of the information submitted and without getting the benefit of the data analysis that could help them in their future actions.

Taking corrective action

Corrective action is not just the result of performance measurement. To take corrective action adequately, correctly, and timely there must be contingency planning. Good management means knowing where the system may break down and what measures to take to overcome problems as they arise. Every programme and project will from time to time run into unexpected problems requiring management attention. To the extent that corrective action is taken on the basis of contingency planning that will specify *who* will do *what*, *if*, management involvement in trouble shooting can be reduced and largely limited to unanticipated developments.

The box 'Achieving Results' in Figure 1 does not require any further elaboration. The only matter that deserves mention with regard to results is that the actual accomplishments should be reviewed in terms of both the objectives specified at the beginning of the process and with regard to the various steps that were taken in the management process. Unless the total process is reviewed upon the attainment of the objectives, the organization fails to learn from the experience so as to improve on its planning and performance in the future.

Thus far two of the boxes in Figure 1 have not been discussed. One of them is the roles, missions and objectives of related organizations. An organization does not work in a vacuum. Every organization has linkages with other organizations that supply inputs, absorb the outputs of our organization, which circumscribe out actions and provide our basic authority and resources. Assessing these interrelationships with other organizations and working out effective relationships with them is an important task of management. Finally, the presentation includes a box marked 'Reviewing and Reconciling'. As indicated by the dotted lines connecting this box with all other boxes in the management process, reviewing and reconciling is a continuous activity relevant to all steps at any time in the process. The results of budgeting may be that changes need to be made in programming or in the objectives, because the budget proves to be beyond the available resources. In the measurement of the performance it may appear that the schedule as established is not realistic and needs to be adjusted, and so forth. What the detailed analysis of the management process indicates is that all steps are interrelated and inter-dependent and that the change in one element or step will necessitate adjustments in others.

Management is the allocation and coordination of human and physical resources in the pursuit of specified objectives. It involves a unique set of skills and consists of an increasingly sophisticated and specialized range of methods and techniques. I have presented here only a very brief and schematic overview of some of the determinants of effective management. In development management it is the structuring of an effective and flexible system, the ability to set specific targets and the systematic pursuit of those targets in an efficient manner that counts.

15 Public Administration in Developing Countries: Some Observations

B.L. Jacobs

In this paper, I shall attempt to do two things. First to try and identify some of the problems more commonly found in developing countries – problems which bear on administrative efficiency. And secondly to attempt to indicate what might be done about the solution of those problems, especially by those of us concerned with study and training in the fields of public administration and management.

My observations do not relate in the first instance to any one country but rather to my own experience in many countries in Africa, Asia and Caribbean. I shall conclude with some very tentative attempts to relate my comments to the Indian scene. By so doing you will be afforded the opportunity if you wish to direct your questions and observations to the implications locally.

I never cease to be amazed at the uniformity and commonness of the areas deemed to be challenging in the field

---

Text of a lecture delivered by Prof. B.L. Jacobs, Director of Studies at the Institute of Development Studies, University of Sussex, Brighton, England at the HCM State Institute of Public Administration on 18 March 1976.

of public administration whichever of those continents you have in mind. My own institution runs short 4-6 week seminars largely for senior public servants and academicians from LDCs. More than 1000 such people have passed through IDS in 10 years – 10 per cent of them from India – the largest single country contributor – as might have been expected. It has afforded me as its Director of Studies an unparalleled opportunity to assess attitudes of this very special group and to estimate what challenges they think they are facing and what steps they are taking in response.

Bear in mind, they come from all over the world. Not merely from British Commonwealth countries, not merely from Anglophone countries. They are divided in roughly equal numbers between Asia, Africa and Latin America. The seminars offer them an opportunity to analyse critically the problems they face in a wide variety of subject areas, to exchange experiences and to suggest tentative solutions or improvements. The subjects of the seminars vary greatly – business negotiations in the public sector, social aspects of population growth, income distribution in an international context, socio-economic effects of the new HYV seeds, irrigation and employment strategies, planning in small dependent economies, financing domestic industry in developing countries, and problems of corruption. The spectrum is wide and embraces most of the problems that are important to LDCs, there are certain themes or threads which occur so frequently, almost despite the subject of the seminar – that I am going to suggest that it is perhaps by examining these recurring themes that we shall begin to understand where the true administrative challenges lie. Let me try and list half a dozen of these leading themes. The number is arbitrary and scarcely exhaustive.

The first theme relates to interference by politicians. We cannot do our jobs properly, says the administrator, because the politician pokes his nose into what are essentially administrative decision taking processes. Politician in this context can mean a military leader – a self-appointed holder of power. Decreasingly it means someone who has come to power through the ballot box. I would only comment that administrators have, all over the world, found it possible to adjust to meet such new situations and so to adapt themselves and their behaviour that their position of power has been remarkably unchanged. In particular we can only marvel at the way civil servants have not merely survived but positively flourished in states where military coups have replaced civilian governments.

The second theme is really the opposite side of the coin. If public servants complain of interfering politicians, these politicians are not less bitter about the failure of entrenched public servants to adjust to the changed demands of new societies and an inability or *refusal by administrators to be sympathetic to the aspirations of the new political masters*. From my own observation in many countries over the past decade, I am obliged to acknowledge that post-independence public servants deplore that they are not able to exercise the same arbitrary powers as the former colonial expatriate officials whom they replaced. In some way they feel cheated of the anticipated spoils of independence. It is understandable that having coveted for so long the seat occupied by one's expatriate predecessor, one finds to one's chagrin that the powers, the new incumbent can exercise, are much less than was formerly the case.

The third theme relates to *administrative reform*. Outdated machinery, often equated with colonial machinery, is the cause of all the malaise. Colonial administrations, it is suggested, were designed only for law and order objectives. Let us instigate major administrative reforms it is suggested, and all will be well. Hence such ambitious and costly exercises as the appointment of prestigious commissions – whose outcomes in LDCs (no less than in industrialized societies) have proved to be at best somewhat disappointing. I do not doubt that administrative reforms are needed: nor do I doubt that administrative

reform is something more than changes in staff and public service regulations. But I doubt very much whether the large prestigious and ponderous commissions tried in India and the UK is the best approach.

The fourth commonly identified theme I shall refer to is one which never fails to stimulate interest and adrenalin production. I refer to *corruption*. No state in the world is free from it. In some it has brought governments to a standstill and has been the downfall of others. The commonest justification given by leaders of military coups has been that corruption had become so bad that action outside the constitution remained the only possible option to be taken.

My fifth theme never ceases to astonish me because it has persisted so long. Indeed I wrote a case study on it over ten years ago. I refer to the *generalist/specialist controversy*. The issue is simple: why should a generalist rather than say a doctor in the Ministry of Health occupy the top administrative seat. My own position in quite relieved even though I am one who has in the past profited from being one of the favoured generalists. One of the 'twice born' as I believe they were known here, 'cock angles' as they were known in the colonial service. I think it wrong that *only* generalists should qualify for such posts as used to be the case.

The last theme I shall mention is not unrelated to the fourth, i.e., corruption. It refers to the suggestion that *public servants are ill rewarded* especially in comparison with their peers in the private sector. Of all the five themes this is the one which strikes least response in my own breast. It has even been pointed out to me that it was deplorable that whereas public service salaries in country X were at a par with UK public service salaries ten years ago, this was no longer so. No amount was paid to relative changes in GNP. The allegations about inferior salaries usually discount such factors as tenure of appointment, pension rights, hours of work and fringe benefits. Most of all they discount the concept of service. I recall having heard so often in the 1950s and 1960s from those wishing to hasten independence, that the throwing off of imperial shackles would itself be the greatest incentive to increased public service output. Once, it was suggested, people knew they were working for their own country and their own people, rather than for a metropolitan colonial power, output would increase, both quantitatively and qualitatively. Alas, in my experience this has not proved to be so. Perhaps it was unrealistic ever to imagine that it would be so. The scene with which I am increasingly familiar is that of a small number of dedicated grossly overworked senior people supported – or rather more often not supported – by an excessive number of ill motivated inefficient subordinates – the *"merchants petits barbonilleurs de paper"* ('miserable little paper scratchers' – so graphically portrayed by Molire).

Let me hasten to add that the inefficiency of this large army of junior officials is often due less to their own intrinsic shortcomings, than to inadequate, unimaginative training programmes.

One fact will not have escaped your attention. Common to all the six themes I have identified are two thoughts. First, none of those are new themes. Secondly, that the shortcomings or failures identified in the administrative machine are the failures and shortcomings of others. Perhaps not surprisingly no group involved – judiciary, executive or legislator – is ready to put its own head on the block and cry *mea culpa* – we are at fault.

To recapitulate then, I have suggested that in LDC's public services all across the world, inefficiency is rife and no one part of the body politic is prepared to accept responsibility. The mote is always seen in the eye of another, never in one's own eye. Departments and ministries are seen as self-contained fortresses. Indeed one could be forgiven at times for having the impression that some departments would rather impart their intelligence to a foreign power than to another department in the same government. The situation is rendered all the more tragic because the technology available for effective government was never greater or more accessible. In short, the administrative challenge exists. It cannot be denied. It cries out to be tackled.

It would be irresponsible of me not to suggest a possible way forward. It would be equally irresponsible of me to suggest that I had a solution of general application. Of course, I do not. I do have two key words which may help indicate a step forward. They are 'dialogue' and 'openness'.

Every opportunity must be taken to develop a dialogue between the parties interested in improved administration – between politician and civil servant; between the civil servant and the public; between politician and public; and between legislator and judiciary (the recent conference of West Bengal lawyers in Calcutta in which ministers participated seemed to me to be an admirable model). Meaningful dialogue is not easy to achieve: for every reason in justification of such a dialogue, ten reasons can be adduced in opposition. I recall my own essays in this direction. The means must not be allowed to replace the end. Or, as one Indian put it to me, "something must be done to prevent standing orders attaining the virtue of religious *mantras*". The end, the aim must never be lost sight of. It can be expressed simply enough, "to make life more tolerable for more people".

Finally, my second key word, 'openness'. The more open a government is, and is said to be, the less likely are the evils associated with corruption to manifest themselves. Open decisions, openly arrived at in public debate, are the best defence against arbitrary power exercised in secret.

What I am suggesting is that those of us concerned with the study of practice of public administration should lose no opportunity to discuss and encourage others to discuss these two concepts. I fully accept that there are other sectors who will decide in the event on the degree and nature of the dialogue and openness.

Finally, let us have a quick look at the relevance of my six themes to the Indian scene. Perhaps my first theme " interference by politicians" is of less relevance than some of the others, though one aspect – politicians requiring public servants to do things not previously considered to be properly civil servantish things is a current issue of some States. Also I suspect that "political interference" in the districts is still an issue in India.

From some of the statements of the Indian leaders quoted in the press recently I am in no doubt that my second theme is of relevance today. I am referring to alleged lack of sympathy of public servants with the aspirations of the politicians. Further, the activities of the Vigilance Commission and other bodies support my thesis that corruption is very much a current issue in India.

Who can doubt that my fourth theme, administrative reform, is of current concern in India. Nor indeed my fifth theme – the generalist/specialist issue, I have noted with interest the way the clock is turning full circle here and the generalist coming back into his own. The Indian Administrative Reforms Commission devoted much time to this issue. The cynic might suggest that this is one area where the lengthy expansive deliberations of the Administrative Reforms Commission did achieve some action.

On my last theme, public service salaries, I note the very peculiar situation which exists here. It would be surprising indeed if it were not a very live issue.

One final comment. And here I unashamedly stick my neck right cut for any one of you to administer the *coup de grace*. In no country have I noted a greater lack of rapport between academic and practical teacher of administration than in India. The very distinction itself is a most unhappy one. It is not uncommon to find academic institutions looking down their collective noses at those concerned with the study and teaching of the nuts and bolts of administration. Not only is the subject often seen as 'unworthy' of an academic institution, but its practitioners, whether they be retired or even serving Chief Secretaries, deemed utterly unworthy of academic status.

"Theory and practice" ought not to be looked upon as two discrete subjects, The shortcomings do not end there. There are cases also where the members of Institutes of Public Administration do not accept that they have any obligation to master the nuts and bolts. Instead they are content to put such matters in the hands of serving officers recruited – and paid – to lecture, on such subjects. I should like to see more give and take – administrators seconded/deputed to serve in institutes and departments of public administration (including university institutes not merely government institutes). I should also like to see even more academics seconded to government departments. In such matters I suspect that the Rajasthan Institute and Government may well be setting examples that could be emulated elsewhere.

A Postscript

I completed these notes two days ago before I had had the opportunity to attend the discussion of Professor Rajni Kothari's book *Footsteps into the Future*. Apart from my interest in the intrinsic subject of the book and its critics I would not fail to be struck by the fact that the discussion reinforced what I have just said about the relationship in India between, as Professor Kothari put it, "the political and intellectual elites". He actually used the word 'conflict' and describes these bureaucrats in his book as the, 'enemy'. In making his presentation he spoke of them as a 'menace'. This is a language which is new to me. It will be of little satisfaction to be told – as I shall be told that the statement is a typical. Certainly it is no more than an extreme statement of a situation which I had already identified from my own – alarming because it echoes much more commonly heard comments heard all over the world from politicians talking about intellectuals. I am old enough to remember the public burning of books in Germany in the 1930s. Thus what needs to be emphasized is that bureaucrats and intellectuals should be mutually reinforcing – even if critical. Epithets like 'menace' and 'enemies' have no place in this debate.

16 Comparative Aspects of Public Administration

R.B. Jain

Public administration, as an aspect of governmental activity, has existed ever since political systems started functioning. This is evident from classical treatises such as Kautilya's *Arthashastra* and Aristotle's *Politics*. Presently, political scientists generally believe that no description of any polity or governmental system is complete without an account of the administrative apparatus of the polity. However, public administration as a field of systematic study is only recent. In the United States, interest in the field of public administration had not really begun until the publication in 1887 of Woodrow Wilson's famous essay, "The Study of Administration", generally considered the starting point of a deep intellectual interest in the field of public administration. Since then, it has become a well-recognized area of specialized interest, either as an aspect of political science or as an academic discipline in its own right. Today the American study of public administration has perhaps gone further than any other field of American political science in the direction of developing a culture-free conceptual framework for approaching its objects of inquiry.

The search for the construction of a science of public administration brought home the fact that this depended, among other things, on success in establishing propositions about administrative behaviour that transcended national boundaries. In his essay, "The Science of Public Administration" published in 1947, Robert Dahl had argued that "the attempt to create a science of public administration with universal or even generally applicable principles was handicapped by the three basic problems of values, individual personality and the social framework".[1] He pointed out that "the comparative aspects of public administration have largely been ignored, and as long as the study of public administration is not comparative, claim for a 'science of public administration' sound rather hollow".[2]

The need for comparison presented many problems. To begin with, any attempt to compare national administrative systems must acknowledge the fact that administration is only one aspect of the operation of the political system. This inevitably means that comparative public administration is linked with the study of comparative politics. Work in comparative public administration has thus closely followed comparative political analysis. In the United States both movements, viz., of comparative politics and comparative public administration have been characterized "by the comparative youth of their participants, by a general commitment to the outlook identified with behaviouralism, by an effort to be interdisciplinary in interests and techniques, and by an effort to arrive at concepts, formulas, and theories that are truly universal, bridging and embracing all cultures".[3]

Interest in comparative public administration also grew out of the fact that beginning with Second World War continuing into the post-War military occupations, and accelerating with the many technical assistance programmes of the United States, the United Nations, and private foundations, the American students and teachers of public administration by hundreds have found themselves engaged in professional work in foreign lands. This exposure to foreign, often non-Western, governmental systems and cultures has stimulated a sense of 'comparativeness' in general, and in particular has raised questions about either the appropriateness or the sheer possibility of transferring familiar administrative devices or applying what had been presumed to be good or scientific principles of administration in diverse settings.[4]

Thus, in order to meet the needs of new policy areas of technical assistance to administration, important strides have been made in the evolution of the study of comparative public administration. Consequently, the students of comparative public administration, aware of the intellectual developments in comparative sociology, anthropology, and other areas, became interested in developing theoretical constructs with a cross-cultural, cross-national, and cross-temporal relevance in their field. They recognized that hypotheses developed in the American cultural context, in order to be valid and part of the success of public administration, should be tested in cross-cultural settings.

The ultimate objective of the comparative public administration movement, as Caldwell observed, has been "to hasten the emergence of a universally valid body of knowledge concerning administrative behaviour – in brief to contribute to a genuine and generic discipline of public administration".[5] Comparative public administration thus delineates an area of concern and a methodological orientation that differs from the traditional approach of merely juxtaposing the description of a number of similar administrative institutions in different countries at one place. It offers to study the administrative processes and organizations for the purpose of answering common problems and questions. It attempts to identify the characteristics of various administrations in terms of certain established analytical categories in the light of which identification of administrative phenomena becomes possible for as many administrative systems as possible. It further purports not only to examine similarities and differences in the norms, institutions, and behaviour of administrations, but also to account for them and aim toward the development of a body of knowledge so that policy recommendations can be made and trends predicted. It is in this sense that it becomes a matrix from which theories emerge. At the same time, it serves as a laboratory for their testing. As Dwight Waldo has put it:

> To compare is to examine similarities and differences simultaneously; the effort is bent forward to two main ends: (i) to discover, define and differentiate the stuff (politics or administration) to be compared, wherever in the world it may be; and (ii) to develop criteria of differentiation that are useful in ordering and analysing the "stuff" once it has been identified. In this task, the contemporary stock of provoked or fashionable concepts in the social sciences (as well as those "indigeneous" to political science) has been drawn upon extensively. The works of Max Weber and Talcott Parsons, structural-functionalism as conceived in various sources, the concept of culture, the decision-making scheme, communications theory and cybernetics, systems theory – all these and several more sources have been drawn upon by both movements.[6]

Trends and Models in Comparative Public Administration

The Comparative Administration Group of the American Society for Public Administration (ASPA) has done some pioneering work in strengthening the comparative public administration movement. A draft statement in 1961 described comparative public administration as "the theory of public administration applied to diverse cultures and national settings – and the body of factual data by which it can be examined and tested".[7] In his paper on "Trends in the Comparative Study of Public Administration", presented in the ASPA meeting in 1961, Fred W. Riggs, one of the leading scholars of comparative public administration, outlined three trends in the comparative study of public administration. The first is a trend from normative toward more empirical approaches (characterized by a growing interest in descriptive and analytical information for its own sake). The second is a shift from ideographic toward nomothetic (any approach that concentrates on the unique case – the historical episode or case study, the single agency or country, the biography or cultural area – is ideographic; by contrast, an approach that seeks generalizations (laws) or hypotheses that assert irregularities of behaviour, and correlations between variables, may be called nomothetic). The third is a shift from a predominantly non-ecological to an ecology basis for the study of public administration. The ecology implies not only a characterization of environments, but rather analysis of the patterns of interaction between the subject of its study and its environment. Riggs described the first trend as fairly well established and the second and third as "perhaps only just emerging".[8]

Such trends in the study of comparative public administration have given rise to problems of methodological concern and of conceptual focus. Scholars have been greatly preoccupied with the construction of models and typologies of political regimes and institutions and the delineation of geographic-cultural areas – an activity prominent also in and shared with comparative politics. The range of concepts associated with the term 'bureaucracy' and its ideal type has been extensively used. The so-called action theory and the concepts and language of structural-functionalism have often been employed. The concept of culture has often been involved, and the related and overlapping but different and broader concept of ecology is also frequently set forth as important. Equilibrium theory, and particularly the idea of a 'system' with 'inputs' and, 'outputs' is prominent. Most of the popular concepts and phrases of contemporary behavioural science are being used, and there is reference, for example, to matters such as communications theory and multivariate analysis.

The Bureaucratic Model

The bureaucratic model has been enthusiastically adopted by students of comparative public administration in developed countries as a means of measuring the actual administrative institutions observed against an 'ideal-type model' of rational administrative organization, that is, organization perfectly developed to fulfil some set programme objective. The model was first developed by Max Weber and has since been further developed, applied, criticized, and altered. The model is so well known that it need not be elaborated here. Following Max Weber, political scientists have generally assumed that only an advanced society with a culture featuring legal-rational concepts of authority would be capable of sustaining administrative structures approximating the bureaucratic model.

Dwight Waldo has found the bureaucratic model useful, stimulating, and provocative, its advantage and appeal being that it "is set in a large framework that spans history and cultures and relates bureaucracy to important societal variables, yet it focusses attention upon the chief structural and functional characteristics of bureaucracy".[9] He correctly points out that not much empirical research has actually been done on the basis of the bureaucratic model.

However, American students of public administration – who had a tendency to resist the abandonment or serious modification of the bureaucratic model as they moved from the realm of advanced, complex nations to that of the nations still undergoing modernization – have been beset by the malady afflicting comparative study in general: the tendency to put the structure first and to assume that the function performed by a given structure in one cultural political context will carry over to a similar structure in another context. This accounts for the frustration of American specialists in public administration when they have attempted to apply their expertise in the role of technical advisers to the governments of Asian and African countries. Invariably, they have found that the structure set up along the lines of classical principles has failed to behave as expected or even to display standard aberrations familiar in the Western settings. Most perplexing has been the difficulty of maintaining stable boundaries between the administrative organizations and the political environment. On the one hand, achievement criteria have been violated, often in a wholesale fashion, as political considerations of personal loyalty, ideological parity, or both have become predominant as personnel policy. On the other hand, administrative agencies have shown a tendency to step beyond the brands of their assigned functions and to seek a role, sometimes in the absence of clear political initiative, in charting the direction and pace of the modernization of their countries.[10]

Among scholars who have contributed to the studies of comparative bureaucratic systems are Monroe Berger, Alfred Diamant, Ferrel Heady, Robert Presthus, and Michael Crozier. The emphasis in most of the writings on comparative bureaucracy appears to be on the interaction between the administrative subsystem and the political system in which it (i.e., the administrative subsystem) exists, although some attention has been paid to other dimensions of administrative ecology.

Riggs's Prismatic-Sala Model

The most prominent model builder in the comparative administrative movement is Fred. W. Riggs. In fact, Riggs, as his thinking has evolved, has developed not only a model but a series of overlapping and interrelated models. Extending Sutton's two ideal models of agraria and industria to illustrate the relationship between societal structures and whole cultures, Riggs set forth his first major model in a lengthy essay entitled, "Agraria and Industria: Towards a Typology of Comparative Administration".[11] He suggested an inductive typology of administrative systems along a continuum between Agraria and Industria. He illustrated two ideal types of public administration systems in 'agraria' and 'industria' and claimed that similar ideal types could be constructed at various transitional stages between the two, with similar categories illustrating the interdependence of administrative systems and societies. As his conceptualization proved too abstract to apply, he turned away from general systems models to middle-range theory based on his empirical research in South-East Asia.

Riggs then came out with his well-known model of 'prismatic society'.[12] In this model, Riggs has changed the key terms from 'agraria-transitia-industria' to 'fused society', 'prismatic society' and 'refracted society' (later redesignated as 'diffracted' society). It is based on the structural-functional approach, and delineates societies according to different social structures.

After examining various societies, Riggs observed that in some societies a particular structure fulfils only one function, whereas in other societies a particular structure fulfils several functions. From this, he argues, we can imagine a purely hypothetical society in which a single structure would perform all the functions necessary for the survival of the society. "Let us call it 'a fused model', just as we call white light fused. In extreme contrast, let us imagine a situation in which every function has a corresponding structure that is specialized for its performance. We call this situation a 'refracted model' just as we say that light is refracted into all the separate coaxes of a rainbow of spectrum." Riggs then explains that if we imagine a midpoint between these extremes (though it would be a mistake to think that any society is fully refracted or fused), we might call it the 'prismatic model' because of the prism that refracts fused light.[13]

The three ideal-typical categories of societies are thus constructed on the basis of the extent to which rules in various organizations are exclusive or overlapping. The fused society has almost no specialization of rules, whereas the refracted society is at a high level of structural differentiation, and the prismatic society forms the intermediate category. In the prismatic society, a high degree of formalism – discrepancies between norms and realities – overlapping and heterogeneity exists. Riggs has argued, therefore, that in a prismatic environment institutional or formal structural analysis is likely to produce a disappointing outcome, since what might normally be expected to result from a particular administrative system on organizational patterns fails to appear because of a big gap that exists between the formally prescribed norms and the effectively practiced action.

These models emphasize ecology, and Riggs is primarily concerned with examining how public administrative functions are performed by different types of structures. His approach emphasizes an open system perspective that has had increasing influence elsewhere in the social sciences. However, his systems models lack the dynamic qualities developed in many other open system models, for in them he has not analysed the process of refraction from a developmental perspective. He also does not appear to have worked out fully the implications of his theory on public administration. This is, however, not to underestimate the value of his theory, which, as Chapman believes, "deepens our insight into some of the underlying problems of administrative development in transitional societies".[14] His prismatic theory may, perhaps, be especially valuable in understanding the pathology of public administration, as it may be useful for diagnosis in the same way that principles help in the diagnosis of certain administrative malfunctions. What is noteworthy in Riggs's provocative suggestions is that he is attempting to place the administrative subsystem into a larger system and to show both its functional relationship thereto and its conceptual consequences. To the extent that Riggs and others sharing his assumptions have provided a framework for further undertaking in the field, the study of comparative public administration has moved further to date than have the other subfields of comparative political systems.

Dorsey's Information-Energy Model

John T. Dorsey's 'Information-Energy' model is based on a synthesis of concepts of general systems theory, of communication and cybernetics, and of energy and energy conversion. Dorsey's model conceptualizes individuals, groups, organizations and societies as complex information – energy converters. Energy is defined as the ability to effect some change of form, time, or space in physical relationships – that is, to do work. Energy conversion, consequently, is the manifestation of this capacity, or the process of effecting such changes. Information can be viewed as energy in certain forms or configurations. A system converts inputs, such as demands and intelligence, through various conversion processes of screening, selecting, and channelizing into outputs. Generally, high levels of information input, storage, and processing permit a high energy output. An administrative system produces outputs in various forms, for example, regulation of services for other subsystems and systems forming part of its environment.

Dorsey has presented certain general hypotheses that help explain the administrative problems of developing countries in terms of the non-availability of surplus information and energy. His basic hypothesis is that a society's degree of development is a measure of its information and energy surplus. Developing nations' administrative systems usually have scarcity of information input, storage, and processing. This results in relatively smaller energy outputs, which, in turn results in an ineffective administrative process, ritualistic procedures, conservatism, and a lack of rationality.

Dorsey has stressed that research in comparative public administration should focus, if possible, on all of the input, conversion, and output aspects of the administrative system, though, he adds, in particular cases of study, much would depend on the needs and orientation of a scholar. Since his approach views administrative system in the context of their environment, it is essentially ecological. Moreover, as noted previously, it has certain elements of a developmental perspective. However, it is probably because of the model's complex variables and the operational problems associated with them that other scholars have not used this approach in their analyses.[15]

The Developmental Model

Closely related to the study of comparative public administration is the study of developmental administration. Developmental administration, an indispensable tool in the attainment of the goals of the 'good' society, has attracted the mainstream of comparative administrators seeking ways and means to improve administrative performance and to strengthen the planning and execution of development programmes. The idea had its origins in the desire of wealthier countries to aid poorer countries and more especially in the obvious needs of the newly emerging nation-states to transform their colonial bureaucracies into more responsible instruments of social change.

It should be noted, however, that developmental administration is not the same as administrative development. Essentially, it is that aspect of public administration that focusses on government influenced change toward progressive political, economic, and social objectives, once confined to recipients, of foreign aid, but now universally applied.

Developmental administration thus encompasses the organization of new agencies such as planning organizations and development corporations; the reorientation of established agencies such as departments of agriculture; the delegation of administrative powers to development agencies; and the creation of a cadre of administrators that can provide leadership in stimulating and supporting programmes of social and economic improvement. It has the purpose of making change as attractive as possible.[16] Strictly speaking, it may not be referred to as the 'applied side' of comparative public administration, as there is no sharp distinction in intent, concepts, and involved personnel between the two. Those interested in developmental administration are interested in and draw on many sources other than comparative public administration; and some of them are trained in (and identify themselves with) disciplines other than political science or public administration.[17]

Developmental administration is related to goal and action-oriented administrative systems. Since most definitions of the word 'administration' connote the aspect of goal attainment, the inclusion of the word 'developmental' might at first seem to be redundant. Nevertheless, the term refers to a particular focus on certain key aspect of socio-administrative change. Also, to Edward Weidner, its foremost proponent, the concept of developmental administration "refers to the process of guiding an organization towards the achievement of progressive political, economic and social objectives that are authoritatively determined in one manner or another". Weidner has urged a separate focus on development administration whose end objective is "to relate different administrative roles, practices, organizational arrangements and procedures to the maximizing of development objectives. In research terms the ultimate dependent variable would be the development goals themselves".

The concept of developmental administration has two important dimensions. First, it is concerned with the processes through which a public administrative system directs socio-economic and political change in the society, and, second, it studies the dynamics of change within the administrative system, that is, the way the system enhances its capabilities to withstand undesirable change coming from the environment and to direct desired change. The first phase refers to the 'administration of development', whereas the second is related to the process of 'administrative development'.

Problems in the Application of Models

The foregoing brief review of some of the models constructed by American public administrationists for the study of public administration on a comparative basis raises a number of questions about their application in understanding the administrative systems in the developing world.

Which particular model is most appropriate, and for what purpose, and where should it be applied? The central problem in the study of comparative public administration is that it is large enough to embrace all the phenomena that should be embraced without being, by virtue of its large dimensions, too unwieldy. The second problem is of relating the universal and the unique in one system. The idea of universals runs through administrative study, for example, in the assertions of the 'founding fathers' to the most sophisticated of our contemporaries in the field. But to make comparisons implies not only the identification of the universals but also discovering a criterion of differentiation.

The choice of models thus is intimately related to the choice of a research strategy and to the most effective employment of limited resources. None of these models listed previously may present a perfect analysis of contemporary administrative scenes in diverse cultural settings. But if carefully used, they do serve as a framework for analysing different aspects of administrative phenomena in a comparative perspective. These models may be useful in revealing more clearly the social, economic, and political basis on which administrative institutions depend. In public administration they are impressionistic and non-quantitative; it is only when we understand their limitations that we can use models intelligently and safely to help us toward an understanding of administrative behaviour.

Comparative Methodology in the Study of the Indian Administrative System

A brief survey of the literature on comparative public administration undertaken by the author sometime back indicates a very limited use of the comparative method of research in a scientific and comprehensive manner by Indian scholars.[18] It seems that, barring the bureaucratic model, other models have not been used in the study of administrative phenomena in India. The three dimensions of comparative research, namely, the vertical comparison (comparison between national administrative phenomena and regional or local administrative phenomena), the horizontal comparison (analysis of administrative processes over a period of time), and the study of administrative institutions and processes across national boundaries with a new orientation and approach, have yet to be explored fully by Indian scholars of comparative public administration.

It is fitting to mention here the findings of one of the research studies that has used the bureaucratic model to understand the differences in the Indian bureaucratic system. This is an example of how the Weberian model of bureaucracy can be fruitfully employed to understand the bureaucratic phenomenon in a cross-national perspective.

A basic conclusion emerging from the study conducted by Panandikar and Kshirsagar is that the general constructs of bureaucratic theory as evolved by Weber and others provide a useful basis for both practical and broader theoretical and comparative purposes.[19] To the extent that the study identifies the universality of structural characteristics of bureaucracy, it also supports Heady's thesis that for comparative purposes bureaucratic structure presents a meaningful starting point.

The above study reveals, however, that structural and behavioural characteristics in India bureaucracy are only moderately interrelated and that the functional content of the bureaucracy, the type of office and its level of mass contact to meet programmatic needs, and the level of its skill composition, have a significant bearing on the behavioural characteristics. This finding has theoretical as well as practical implications.

Theoretically, it implies that bureaucracy is not a static phenomenon with certain standard structural and behavioural characteristics in more or less comparable proportion. Bureaucracy is a far more dynamic phenomenon in which its functional content, and the mass contact inherent in its objective, and several other factors influence its behavioural characteristics. What is more, the behavioural characteristics appear in turn to modify or alter the bureaucratic structure itself.

In other words, the existing theory of bureaucracy based essentially on the Weberian model, though extremely useful as a starting point, appears to be somewhat static. Even Heady's idea of using the structural postulates of Weberian theory appears to be restrictive. Although Heady's approach may make comparative study in bureaucracy relatively easy, it would not help adequately in the development of a more rigorously based bureaucratic theory for either academic or policy-making purposes. The main limitation of Heady's approach is that it makes structural postulate of bureaucratic theory independent of behavioural postulates. The present study suggests that the structural postulates are not after all so independent as to build bureaucratic theory around them; that it is necessary to examine structural and behavioural postulates together to formulate a more valid and useful bureaucratic theory even though this creates many research problems.

The findings of the present study also suggest that what we need is not only a generalized bureaucratic model but also a range of submodels in which the various characteristics of bureaucracy play differing roles, some more powerful and some less powerful, in various combinations. The main considerations that appear to necessitate such a range are that (i) the functional context of bureaucracy differs from agency to agency; (ii) the degree of mass contact the bureaucracy is involved in, especially to achieve its objectives, varies; and (iii) the skill composition, including the levels of education of the bureaucracy, itself undergoes major alterations between agencies within the same governmental apparatus.[20]

Western Bureaucracies and Comparative Methods

By far the most comprehensive study using a comparative historical methodology in a cross-national perspective within the framework of the bureaucratic model is *The European Administrative Elite* by John A. Armstrong.[21] He has combined a method and a subject matter resembling historical sociology with a conceptual focus derived from social psychology. The study provides a theoretical framework with a focus on social psychological categories and a judicious blend of the sociological approach and the application of theory to history in as coherent and substantive a comparison as possible.

The Communist Bureaucracies

Today, the Communist bureaucracies provide most valuable objects for comparison with Western public as well as private bureaucracies. Their value is greatly enhanced for this purpose by the close convergence of technologies. The question "Is communism possible?" asked in a multitude of forms by both Western observers and the Communists themselves, has provided fruitful focus for research on administration. It has provided new evidence - about whose interpretation, agreement may not always be there - on the relation of economic incentives to productivity, and on the behaviour of planning and pricing mechanisms as coordinating instruments.

Administration in Developing Countries

The new nations of Africa and Asia are having an even greater impact on applied administrative science than is Eastern Europe, The reason is plain: In these new countries, American political scientists are not only observers but frequently have also been advisers. Unawareness of ethnocentrism - a major deterrent to losing it - can sometimes survive a two-week consulting trip to a foreign land, but less easily a year's immersion in its affairs. (Some handy data on this point would be extremely valuable for the applied science of administration). The new nations have given impetus to studies in comparative administration but have also posed severe methodological problems. Here no easy assumption can be made that 'all other things are equal', and tracing cause-and-effect relations is correspondingly difficult.

As with other institutional changes we have mentioned, the emergence of the new nations emphasizes new facets of administration. Although there may be little mention of the 'scientific estate', there is much talk about the 'technical estate'. The presence in a society of military and development experts as almost the only trained cadres makes the problem of political responsibility of the specialists focal and gives the problem a special flavour. Balanced against the difficulties of political control are the urgent needs to acquire technical and managerial competence where none has existed before.

The particular problems of neutrality arising from recruitment have been relatively minor problems in the American bureaucracy, though the civil rights movement has revived them. We would expect them to be far more severe in developing countries, where requirements of technical competence, and sometimes even of literacy, lead to vast over-representation of upper-class strata. Where class is also closely related to special forms of economic interest (e.g., landholding), as it is in many developing countries, the class composition of the bureaucracy is a central and not a peripheral issue. This is reflected in the emphasis placed on this issue in the growing literature of comparative administration.[22]

Problems of Comparative Research

Evidently, this kind of approach to the study of public administration is fraught with many difficulties. The basic problem is one of competence in comparative research methodology. But that is not the only problem. Even if it is assumed that a researcher knows the techniques of comparative methods of study, there is always the difficulty of 'models building', that is, to choose between various concepts and models of comparative research or to develop a theory or hypothesis around which a generalization applicable to many administrative systems can be built and tested.

An Indian scholar, in particular, faces difficulties with respect to the non-availability of data and material, particularly across national frontiers. The prohibitive cost and the time involved may itself deter a researcher from venturing in this direction. Further, there are difficulties arising from the nature of the data, which some governments may regard as confidential and which, therefore, may not be easily available to a researcher. There are other difficulties that arise from the range and nature of variables that must be used in the study of comparative administration. Some variables are simply not capable of being measured precisely. A researcher may use certain general or cross-national variables (e.g., psychological or socio-economic variables), but the unique character of each administrative policy and organization must, in some form, be measured if comparisons are realistically to account for the presence of a particular type of administrative phenomenon. Difficulties also arise from the interplays and interrelationships among the norms, structures, and behaviour of the administrative systems. Models and theories must take into account all of these factors. Further, any meaningful comparative research must take into account the study of the societies as wholes, so that they may be subjected to comparative analysis. Obviously, this requires an interdisciplinary approach to the study of administrative phenomena. In India, the study of public administration through an interdisciplinary approach has yet to begin on a serious footing. Models are difficult to build, and researchers have found the comparative method of research more difficult than the empirical or behavioural approach, techniques that have, to some extent, been perfected.

Agenda for further Research through the Comparative Method

The list of difficulties just presented does not suggest that comparative research in India is not possible, nor that there are no avenues open to research on a comparative basis. Indeed, the national frontiers of India present a veritable paradise for researchers in comparative administration.

In the first place, there is ample scope for comparative research in various administrations of the States and Union Territories in India. The socio-economic and cultural factors, which have both similar and dissimilar features in various regions of the country, present a challenge to a researcher to make a scientific inquiry into the study of administrative institutions, programme administration, and policy implementation on a regional basis. An inquiry into the causes of dynamism through which the same institutions work in a particular Union Territory or State and the slow pace at which they work in other regions would be a worthwhile area for study as a means of improving administrative organizations in various regions. The more often the States or Union Territories are included in the survey, the greater the possibility of "administrative theory-building through empirically tested generalizations about Indian administration". Such research, if undertaken by Indian scholars, would also obviate the subjective element that is likely to crop up in researchers who have been exposed to only their own political culture, for example, of the Western type. With some imaginative and concentrated efforts on the part of professional institutions and universities, a unified programme to study various administrative phenomena on cross-regional bases could perhaps be drawn. This will help build up a substantial amount of literature on the basis of which future researchers may develop improved research models for comparative study.

Secondly, there is considerable scope for researchers with a comparative approach in respect to policy and programme administration in public and private settings. This will be especially fruitful in comparing the performances of public and private enterprises, particularly with reference to the same industry. The development of the public sector on an unprecedented scale has confronted the government with the problem of running those enterprises on a basis in which they could generate sufficient dividends necessary for the establishment of a socialist welfare state. Horizontal studies over a period of time of nationalized industries (e.g., it would be interesting to compare the performance of the banking industry before nationalization and after nationalization over a period of time, along with a comparison of, say, consumer satisfaction with banks in the private and public sectors) would indeed be logical and meaningful.

Thirdly, vertical comparisons of various aspects of functional administration between the national, regional and local government open an extensive field for researchers. It is generally admitted that administration at regional and local levels is weaker when compared with that at the national level. This may perhaps be a universal phenomenon. In the Indian context, however, it would be beneficial to undertake such exercises with a view to locating the factors that hamper the growth of sound administrative practices in many areas. The combination of comparative method and empirical analysis will, it may be hoped, open up many bottlenecks of administrative processes.

Finally, comparative studies, on a cross-national basis, provide vast potentialities for scientific and meaningful research toward the identification of a universal administrative plane. Admittedly, such studies would have to be undertaken with considerable planning, insight, and an adequate knowledge of the unlimited range of variables that is involved in the interplay of administrative processes across national frontiers. However, the difficulties are not altogether insurmountable. To begin, cross-cultural studies can be undertaken on a regional basis (e.g., with respect to administrative phenomena in South Asian countries) with a little systematic effort. For instance, a common theme for a comparative analysis could be the impact of public administration on the developmental process with reference to South Asian countries or with reference to Latin American countries or East African countries. Another theme for comparative and historical exposition could be the impact of the British administration on the development of public administration in various erstwhile colonies. Yet another comparative study could be an analysis of the planning and decision-making processes in various countries.

Research Areas in Comparative Administration

Comparisons can also be made between various aspects of administrative processes in India and some other developed countries like the United States, the United Kingdom, France, the Scandinavian countries, and so on, with a view to testing the validity of administrative generalizations evolved through regional comparisons, and for the purposes of determining the overall performance of an administrative system in terms of goal achievements. For instance, a common framework in this context can be an analysis of the administration of social services and welfare activities with respect to as many systems as possible.

Some other suggested topics are as under:[23]

1. Impact of social structure on the development of bureaucracy and its procedures.
2. The natural calamities and the administration.
3. Technological developments and public administration.
4. Public administration and political development.
5. Social, economic system and administration (ecology).
6. Imperial traditions: their impact on administration.
7. Political agitation and administrative response.
8. Administrative load and popular demand.

However, all these suggestions are based on the assumption that the research will be undertaken with reference to a common framework to point out similarities and dissimilarities and to account for them or to test the validity of certain generalizations through empirical studies of as many systems as possible. Only then can comparative studies be scientific and more meaningful.

Conclusion

Since post-World War II tendencies in comparative public administration are still being analysed and illustrated, we cannot really conclude the survey of public administration. In the contemporary development of the discipline nothing has really concluded. There is still some vagueness and dilemma as to the claim of public administration to be a self-contained academic discipline. At this point we can only say that the study of comparative public administration, in spite of its many vagaries, has reached at last a new consensus upon concepts, methods, and analytical approaches capable of yielding a broad and precise science of administrative institutions. It is possible that at a later stage we will be able to develop better research strategies for comparative public administration, once we have been able to gather enough empirical data about administrative behaviour in as many systems as possible, particularly relating to the developing world, which has very little empirical data to offer for any meaningful comparative study leading to theory construction.

Notes

1. Robert A. Dahl, "The Science of Public Administration: Three Problems", *Public Administration Review*, VIII (1947) pp. 1-11.
2. Ibid.
3. Dwight Waldo, "Public Administration", in David E. Sills, ed., *International Encyclopedia of Social Science* (New York: The Macmillan Company and The Free Press, 1968), XIII, p. 151.
4. Ibid.
5. Lynton Caldwell, "Conjectures on Comparative Public Administration", in Roscoe Martin, ed., *Public Administration and Democracy: Essays in Honour of Paul H. Appleby* (Syracuse, N.Y.: Syracuse University Press), p. 230.
6. Dwight Waldo, "Comparative Public Administration: Prologue, Performance, Problems and Promise" (*Symposium on Business Policy*, April 8-11, 1963, Graduate School of Business Administration, Harvard University), pp. 11-12 (mimeo).

7. Ferrel Heady and Sybil L. Stokes, eds., *Papers in Comparative Public Administration* (Ann Arbor, Mich.: Institute of Public Administration, 1962), p. 4.
8. Fred W. Riggs, "Trends in the Comparative Study of Public Administration", *International Review of Administrative Sciences* XXVIII (1962), pp. 9-15.
9. Waldo, "Comparative Administration", pp. 28-29.
10. David M. Wood, "Comparative Government and Politics", in Stephen L. Wasby, *Political Science. The Discipline and its Dimensions: An Introduction* (Calcutta. Scientific Book Agency, 1970), pp. 516-17.
11. See W.J. Siffin, ed., *Toward the Comparative Study of Public Administration* (Bloomington: Indiana University Press, 1957).
12. For an introduction to the prismatic-sala model, see Riggs, "The 'Sala' Model: An Ecological Approach to the Study of Comparative Public Administration", *Philippine Journal of Public Administration*, VI (1962), 3-16 and his *Administration in Developing Countries* (Boston. Houghton Mifflin Co., 1964).
13. For an exposition of Riggs's prismatic theory, see Riggs, *Administration in Developing Countries and The Ecology of Public Administration* (Bombay: Asia Publishing House, 1961).
14. Richard A. Chapman, "Prismatic Theory in Public Administration: A Review of the Theories of Fred W. Riggs", *Public Administration*, Winter, 1966, p. 423.
15. For a detailed study of the model, see John. T. Dorsey, Jr., "An Information Energy Model" in Heady and Stokes, *Papers in Comparative Public Administration*, pp. 37-57.
16. G.F. Grant, "A Note on Applications of Development Administration", *Public Policy*, XV (1966), pp. 200-1.
17. See John. D. Montgomery and William J. Siffin, eds., *Approaches to Development: Politics Administration and Change* (New York: McGraw Hill Book Company, 1967) and F.W. Riggs. ed., *Frontiers of Development Administration* (Durham, N.C.: Duke University Press, 1970).
18. See R.B. Jain, "Research Methods in Public Administration: A Critical Survey of Important Works in Historical and Comparative Methodology", *The Indian Journal of Public Administration*, XVII (October-December 1971), 698-725, undertaken for the Indian Council for Social Sciences Research, New Delhi.

19. V.A. Pai Panandikar and S.S. Kshirsagar, "Bureaucracy in India: An Empirical Study", *The Indian Journal of Public Administration*, XVII (April-June 1971).
20. Ibid., pp. 206-7.
21. John. A. Armstrong, *The European Administrative Elite* (Princeton, N.J.: Princeton University Press. 1973).
22. Herbert A. Simon, "The Changing Theory and Changing Practices of Public Administration", in Ithiel de Sola Pool, ed., *Contemporary Political Science: Toward Empirical Theory* (New York: McGraw Hill Book Company, 1967), pp. 92-93.
23. This list of topics, among others, was first suggested by the ICSSR Group on Research Methodology in their meeting held at Bombay in October 1971. See Indian Council of Social Sciences Research, *A Survey of Research in Public Administration*, Vol. 2 (Bombay: Allied Publishers, 1975), p. 510. The author was a member of that group.

17 New Dimensions in Management Theory: The Japanese Contribution

K.D. Trivedi and Ravindra Sharma

At a time when Japanese productivity is the highest in the world and the productivity in the western nations is declining, there is clearly a great deal that we can learn from Japan. A great many statistics testify to the Japanese economic prowess and decline of western world's industrial standing.

In 1980, Japan's GNP was third highest in the world and if the current trend persists it would be number one by the year 2000.[1] Japan supports a population of over 115 million people (half the population of the United States), exports $ 75 billion worth more goods than it imports, and has an investment rate as well as GNP growth rate which is twice that of the United States. Japan has come to dominate in one selected industry after another – eclipsing the British in motor cycles, surpassing the Germans and the Americans in automobile production, wresting leadership from Germans and the Swiss in watches, cameras, and optical instruments and overcoming the United States historical dominance in businesses as diverse as steel, ship-building and consumer electronics. Today, Japanese wages are slightly higher than those in the United States. The Japanese standards for occupational safety and pollution control are now among the most stringent in the world.[2]

It is often thought that Japanese success is mainly due to its peculiar socio-cultural milieu. Japan no doubt has the advantage of homogenous population with widely shared cultural traits. It is also said that perhaps Japanese techniques like lifetime employment are responsible for the major achievements. These factors have certainly contributed towards the Japanese success story but the major reason for the superiority of Japanese is their managerial skill. It is therefore necessary to understand the major ingredients which have gone into the making of Japanese managerial culture.

At the outset there is a need to underline the Japanese belief that technology, technique and innovative ways of thinking move across national boundaries more readily than ways of perceiving, believing and behaving. The Japanese, therefore, have been extremely effective in borrowing from the West in areas where it excels. They took the best that the United States had to offer and adapted it to their conditions.

Organizational and Behavioural Aspects of Japanese Management

Japanese management practices have attracted worldwide attention. Academicians and practising managers all over the world have been very keenly observing Japanese management scene these days. Several studies of Japanese management practices are now available. One of such studies is by William G. Ouchi[3] who has spent years in researching and examining major corporations in Japan. On the basis of his in-depth study of the Japanese industrial and economic development he has added what is now quite well known as Theory Z to the existing postulates of Douglas MacGregor[4] known as Theory Y. Another important study done by Pascale and Athos[5] gives us an inside view of Japanese management style and culture. It has taken up Matsushita Electric Company, an industrial giant for an in-depth examination of Japanese management skills.

Theory Z

As a result of his studies of Japanese corporations, Ouchi has come to believe that productivity is essentially a problem of social organization and only in a limited way of managerial organization. He stunned the western business world by saying that productivity and trust went hand in hand. According to him, it is a history of mutual distrust between union, government and management during the twentieth century that paralyzed the British economy and lowered the English standard of living to a dismal level. On the other hand, the basic assumption in Theory Z is to structure the organization around a powerful bonding attachment between workers and their firms; where everyone from top to bottom plays one's part in an integrative unity of business and in the long-range planned growth of the organization. Theory Z style companies are not simply business school models. They are said to be the real secret of Japan's spectacular economic success.

In Japan, most of the companies are covered by 'lifetime employment' practice as distinct from the principle of 'hire and fire' widely prevalent in the industrialized countries of the West. Theory Z believes in the old adage that a job is more than just a job. Our occupation defines the major part of our lives. Theory Z culture assumes that any worker's life is a whole and not half machine from nine to five and half human in the hours preceding and following. The main plea of Theory Z is that humanized working conditions not only increase productivity but also the self-esteem of employees. Until now it was a common belief amongst the western managers that technology made for increased productivity. What Theory Z calls for instead is a redirection of attention to human relations in the corporate world.

As a natural corollary to this management philosophy, emerged a participative approach to decision-making which is now one of the best known features of Japanese organizations. The process of decision-making by consensus building is tedious and time consuming but once the agreement is reached no one attempts to sabotage or slow down the project. When a Japanese joins an organization he becomes a member of a larger family He grows with it and continues to share its successes or failures as an equal partner. When the times get tough for the organizations, instead of resorting to lay-offs of the workers, company managers will stop the increments and cut down pay hikes for everyone including themselves till the climate changes for the better; such actions foster a sense of belonging and of shared experience by everyone and lead to collective work ethic. To put it simply Theory Z suggests that involved workers are the key to increased productivity.

The Matsushita Case

Pascale and Athos study of Matsushita one of the fifty largest corporations in the world, illustrates how Theory Z has been operationalized in a corporate setting, The products of Matsushita are sold under the brand name of National Panasonic now a household name for quality consumer electronics all over the world. The factors that have contributed to Matsushita's growth and current position as a leading enterprise shed a great deal of light on the art of Japanese management in action.[6] Matsushita today employs more than 2,00,000 people with an annual sales of Rs 10,000 crores. It has consistently invested four per cent sales in R & D of which the major portion goes to production engineering.

The founder of the organization Konosuke Matsushita was a commoner who started as an apprentice in a bicycle shop earning twenty-five cents a day in the early years of the present century. In 1918, he started toying with the idea of producing small electrical appliances after he heard the news of Thomas Edison's remarkable discoveries. He went ahead with his projects and within a decade Matsushita Electric Company emerged as a leader of fledgling appliance industry. Between the Second World War and 1973, the year of the retirement of its Chairman Matsushita, sales in constant dollars multiplied over

4000 fold, profits increased at even greater rate.[7] Despite considerable diversification and enormous increase in size, product complexity and geographical dispersion, Matsushita increased efficiency substantially.[8] Konosuke Matsushita, the founder of the company, is still active at the age of eighty-eight.

The success of Matsushita rests mainly on two pillars, first the innovative business strategy and secondly, adoption of a style of management rooted in the finest traditions of Japanese culture.

Managerial Strategies

Some innovative market and sales techniques adopted by Matsushita related to the creation of their own channels of distributions and their direct approach to the retailers. The second element of the Matsushita strategy gave explicit recognition to the importance of market share. As soon as higher production volumes generated cost savings, these were passed on to the customer via reduced prices; thereby establishing barriers to entry for competitors. Thirdly, from the outset Matsushita did not attempt to pioneer new technology but emphasized quality and price. The dominance which Matsushita came to acquire in video tape technology is a good example of its market strategy. Sony, another Japanese consumer electronic giant only pioneered this technology but had established its brand name Betamax as synonymous with video-tape recorder. Given Sony's initial leadership in this market, one might have thought that its position was unassailable but Matsushita looked for a means to leapfrog competition. Market surveys indicated that consumers wanted longer (4 to 6 hour) video capacity versus the two-hour capacity for Betamax. Matsushita designed a more compact VTR system that met this need and was highly reliable, and priced the product 10 to 15 per cent below the Betamax. Today Matsushita selling under the Panasonic and RCA labels, manufactures two out of every three video-tape recorders sold.[9] At the heart of Matsushita's strategy is production engineering.

It also explains as to why Matsushita invests four per cent of its total sales in R & D. Matsushita's underlying strategic assumption is that profits are linked to growth and that investments which promote growth will eventually pay off in profits over the long term.

Matsushita's organizational strategy presents a unique blend of centralization and decentralization. As the business grew, specialized divisions were established for each product line, but at the same time Matsushita counterbalanced this thrust towards decentralization by centralizing four key functions. First, he created a cadre of controllers reporting to headquarters. Second, he instituted company 'bank' into which divisional profits flowed and from which divisions had to solicit funds for capital improvements. Third, he centralized the personnel functions. Matsushita viewed people as the critical resource of his company. To this day, no employee above a junior high school graduate is hired without central personnel screening. All managerial promotions are carefully reviewed by headquarters as well. Fourth and finally, Matsushita centralized training. All Matsushita employees flow through a basic training system that includes a heavy emphasis on Matsushita values.

Style Component

A fundamental tenet of Matsushita is "to develop extraordinary qualities in ordinary men". The major emphasis is on training and building competence. Senior management interventions are never done in the spirit of inquisition. This underlying goal interjects human objectives into superior subordinate relationship.

Another feature of the Matsushita style is its pragmatic approach to conflict. Japanese organizations have introduced the concept of 'acceptance time' as a powerful antidote to conflict. The underlying idea of this concept is that when new ideas or facts come along it is felt that people need time before they can get rid of the old and accept the new. To quote a

Matsushita manager: "You can't force people to accept your ideas – we try insofar as possible to expose them gradually and win their acceptance".[10] One is reminded of Chester Barnard's concept of zone of indifference which comes very near to the concept of 'acceptance time'.

It is interesting to know how Matsushita incorporated some of the religious values into the corporate structure. He once said: "It comes clear to me that people need way of linking their productive lives to society... A business should quickly stand on its own based on the services it provides to society. Profits should not be a reflection of corporate greed, but a note of confidence from society that what is offered by the firm is valued".[11] How close he is to the Gandhian concept of trusteeship? Such calls for values are not just thinly disguised manipulation but a part of the belief system for thousands of people who work for that company. The Matsushita philosophy provides a basis of meaning beyond the products it produces. Matsushita was the first company in Japan to have a song and a code of values. "It seems silly to Westerners", says one executive, "but every morning at 8.00 a.m., all across Japan, there are 87,000 people reciting the code of values and singing together. It's like we are all a community".[12] Some Western minds, will find these ideas rather strange but for Japanese such a connection between philosophy and hardheaded business objectives looks natural.

Matsushita's belief in developing people reaches rank and file as well. He works on the philosophy that a lot of, 'little' brains are superior to a few 'big' brains when it comes to making organizations work properly. To give practical shape to this principle, Japanese firms have suggestions, programmes and most view them vital for success. Matsushita not only rewards suggestions but maintains statistics on the number and quality of suggestions from each division. Japanese way of communication has also certain marked features which are quite distinct from the western ways. The Japanese, it is said, conduct their dialogues in circles, widening and narrowing them to correspond to the others' sensitivity to feedback. A Japanese manager might say: "I'd like you to reflect a bit further on your proposal". Translated into Western thought patterns the same sense might read: "I think you're wrong and you should come with a better idea".[13] The first approach as opposed to the second, allows the recipient to exist with his self-esteem intact. Verbal communication is also very important in the Japanese scheme of things. It is said that the Japanese have nineteen ways of saying 'no', the major aim being avoiding conflict if possible. Japanese are also generally suspicious of too much logic. They use 'too logical' in a pejorative, sense analogous to the way we use the term, 'legalistic.' Ambiguity, uncertainty and imperfection are not always undesirable attributes for the Japanese.

Linguist Frank Gilmey has pointed out Japanese penchant for using double negatives, He says: "Japanese shuns flat commitments and dotes on double negatives. A Japanese response to a question rarely is either 100 per cent acceptance or 100 per cent disagreement. He prefers to examine the proposition discussed and suggest various approaches that could be made of it".[14]

For example, one Japanese will say: "It isn't that we can't do it this way".

"Of course," replies the other, "still, we couldn't deny that it couldn't be done, could we?"

And so it continues. An exchange has begun and the two are exploring a problem from different perspectives. They try to avoid aggressiveness and brutal use of words.

Perhaps much better than others the Japanese seem to understand the basic dilemma of human existence, i.e., the inherent preferences of organization are clarity, certainty and perfection, the inherent nature of human relationship involves ambiguity, uncertainty and imperfection. The real trial of management lies in honouring, balancing and integrating the needs of both.

While comparing the Western and the Japanese systems of management, Pascale and Athos observe: "It is a matter of seven Ss. Western companies have tended to favour these three Ss

Strategy
Structure
Systems

When an American manager wants to make changes, the odds are that he will reorganize structure, introduce a new strategic direction and impose a new control system,

Our emphasis on the first three Ss produces an arid world in which nothing is alive. An organization is often given its life through the soft Ss

Staff
Skills
Style
Superordinate Goals

The tremendous success of many Japanese companies through meticulous attention to soft Ss, which act as a lubricant in the organization machine to keep the hard Ss from grinding one another away".[15]

Lessons to be Drawn

The Americans are trying hard to learn from Japanese techniques of management. In fact, some of their big and more successful companies like IBM have already incorporated some of these concepts in their management philosophy. At the same time one must admit that the Japanese technique cannot be directly copied either in the West or in an oriental setting like ours. It would be better to look at the Japanese as if they were a special kind of mirror one which might allow us to see ourselves in some new way that may suggest directions for careful changes.

Theory Z may not be the last word on motivation. While it is true that with the delineation of Theory Z we have reached the ultimate in alphabet, it is difficult to say whether with this we have reached the ultimate in the theories of motivation and management. Numerous experiments in participative management abroad testify to a greater awareness of the intricacies of motivation. They have clearly established that people are complicated intermixtures of wants, needs and abilities from which it would be impossible to isolate specific motives or preferences. As a result, recent thinking amongst more and more psychologists and sociologists has been veering round the views that no single theory of human behaviour whether X, Y or Z can be applied with equal success to all people at all times. For us in India the Japanese experience is of special value. We both claim to be adherents of an ancient culture while Japanese have been successful in incorporating some of the finest aspects of their traditions and culture as an integral part of their management skills which has made them the industrial giants of today and we are still groping in the dark and are chary of such innovation in our management techniques and skills which suit our culture and social milieu. We imitate but cannot innovate. How striking is the similarity between Matsushita's views about the social responsibility of business and those propounded by Gandhiji? This comparison becomes all the more meaningful when one is reminded of the fact that Matsushita is the founder leader of one of the biggest and most modern industrial enterprises in the world.

Theory Z may not work in India in the climate of declining productivity and employee alienation. Consensus building, which is one of the key features of Japanese management, is not possible under these conditions. But we can certainly keep reminding ourselves what Japanese have proved by their achievements, i.e., West is certainly not the last word in management.

Notes

1. Herman Khan A. and Thomas Pepper, *The Japanese Challenge: The Success or Failure of Economic Success* (New York: Crowell, 1979).

2. Ezra F. Vogel, *Japan as Number One: Lessons for America* (Mass.: Harvard University Press, 1979).
3. William G. Ouchi, *Theory Z: How American Business Can Meet Japanese Challenge* (New York: Avon Books, 1982).
4, Douglas McGregor, *The Human Side of Enterprise* (New York: McGraw Hill, 1960).
5 Richard T. Pascale and Anthony G. Athos, *The Art of Japanese Management Application for American Executives* (New York: Warner Books, 1981).
6. Rowland Gould, *The Matsushita Phenomenon* (Tokyo: Diamond Sha., 1970).
7. Ibid., p. 5f.
8. Ibid., p. 5f.
9. Peter Nulty, "Matsushita Takes the Lead in Video Recorders", *Fortune* (July 16, 1979).
10. Pascale and Athos, op. cit., p. 71.
11. Gould, op. cit., pp. 15-19.
12. Pascale and Athos, op. cit., p. 73.
13. Frank Gilmey, "The Japanese and Their Language", *Encounter* (March 1975), p. 33.
14. Gilmey, op. cit., p. 32f.
15. Pascale and Athos, op. cit., p. 1.f.

Section IV

ORGANIZATIONAL CHANGE

18 Introducing Change in Bureaucracy: A Framework

Udai Pareek

Bureaucracy is an extremely important system in the country, as it determines the major administrative styles and influences a large section of society. 'Bureaucracy' here is used as a descriptive term to denote the government systems which govern most of the country.

Bureaucracy has a vital interface with the political system of the country. The political system consisting of the political party in power, elected representatives in the Parliament and State Legislatures, exercises a great deal of influence in policies, and in many cases even in the procedures of work. This interface, both produces problems as well as provides opportunities for easier introduction of change in the system.

Indian bureaucracy has deep roots in the British administrative system introduced in the last century. It was primarily meant for maintaining law and order in the country and for carrying routine administrative functions. Although Indian bureaucracy has taken long strides in the direction of developmental work, the basic character continues to be oriented towards maintenance. This goes against the spirit of experimentation and change.

Bureaucratic system (i.e., the various departments of bureaucracy) have a transient membership. Excepting the secretarial staff who usually do not move from the place where they live and work, administrative officers are mobile. This is true of those who are selected in the Indian and State Administrative Services. Such officers remain with a department only for some time and are transferred to some other departments, to enable them to have a variety of experiences. This transient membership creates special problems for the introduction of change. An enthusiastic officer who introduces a change in a system may soon leave the system, and somebody else who succeeds him may, in the absence of proper understanding of the experiment, wipe it out.

These characteristics of bureaucracy may be taken into consideration while planning change. Here, three major dimensions of bureaucracy are used to suggest a model for introducing a change.

Major Dimensions of Bureaucratic Change

Various dimensions of bureaucracy are important, when we consider the change to be introduced in it. As already stated, one of the main characteristics of bureaucracy is its vast size. Its system (with the contextual factors) and several dimensions of that system that are important are: the systemic structure of bureaucracy, its systemic dynamics, and the change process which occurs in bureaucracy. Following is a discussion of these factors, their main properties and how they interact.

Systemic Structure

Various aspects of the structure in bureaucracy are important in relation to change. Bureaucracy is divided into several departments or parts of a larger system. At one level, bureaucracy as an aggregate government machinery, consisting of all the departments of which the government is constituted with its various sub-parts, spread over the whole country, can be considered as a system. At another level, each department is also a system. Usually a department is regarded as one unit. For example, the Department of Education, in a particular state, may be regarded as a basic unit of bureaucracy. We shall call it the focal system – the system in which change is being introduced. Other departments within the bureaucracy are equally significant for change. These we can call as proximate systems. The third important system is the political system, determining the direction for bureaucracy and the way in which the change will be introduced and implemented. Representatives of the Assembly or the Parliament constitute a system, because they make policies, and because their representatives as Ministers have direct roles in the bureaucracy. The Ministers who head the various departments in the government, although not part of bureaucracy, have a legitimate role in determining many things. This system we shall call the political system. These are the three important aspects of the systemic structure. Here, we shall briefly consider each of these.

The Focal System

It is in the focal system that change is implemented. The significant dimension of the internal system can be said to be that of conformity-creativity. If the change is properly implemented the persons working in the system will be creative, they will use the change effectively, and will also conform to the minimum necessary level required. Both conformity and creativity will be balanced. However, if change is not accepted by them, they may either not conform or passively conform and may cease to be creative. Creativity, therefore, becomes a relevant aspect of the internal structure.

The focal system consists of those who are operating within the system, where the change or experiment is being attempted. These people do not remain with the system for a long time. They are in a particular department or part of bureaucracy for some time, and then they leave that department and go to some other department, so that their commitment to a particular department or subunit of bureaucracy is not as high, as it may be in the case of an independent unit, which people may join and where they think they will continue for a fairly long time. Because of this transitory membership of a system, the motivation of the people who live in that system would depend on how much they feel themselves as a part of it. Their conformity and creativity will also depend on this factor. If people within the system are not in favour of the experiment, they can very easily thwart that experiment, by either not adhering to the requirements of the experiment at all, or even if they do what is required, this may be a passive response. They may patiently live out the time in the hope, that in due course of time they will have a chance of going to some other department. This may affect the success of the experiment.

The Proximate System

A unit of bureaucracy is a part of a complex network of several ways. A change which is being brought about in one part of the bureaucratic system has implications for the other parts also. If the experiment succeeds, there may be pressures for such change in other parts of the bureaucratic system also. Therefore, the main property of the proximate system is that of diffusion and spread of the change which occurs in one system; depending, of course, on the success achieved in that process of change. If the change threatens the proximate systems, it can again prevent the change from spreading. Not only the boundary systems may attempt to contain it within the focal system (the system in which the experiment is being made), but may even prevent it from growing in the focal system itself.

No change can remain confined to one section of the bureaucracy for a long time. It will have implications for other parts of the bureaucracy. So the eventual choice for an experiment of change being introduced is, either its diffusion or its ultimate death in the system in which it originates. The proximate systems are significant in influencing this decision. It may be useful, therefore, to consider various factors, which contribute to the attitudes of the proximate systems towards a change being attempted in any department.

The Political System

The political system provides support for any experiment or change. The political system consists of elected representatives, mainly the Ministers and members of Legislatures or Parliament. They wield power in the bureaucracy and are concerned about policies and general matters. The main role which they can play is to provide necessary support for the experiment to grow. Lack of such support may eventually result in problems for the experiment. If the political system is in favour of change, it can provide opportunities for the experiment to continue and even spread. However, if somehow the political system is not in favour of change, or if the change threatens the political system in some way, it may not provide support for such change and in the absence of that support the change may not take root. The political system may use several ways of providing, withdrawing, or not giving the necessary support for the successful implementation of a programme of change.

These three main systems which operate in the bureaucratic context are all equally important for making the change effective. A discussion of the other two dimensions follows.

Systemic Dynamics

The dynamics of bureaucracy revolves around power. And in that sense, it is power dynamics. There are three main aspects of power dynamics. Power is wielded through influence in decision-making, through the monitoring role (control systems); and through the knowledge and skills relevant to the tasks. The absence of any of these may produce a threat and a fear. If one cannot influence decision, one may feel irrelevant to the system. If one loses control, because of lack of the monitoring mechanism, one may feel impuissant. If one does not have the relevant knowledge and skills, one may feel obsolete. The three fears, therefore, arising out of the three dimensions of power in a system (influence, monitoring, and knowledge) are respectively irrelevance, impuissance, and obsolescence.

The main function of systemic dynamics, is to deal with the problem of defensive behaviour (arising out of the fears), when change is introduced. If the proposed change threatens the power or influences members of a system who exercise power, the fear of irrelevance may produce aggressive behaviour, which may result in rejection of the proposed change. If there is a threat to the monitoring of change and to the possibility of knowing what is happening, the fear of impuissance is likely to produce regression, or a going back – a tendency to suggest that the older method was a better one and a feeling that the system should go back to the previous method. If people feel that they do not have enough knowledge and skills which are required to properly understand and go along with the change, the fear of obsolescence, or if a change makes a particular system or members obsolete because of the involvement of new skills; it is likely to result in rationalization of the merits of the previous system, with people giving arguments as to why the previous system was a better one. People do not want to face the realities or obsolescence. One way to deal with the resistance to change is to find proper reasons for not going along with the change. Therefore, to deal with these aspects of the dynamics of change, it is necessary that enough attention should be paid to all the three aspects, so that the various systems continue to have some influence. As they have ways of knowing and monitoring what happens, the necessary knowledge and skills to be able to understand what is involved in the new change and how this will benefit various aspects of the working of the systems.

Process of Change

The process of change has several stages. Change cannot be introduced all at once. Various stages have been identified in various studies. Most of these are some form of adaptation of the classical explanation which Kurt Lewin gave about the adoption of change. Taking an example from the changing shape of liquid into another shape, he proposed three main stages of the change process: unfreezing, moving and refreezing. The first stage of change is when the current state is disturbed and the system is ready for change. The second stage is the actual adoption of change, and in the third stage the change gets stabilized in the system. Various other authors have proposed more elaborate stages, breaking down the three main stages into several parts. For example, Waston, et al., have suggested five stages of change. Rogers has also suggested five stages while Pareek and Singh, reviewing various studies in India and critically looking at the conceptual framework of the process of change, have suggested seven stages of change. But basically, the three-stage model seems to hold well. We can use a three-stage model of change in bureaucracy, the stages of acceptance, action and stabilization. All the three stages are important for the final adoption of change in the focal system. Let us take each step and consider what it involves.

Acceptance

In the first stage of change, the change has to be accepted by all the three systems: the political system, the proximate system, as well as the focal system. The acceptance of change is the initial stage of motivation, when there is enough motivation amongst all the three systems in favour of change. Such motivation comes about, when the three main factors which we have considered in power dynamics are not disturbed, viz., when those in power feel, that their influence is not (nor will be) affected, that they will have enough monitoring control over what happens in the system, and that the change is not beyond their own knowledge and skills. Acceptance will be more when the need for change is high, and the concerned system sees change as an instrument in increasing the various important dimensions of their own competence and control over it. At the stage of acceptance, if the concerned systems are dissatisfied with the present ways of working and they perceive the experiment as a potential way of improving things, the motivation for change will be high.

Action

After the necessary acceptance and planning, definite action is taken for the implementation of the change being introduced. When the change is actually being implemented, again all the three systems are involved in some form or the other. Involvement, therefore, is the main process dynamics at this stage. This involvement comes about, because the change is promising in terms of solving some problems, as well as the change provides an opportunity for various persons involved in the system to retain their power; and in fact to increase it. When they feel that they are partners in the process of change, their involvement is continued. They watch with interest and continue to get involved in what is happening as a result of change.

Stabilisation

This is the stage when the change, which has been introduced and for which action has been taken, becomes a part the system, and the system is able to internalize it and make it more or less a permanent part of its working. Change does not remain a new thing any more. It is regarded and accepted as a regular part of the system. This is the process of legitimization of change. All the three systems regard the change as a legitimate part of the system; they do not consider it as new, or anything yet to be experimented. The three aspects of dynamics are important in this also, viz., to what extent the power and control is retained or threatened, and to what extent the three systems feel that it is still within their knowledge and skills to be able to contribute to the understanding and implementation of the change.

Bureaucratic Change Cube

Considering the various aspects discussed so far regarding change in bureaucracy, a three-dimensional cube emerges which depicts the different aspects of the change. This appears in the Figure 18.1 given ahead. Figure 18.2 gives the underlying processes.

Figure 18.1
Dynamics of Change in Bureaucracy

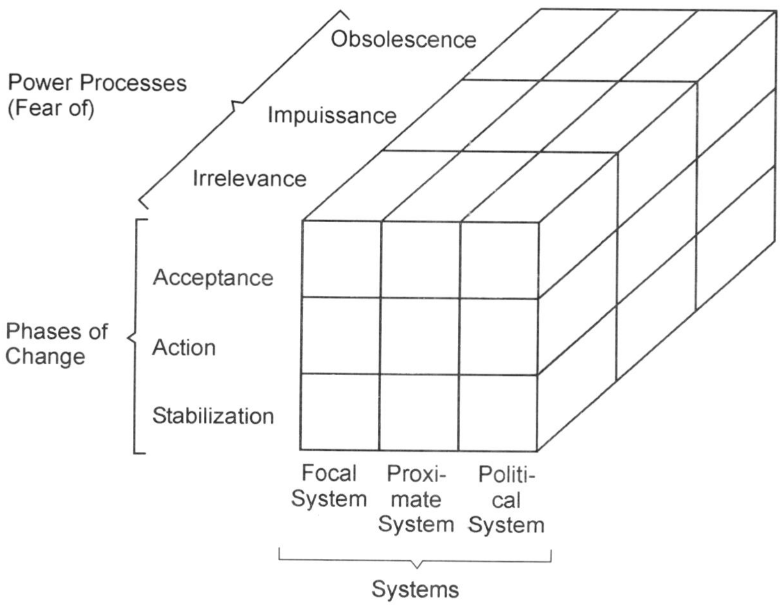

Figure 18.2
Underlying Processes of the Change Cube

Elements	*Underlying Processes*
Systems	
Focal system	Creativity-Conformity
Proximate system	Diffusion
Political system	Support
Power Processes (Fear of)	
Irrelevance	Aggression
Impuissance	Regression
Obsolescence	Rationalization
Phases of Change	
Acceptance	Motivation
Action	Involvement
Stabilization	Legitimisation

Three dimensions along with the key processes are mentioned in the figure above. The combination of the three dimensions may produce 27 cells in the cube, suggesting 27 elements. Each element can be discussed to know what happens when the change is introduced in the system. However, instead of discussing them separately, we shall use the three main dimensions of power dynamics, namely, influence, monitoring, and knowledge (the related fears of irrelevance, impuissance and obsolescence), discussing how these operate at different stages of change, in relation to the different systems.

Influence (Fear of Irrelevance)

Political, proximate or focal systems all feel it necessary to have influence in and be relevant to the system. If the system threatens the power which different people have, there will be an aggressive reaction by the people concerned and these can be expressed in several ways. It may, therefore, be assured that power is not threatened.

Let us take the political system first. The political system influences what happens in the focal system in which any experiment or change is being tried out. In the initial stage, therefore, it is necessary to ensure that the external system not only does not feel threatened, but perceives that the influence it has, in fact is enhanced by the new experiment. The perception of power can be in various forms. In the absence of a positive concept of power, the people involved are likely to consider only that aspect which gives them importance in the system.

One way to increase the power of the political system is to involve it in the process of change itself. The various ideas of change can be discussed with the political system, and the political system can be helped to feel, that it is not only approving, but in fact is generating ideas for such experiments. When a prestigious idea is implemented and when such an idea succeeds in a system, the persons who feel that they participated in originating that idea and in giving shape to it, feel very proud of it and quite powerful. Power can therefore be enhanced by involving the political system.

If the idea which is being implemented, relates to an important aspect of the system, the political system can be involved in presenting the arguments in favour of that system, whenever such an opportunity arises - either in the Central Government, or when there is a meeting of the experts, where the case is to be presented for such a change. If people in the political system, such as Ministers, are involved in arguing for the experiment and for the change, their involvement and commitment to that change is higher It also enhances their influence. In the initial stages, if the persons belonging to the political system are able to understand the process of change; know why it is necessary, feel that the change will be a feather in their cap, and have an opportunity to advocate that change and argue for it whenever there are opportunities available, the possibility of getting their support will be high and their motivation to provide that support is ensured.

When that change is being implemented, it is necessary to make sure, that the people in the political system continue to feel powerful in relation to that change. This is possible, in the first place, by providing necessary information to these people. Their continued involvement in the change is necessary. They feel powerful when they continue to own the change which is being introduced, and are able to provide necessary ideas and participate in some aspects of the discussion. Secondly, the political system can be given some feeling of power, when the various difficulties which people come across are discussed with them and they are involved in removing these difficulties. A person also feels powerful when he is able to use his expertise, abilities and skills to contribute to the solution of problems. This is a positive aspect of a person's power. In fact, the political system people have a lot of power in that sense. It may be in the interest of the experiments being tried out, that this aspect of their influence is properly utilized. When we use this power, we are in fact involving them more and more in the change process.

Similarly, the political system can be involved even at the stage of the stabilization of change. After the change has been introduced, has been found to be effective and is becoming a part of the system, the necessary support from the political system for its legitimization is very important. Here, the concerned persons from the political system, can provide a lot of support, by initiating discussion of legitimization with other members of their system. So that change becomes a part of the regular procedure. In this process, not only are the Ministers or the concerned people directly dealing with the department helpful, but also others, who deal with other departments. Persons in the political system dealing with the department may become instrumental in this process. It may, therefore, be useful to continue to involve the political system people in providing such support. Power can also be increased, if the new experiment which is being tried out, is able to solve some problems which the public is facing in relation to a particular department. The possibility of acceptance of the systemic change increases, if the change is seen as a very useful instrument of problem-solving.

As it is important to take care of the power which the political system feels in relation to a particular change; it is equally useful to see that the proximate system's power is not threatened by the experiment, or the change being introduced and tried out. Again, this can be considered in relation to the various stages.

At the stage of acceptance, the power of the proximate system can be threatened, if the experiment is seen as deviating too much from the normal practices followed in the proximate system. In such a case, there may be a complaint that the change does not conform to the norms, which leads to lack of uniformity in the various departments. One way to let the proximate system feel powerful, is to have a committee which is able to discuss various dimensions and raise questions from time to time. If such a monitoring committee can be devised, for looking at the change which is being tried out and seeing what are the different dimensions which require consideration, some people from the proximate system can feel a part of the process. However, this has to be balanced with autonomy. If such a committee is given all the power to intervene and make the necessary adjustments in the experiment, or the change which is being tried out, it can also result in unnecessary interference and subtle ways of preventing the change to assume significance. However, if the people belonging to the proximate systems, are able to raise questions, but do not necessarily go into the details of what is being done, they can serve a useful purpose. In one department in Indonesia, where some change was being introduced in one system, people from the proximate systems, were appointed members of the steering committee and even while the steering committee raised several inconvenient questions from time to time, the collective decision taken helped in making the change more acceptable, although this process slowed down the progress of change. It may be worthwhile to make an initial investment of time, in helping the various agencies to perceive that their power is retained and in fact, increased as a result of the proposed change. The main advantage the proximate systems can derive, is to see that the practices which the change introduces or produces, can also be tried out in their system. This is facilitated, if they are involved in the change programme from the beginning.

The power of the proximate systems can be threatened at the action stage also. If the experiment is proving very effective, they may feel that there will be pressure for similar change in their own system. This feeling may arise mainly, when they do not have sufficient knowledge about the innovation, and what is happening as a result of that change. These threats can be reduced both by their continued involvement and at the same time by discussion of what is happening with some important members of the proximate systems. Some diffusion of information from time to time amongst the proximate systems may help in reducing such a threat at the action stage. Mostly, threat is produced due to lack of knowledge, and because of some rumours which may float around. To reduce these rumours, it may be useful to have some legitimate ways of diffusing information about what is happening. But this should not be done as a part of publicity. Publicity may, in fact, become a threat to the proximate systems and as a result, the experiment may be adversely affected.

If the power of the proximate system is threatened at the action stage, there may be opposition to the experiment being planned. Power can be threatened at the action stage, if there is a feeling in the members of the proximate systems that the experiment which is being tried out, is likely to reduce their power in their own systems. Again, several factors may contribute to this. At the stage of acceptance, one factor which is likely to contribute to this feeling is lack of proper knowledge about the experiment. If the members of the proximate system do not really know what is being tried out, and as a result different rumours are floated, through those members of the focal system who feel less secure with the experiment and therefore spread both rumours and distorted information – the proximate systems' members are likely to exaggerate the rumours if they also feel threatened by the experiment. Continuous, but carefully planned information sharing, therefore, may be useful throughout the experiment with the proximate systems. This can be done in various forms. There may be open seminars on the experiment, in which several members of the focal system may be able to participate and speak about the results they are achieving; share some of the problems they are coming across and also how these problems are being solved. This may help in clearing misgivings amongst members of the proximate systems. Secondly, the members of the proximate systems can be helped to feel some increase in the power, if their own expertise is utilized for solving some problems which the focal system is facing, in relation to the change being implemented. For example, the members of the proximate systems can be invited to give their ideas and contribute to the solution, either as members of a task-force, which may be set up to solve some difficulties, or as advisers on some aspects of the change-experiment. This may help the members of the proximate systems to feel important. In the third place, the experiment should not do anything, which is likely to affect the proximate systems directly. Threat to the proximate systems can also be produced, if the experiment invokes a great deal of enthusiasm in the members of the focal system; and they may perceive the experiment as a crusade against some general defects of bureaucracy. Once that happens, the proximate systems are likely to feel threatened. Care may, therefore, be taken to see that the experiment does not pose any threats to the proximate systems in terms of exposing their weaknesses.

The power of the proximate systems may be threatened even at the stage of the stabilization of change. After the change has been well tried out, and it becomes obvious that the change will be helpful, and when it is becoming a part of the system, the proximate systems can withdraw their support and may ensure that the change is not legitimized in the system. This can happen when they feel that if the system gets stabilized, they will also have to undergo similar change. One way to help in reducing this threat, is to involve at this stage, a group of people from the proximate systems who are able to study the change and discuss in what different forms their systems can accept some of the ideas. This process of diffusion may not be regarded as the process of acceptance in toto, of what has been tried out and has been found useful in one system. This is a wrong concept of the diffusion of change. A more functional concept of diffusion is that change is seen as an important way to respond to the needs and fulfils the needs of a particular system. Learning from the experience in the form of diffusion of ideas in another system, may be in the form of adaptation, accepting various aspects which have been tried out with some modifications to suit a particular system. At the stage of stabilization, therefore, it may by useful to have an arrangement for members from the proximate systems to come and discuss, the various aspects of the change and also see what modifications need to be made to use this experience in their own system. It is unfortunate, that in bureaucracy, the tendency towards a uniform procedure is very high. Uniformity should be reinterpreted to mean the minimum common approach, but at the same time with enough variations to suit the needs of the subsystem, of course, without sacrificing the main advantages of a particular practice. This approach may help in reducing threat to some extent.

Monitoring (Fear of Impuissance)

The need to have some monitoring mechanism, to get the necessary information from time to time, for various purposes is a legitimate need of all the three systems. In the absence of good monitoring mechanisms, members of a system may feel weak. The fear of impuissance has to be reckoned with. Let us take the political system first. In the political system, the feeling that the necessary information which the political system wants, may not be available as a result of the introduction of the change, can produce, some difficulties and the acceptance may be greatly reduced. It may be useful to find out what information the political system people want and whether the flow of such information to the political system will be affected. There can be two approaches to this problem, In the first place, it can be seen as what is essential for the political system people to know, and such essential information can be provided. Sometimes, the members of the political system may want information which is not essential and gives them satisfaction only because they have a greater volume of information. If such information is not crucial for monitoring and control purposes, the information may only be a burden. In such a case, they may be helped to understand, how a different but simple system of information may be more effective for them to have control over various aspects. This may be an educative approach, helping them to identify, information which may increase the control functions. They may be helped to see how the new system may provide them such information in a more efficient and faster way, than what they were getting before the new system was introduced. Necessary modifications may also be made in the proposed experiment in such a way that whatever information the political system wants, can be provided by making slight readjustment in the change.

This may also be necessary at the action stage. If the political system feels during the experiment, that as a result of it, they are not having the same monitoring control over the information they want for various purposes, some threat may be produced and the support may not be forthcoming. The continued involvement of the political system, and discussing with them as to how the new change or the experiment can help them in better monitoring the crucial information, can be of help. Even when the action is being taken, change in the experiment itself can be brought about, or more information can be provided to the members of the political system. For example, when a new system of performance appraisal is being introduced in a particular department, the concerned Minister may feel that the information which he wanted about the people who are working in the department is not reaching him, because according to the new system, most of the information remains only with the immediate boss of the employee, after the assessment has been made. In the first place, it may be discussed with the Minister, why such information may be required at his level. It may also be sorted out with him, what kind of information he would like to have. For example, if he is interested in knowing how the various persons at a particular level in his own department are doing, a form can be devised for collecting such information in a summary, to be sent to the Minister. It may be useful to ensure that this information goes much faster than what the Minister was getting before, and that the information is also in a more usable form. For example, instead of all the files of all the people going to the Minister, a summary-statement can be prepared which gives the necessary data of several people on the same sheet so that one can have a comparative view of the performance of the various people. If the performance appraisal procedure can be linked with the computer system, a summary printout sheet can be designed and this can quickly go up to the Minister. Thus, if the Minister is helped to see that the experiment which is being implemented, not only gives him the crucial information; but gives it much faster, and in a manageable form, which can be quickly looked at and used, rather than the huge data which he was getting previously; he may in fact become convinced that this may be a more efficient form of monitoring at his level. He is likely to provide support and get involved in ensuring that the experiment succeeds.

The problem of monitoring at the stage of stabilization is also important. When a change is getting stabilized, it may be seen what problems of monitoring or control remain unresolved for the political system and can be resolved at this stage. The follow up at the level of the political system may also be necessary. One important action which can be taken at this stage is to follow-up and see what kind of information is needed, how much time the information takes to reach the

Minister, how that information is being made use of and so on. At the stage of stabilization, the follow-up programme is useful, not only within the system, but also at the level of the political system.

Let us consider the monitoring dimension in relation to the proximate systems. Proximate systems may also have the need of having some monitoring control over various kinds of information they may want. This may be useful in several ways. At the stage of acceptance, if the proximate systems feel that necessary information is not being provided as a result of change, they may not have enough motivation to pay attention to the system, and in fact may come in the way of the implementation of change. As with the political system, an attempt may be made to find out what information is needed by different proximate systems, which have interface-relationship with the focal system and how that information can be facilitated, both in terms of the systems getting the information much faster, as well as the information being given in a better form. This applies to all the three stages of the change process at the stages of acceptance, action and stabilization. Three aspects which are important in relation to the monitoring system should be attended to at all the three stages, viz., getting information in time, whether the information they are getting is sufficient, and whether the form in which they are getting information is usable.

The problems of monitoring are equally important within the focal system, in which the change is being introduced. The focal system also has various problems. People, who are important at various levels in the focal system, also want information from time to time; and if they feel that a system would deprive them of such information, they would resist it. As far as the focal system people are concerned, a continuous discussion of what information is needed by whom and why, may be very useful. More often, people want information which they cannot use. Sometimes, information is a source of power. It may be found out what information is functional and for what roles, then it may be ensured that such information reaches those roles in proper time. If people do not have enough information, they may not be able to act effectively. But at the same time, it may be necessary for people to understand that information-overload is equally dysfunctional and may not be helpful. At the same time, the necessary information needed for monitoring purposes, by several people in the internal system, may also lead to modification of the change, so that the experiment can also help in providing necessary information to people to take decisions. This may provide the necessary support from inside the system and people are likely to become more creative in their approach, as well as accept the change to a great extent.

Knowledge (Fear of Obsolescence)

The last dimension of power dynamics is the feeling of having relevant knowledge and skills. People have fear of obsolescence in relation to a change. When people in any of the three systems feel that the new system which is being devised is beyond their comprehension, or that they do not have the necessary skills to use it, they are likely to feel threatened.

Let us take the political system first. If the change which is being tried out is too sophisticated and beyond the comprehension of the people in the political system, it is likely to pose some threat. They may lack understanding of the proposed change and may complain that the system is too sophisticated, and it may not be practicable for the Indian conditions or the conditions in a particular state.

At the stage of acceptance, obsolescence will play an important role in preventing innovations to be effective. Let us take the political system. If the members of the political system feel that an innovation which is being introduced is something about which they do not know, and that it poses several problems which their present knowledge is incapable to cope with, there will be resistance to the introduction of such an innovation. This is true of proximate systems also. For the political system members, it may be useful to organize some demonstrations and explanation of the innovation and its effectiveness to solve some problems. Where it is possible, persons of similar background may be brought to explain the implications of the change as experienced by another system. For example, when a particular change is being introduced in one State, and if there has been experience of a similar nature in another State government, the Minister from the other State who knows about such a system, may be invited to talk to the ministers of the State, where the system is being introduced explaining how the change was brought about and with what results. When a member of the political system may be able to gain more knowledge, he may not resist the change.

This holds true for the proximate systems also. If members of the proximate systems feel that their present knowledge and skills are incapable of coping with the proposed system of change, they are likely to create noises which will adversely affect the initial stages of the programme of change. For example, if it is proposed to introduce a computer system for handling some problems, the members of the proximate systems may be against the idea because they do not know how the computer operates. But if the proximate system members are given a short exposure to such a programme, they may be motivated to accept it.

This applies equally to the focal system. In one case, a programme of using computers for transfer of teachers was proposed. This was laughed at because the important persons in the focal system did not think this would be possible. Their knowledge about computers was very limited. In order to deal with this problem, a special programme was organized at the Indian Institute of Management, Ahmedabad, where a case was given and they worked with the data of the case on the computer. They handled the data, used several alternatives and worked out the results of their alternative proposals on the computer. This experience thrilled them. They were very enthused and asked for the Institute's help in the experiment with the new system. They requested the Institute to send some persons to visit their State and look at the data available to see if such a computer programme could be worked out. Their knowledge to some extent and in a limited way their skills to use the computer as an aid in decision-making for complex problems, was helpful in the acceptance of change.

Similarly, if at the stage of action there is a fear of obsolescence in any of the three systems, the programme may not go ahead and problems may arise. While the programme is being implemented, obsolescence may be in terms of specific elements, when the details are to be worked out and are being implemented. Obsolescence may greatly affect the programme. If the members of the focal system feel that their present knowledge or skills are not adequate to cope with the change being introduced, they are likely to resist the change a great deal. For example, if a system of performance-feedback and counselling to the employees is to be introduced, the members of the focal system are likely to resist this change at the stage of implementation, if they do not have adequate skill of providing guidance and counselling to their employees. They are likely to raise doubts and indicate that such counselling may be dysfunctional. The most effective way to deal with the problem of obsolescence is, of course, by providing adequate training and using other ways of developing the knowledge and skills of the people involved; to help them realize that they have adequate knowledge or skills to deal with the problems which may be thrown up by change. People, who do not have the necessary knowledge or skills, feel threatened when they think of coping with problems which are likely to arise, as a result of the introduction of the change.

At the stage of consolidation or stabilization, the problem of dealing with obsolescence may still continue. This is particularly important as more and more people would be involved at the stage of stabilization. If most people at the stage of stabilization, fear that the change introduced in the focal system may eventually make them obsolete, they are likely to resist the change. As long as the proposed change is at the experimental stage, the threat to the three systems is not as high as at the stage of stabilization of the change. The fear may be that once the change becomes a part of the system, it would be difficult to go back. This would be particularly so, if the change requires increasing sophistication, and is likely to become a problem with the members of the focal system, who may be apprehensive of being irrelevant in due course. For example, if a new potential appraisal and promotion system like the assessment centre has been tried out in an organization and is now becoming part of it, persons administering appraisals and promotions may feel uneasy, because the new system would require increasing sophistication, and their present level of knowledge, skills and experience may be inadequate to cope with the requirements. The proximate systems may also disturb the stabilization process if they feel that once the change is accepted as a part of one system, they may also be under pressure to adopt it. In both cases, it may be useful to organize programmes to update the knowledge and skills of the members of the focal system, and also of the proximate systems. It may be better if such training precedes the stabilization stage so that the members feel confident and positive about the change being internalized in the system.

19 Re-engineering Public Administration

K.B.C. Saxena

The last two decades or so have witnessed a remarkable change in the structure and culture of government and public service organizations in the industrialized countries. There is an increasing demand by citizens for social actions and public services that have to be funded and monitored by government, coupled with their unwillingness to pay more taxes. Further, the need for government regulation of economic and social development and the growing complexity of the society is confronting public administration with a great deal of complex problems and tasks, such as improved health care for the aged and housing for the lower income groups, etc. Solving these problems need more resources, which the public sector has to provide only through "working better and costing less".

As for developing countries, many of them such as India have made economic management their prime agenda. They are going through a process of restructuring their economy to emphasize competition, integration with global markets and an increasing level of privatization. Such restructuring has also brought out the need to review the role of government in economic activities. Increasingly, the role of government is moving away from producing goods and services through public enterprises, to that of creating an enabling economic environment through policy changes and more effective policy implementation. To realize this goal, there is a strong need for the public administration in these countries to be efficient and cost-effective.

Unfortunately, the public administration in developing countries is, in general, highly bureaucratized and extremely centralized, based on an authoritarian legal system (Avegerou, 1990). It has been shaped under conditions of domination from outside centres (under colonial regimes or under the influence of 'protecting' superpowers), and has been assigned a significant and highly political role of planning and implementing the development process. Many developing countries are in general characterized by a combination of factors such as population growth, weak infrastructure, foreign indebtedness, asymmetric world relations and increasing inequalities between individuals, groups and regions, which hamper their socio-economic development. Therefore, efficiency and cost-effectiveness of public administration is of utmost importance in order to effectively manage the development process.

Thus, public administration in both industrialized as well developing countries is increasingly entrusted with the responsibility of high performance level as well as cost-effectiveness. At the core of this dilemma is the increasingly felt need for a *radical transformation* of public administration than in the earlier periods. Whereas the concepts of unity, cooperation, coordination and (increased size have guided the attempts to change the public sector in the 1960s to 1980s, the present themes guiding public sector change are of decentralization, disaggregation, competition and markets, efficiency strategies, reduction in size of units, emphasis on, 'proper' management practices, customer orientation and performance measurements. *Re-engineering* is an approach to facilitate such a trans-formation, and such efforts are already in progress in many industrialized, newly industrialized and less-developed countries such as Australia (Parker, 1994), the Netherlands (Snellen, 1994), UK (CCTA, 1994), USA (Carr and Littman, 1990; Gulledge, et al., 1994; Katz, 1994; Osbrne and Gaebler, 1993); Singapore (Neo, 1994); and Slovenia (Bavec, 1992).

Business Process Re-engineering

Engineering may be defined as the systematic design and building of a, 'process' or 'artefact' from a concept that has been converted into an implementable specification with the application of science and mathematics. Re-engineering thus involves taking an already existing process or artefact and improving it in its critical, contemporary measures of performance, such as cost, quality, service and speed.

Business process re-engineering (BPR) refers to an integrated programme and perspective on organizational change focusing on business processes rather than *business functions*, in order to significantly improve their performance. In this context, a business process refers to a set of interrelated work activities and value-added tasks that convert business inputs into business outputs. A process corresponds to a natural business activity and often cuts across traditional functional structure of organizations. Examples of such processes could be product development, service delivery, or order fulfilment.

The traditional functional (hierarchical) view of organizations optimizes individual business functions (such as finance, production, marketing, etc.) sometimes at the expense of the entire business. The narrow scope of a function attacks symptoms (of a problem) in one function but misses the causes rooted in another. It can also fail to prioritize problems which although small for any individual function, might be large in aggregate. As a result, operational improvements occur piecemeal and independently of one another. Consequently, their impact is substantially lower than is often required.

BPR has been perceived as a business process focussed initiative involving simultaneous change to organizational design, culture and information technology (IT), to enable radical performance improvements. BPR is not merely downsizing, restructuring, computerization, continuous improvement, although all these can be parts of BPR. Benefits from a BPR exercise can be expected to include (Saxena, 1998):

- clearer focus on the customer's needs,
- reduced cost of operations,
- improved quality of service,
- reduced delivery/response times, and
- improved responsiveness to customer demands.

In summary, the major benefits to an organization of undertaking BPR can be:

- a radical improvement on current process performance,
- better alignment of business process with strategic objectives and key performance indicators,
- focus on outputs that the customer wants rather than inputs to the organization, and
- Increased job satisfaction leading to better individual performance.

Thus, BPR aims to refit or revamp an organization to survive today's economic downturn and to emerge, refreshed and revitalized, to meet its social obligations and accept its economic challenges into the next century. It provides a way to enhance the efficiency as well as effectiveness while resources are declining.

Public Administration Re-engineering

BPR is common in the private sector, and the public sector cannot insulate itself from new management cultures that evolve from innovative practices. However, because of the differences in the nature of private and public sectors, the BPR concepts as applied in the private sector may need some modifications before they could be applied in the public sector. We would refer to the application of these modified re-engineering concepts to public administration as "public administration re-engineering" (PAR).

PAR involves a total replanning and concurrent redesign and implementation of administrative processes, organizational structure and the supporting information system in direct or indirect response to external forces in order to achieve some objective (such as cost-effectiveness, time service quality or customer satisfaction), which are usually not easy to achieve given current conditions of the public organizations (Saxena, 1996).

PAR is particularly relevant in those areas which involve extensive contact with the public, with record keeping and/or claims processing following customer contact or involving financial transactions. This is because the statutory basis, authorization or rationale of many of these services will often specify the outcome sought, but allows the organization concerned considerable freedom to determine how the service outcome is to be achieved. These are areas where the basic business transactions are similar, so giving scope for a repeatable process. The work is usually of a relatively routine nature and the amount of discretion to take decisions can justifiably be limited.

However, re-engineering public administration requires innovative management and a willingness to change. Unfortunately, the nature of public administration itself is so different from business administration that it may inhibit the re-engineering effort. For example, consider the following characteristics of public administration (Morgan and Murgatroyal, 1994; Osborne and Gabler, 1993):

- Public administration is more resistant to change, being highly bureaucratic in terms of an overcommitment to regulation and enforcement of precedent and rules.
- Public administration institutions are typically paid out of an allocated budget, which is not based on their results and performance. Thus, there is apparently no pressure on them to perform better.
- Public administrators' and managers' pay has traditionally not been related to performance. Promotion, rewards and

recognition systems in public administration are, by and large, based on seniority classification systems for positions rather than any pure merit-based classification. This may demotivate those managers who are willing to be champions for re-engineering projects.

- Public administrators and managers are not free to enact management in the way managers in a business are. This is often due to political control, as politicians do not necessarily restrict themselves to policy making: they often wish to involve themselves in the execution of policy.

Principles of Public Administration Re-engineering

PAR is not an easy concept to apply due to the absence of forces which promote mechanisms for change in the private sector environment. However, whatever the scale, there will be a set of common principles in a PAR exercise, which are listed below:

Create Customer Focus

A common assumption in re-engineering is that every organization has customers and if their needs are not met, they may be able to go elsewhere, or create pressure for change. However, in public administration, customer is a more problematic concept. The benevolent paternalism of traditional government bureaucratic provision has not sought the voice of the 'customer' in the past. Given that the public sector provisions were supplying monopoly or near monopoly services, there was in fact no incentive to do so because no challenge of having to retain or attract customers existed. However, in the last decade, government provisions in countries such as UK and USA, have seen the effects of two forces. On the one hand, there has been the growth of *consumerism*, and the fact that people accustomed to the modern, 'supermarket' range also want more choice and better service in government provisions; politicians have been swift to respond to this. On the other hand, there has been the reshaping of government provisions organizationally to give greater financial accountability and measures of performance. Even, in India, the recent court judgments related to services provided by Indian railways and health care agencies show that public service agencies are increasingly deemed accountable for the quality of their 'services'. Thus, the customer might have been a problematic concept in public administration of the past, we see this as being less and less the case as we move into the future. Once the customer is identified, there will be a need to focus on what is of most importance to the customer and necessary to the running of the organization, including public accountability requirements.

Rethink Functions and Processes

Traditionally, all public organizations are structured as a hierarchical bureaucracy. Therefore, the move from a functional to a process-oriented organization needs to be planned and managed. This will be based on the value-adding service activities provided for the customer rather than for the top bureaucrats of the functional departments.

Challenge Organizational Principles

Assess reasons for, and ask what is the cost and value of activities.

Simplify and Discard Activities

Keep only those processes which add value and those which are absolutely necessary.

Measure the Organizational Performance

The most common basis for defining performance of a public administration process is the concept of 'value for money'. Value for money is most easily defined as the economic acquisition of resources and their efficient utilization in the realization of the purposes of the organization – with the simultaneous achievement of economy, efficiency and effectiveness.

Here economy is defined as the resources used at the lowest possible cost; *efficiency* as the ratio of actual input to actual output; and *effectiveness* as the extent to which the impacts of a policy or programme meet its objectives. These three concepts are essentially interdependent and the relationship between them is shown as follows:

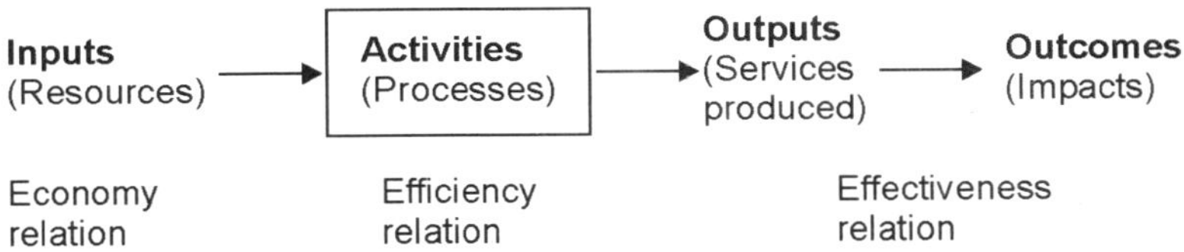

Performance indicators have two main roles. First, they can provide managers and administrators with information necessary to make decisions which reflect economy, efficiency and effectiveness, thereby assisting them in judging how far their objectives have been achieved. Their second role is to provide those outside the organization, including the auditors, with a basis for judging performance and establishing accountability.

Unfortunately, when public organizations set out to measure performance, their managers usually measure their volume of outputs such as how well they carry out some administrative processes, how many people they serve, how fast they serve them, etc. (Osborne and Gaebler, 1993). But outputs do not guarantee outcomes. For instance, a primary school might pump out more and more successful students. But if these students are not able to achieve the minimum levels of learning (MILL), what good is the education imparted by the school?

Output measures can also be useful as they help the organization get a handle on how they can improve their management. In addition, the outcomes desired by any organization are often very difficult to measure or will not become evident for a long time. In such cases, organizations often choose output measures that appear to be reliable proxies for the ultimate outcome. The problem comes when organizations measure only outputs and none of the outcomes – as too many do.

Therefore, compare the outcome as well as the output of a process to determine actual achievement against the target set. Also benchmark performance, i.e., compare the process performance with the achievements of others.

Set Audacious Objectives

Set performance targets out of reach but not of sight, such as cutting of overhead costs by 50 per cent within 12 months. Ideally, these targets should not be achievable by current improvement approaches alone, thus forcing more innovative thinking.

Empower People

Empowerment refers to the ability of an individual or a team to work in their own way within agreed time-lines and with agreed resources to achieve a goal set by the leadership of the organization (Morgan and Murgatroyd, 1994). The philosophy behind this principle is that people who have the ability to make process improvement should be given the authority to make them.

Utilize IT as an Enabler of PAR

Public administration in most countries shares a belief that the advances in IT represent a major opportunity to accelerate development and a crucial component of their ability to compete. Therefore, there is hardly any need to demonstrate here the importance of IT in public administration. Public administration and services are highly *information intensive* and therefore IT could play a crucial role in improving cost-effectiveness. Unfortunately, IT use in public administration typically lags behind business application. For instance, the tightening of the national budget and an accelerated pace of policy changes would increase the demand for policy analysis, transparence, expenditure control, and programme monitoring and evaluation (Bavec, 1992). This would also heighten the need to reduce transaction costs between the public and private sectors and to modernize major public transaction processing systems such as customs, tax administration, land records administration and state treasury administration. IT use in these areas would provide substantial downstream effects and clearly increase the effectiveness of government operations.

IT system can be a powerful agent both for and against change. They have the potential to simplify a process, automate the mundane, and to give rapid access to relevant information. Requirements change, however, and those same systems which had previously been beneficial may no longer meet customer's needs. A PAR exercise will highlight activities that support that customer's requirement and those that the organization itself requires to manage its operations.

No technology stands out as essential in PAR, the use and type of technology is dependent on the requirements of the future process-oriented public administration. However, given the frequent need to improve timeliness and reduce the time taken to carry out a task, telecommunication networks, including computer-to-computer links such as Electronic Data Interchange (EDI), are often essential in achieving a major improvement. Organizational databases, groupware allowing simultaneous access to a piece of work, cross-functional information systems, etc., will also have a part to play when designing new systems to support a process-oriented administration.

PAR does not necessarily require 'leading edge' IT systems to be useful. The administration will require cost-effective and rapid access to accurate and relevant information in two areas: those that add value to the process of fulfilling the customer requirement and those that provide support to the business to enable it to function. IT of particular value is that which can support network relationship, that is, communicating across organizational boundaries with customers, suppliers and business partners.

Applying Public Administration Re-engineering

PAR is most effective when integrated into a radical reappraisal of administrative activities. This begins with revisiting the objective of the public organization and asking the following questions:

- If starting again, what would we do differently?
- How and why do we add more or less value than our competitors (if any)? Or, if no competitors, do we add sufficient 'value' for the money spent for it?
- What is the current assessment of customer requirements and the trade-offs they make between service, functionality, quality and cost?

Having obtained the answers to above questions, the re-engineering of administrative processes is carried out by:

- eliminating unnecessary tasks or processes and reducing any delays introduced by multiple authorizations, inspections and hand offs between departments;
- automating workflows to minimize delays between processing stages; and
- reducing the amount of paper handling by promoting the use of electronic communications both internally and with customers and suppliers.

Finally, management approaches need to be reconsidered in the light of the proposed changes

- Increasing staffing flexibility by creating a multiskilled workforce.
- Reducing duplication, of effort and investment by forming stronger partnerships with customers and suppliers, sharing key information and undertaking joint development.
- Devolving more responsibility and authority.
- Outsourcing essential tasks which add no value but divert time and resources.

Examples of PAR Applications

Public administration interchanges a majority of data internally between ministries, government agencies and the public sector, but data interchange with the private sector is still minor. Also, public administration makes extensive use of official statistics for supporting its decisions.

Therefore, most of the existing use of PAR is mainly in automatic compilation of statistics, automatic transaction processing or automatic case management. Some of these examples are summarized below to give an idea of the need and benefits of PAR, both in industrialized as well as developing countries.

- *Improvement of Statistical Compilation Process through Automated Statistical Compilation within the European Union.* With the emergence of European Union, there is an increasing demand for reliable statistical information to support decision-making on social, financial and economic issues. Thus, the national and regional statistics organizations (such as Eurostat) are under pressure to enhance the efficiency of the process of collecting and disseminating statistics between economic agencies, regional and national administrations, European institutions and end users. On the other hand, the various economic agencies are becoming increasingly reluctant to complete specific statistical questionnaires in an age when all their other productive, operational or administrative activities are highly automated. Obviously, the data required for statistical purposes can be derived from or communicated by the inter-organizational transactions in the electronic form (such as EDI messages) if the statistical needs are taken into account in the various commercial sectors where EDI technology is operational and related messages are being designed. A number of such projects are either in operation or being planned within the EU to explore this aspect further.

- *Improvement of Case Management Process by Automated Decision-Making in the Dutch Government.* Most ministries of the Dutch government have improved the handling of relevant cases pertaining to residents/citizens through automated decision-making (Snellen, 1994). The extent to which the decision-making is automated depends on the type of IT system used by a ministry. For example, the following ministries use automated systems for the production of the text of a decision:

Ministry	*Application*
Foreign Affairs	Decisions on personnel affairs
Economic Affairs	Decisions related to grants and subsidies
Justice	Decisions on minor traffic offenses
Social Security and Employment	Decisions of personnel affairs
Traffic and Water Authority	Generation of car licenses

The following ministries use automated system for the assessment of the data on the basis of the criteria of the applicable regulation. These systems at least partly take over the process of legal reasoning in automatically assessing the factual data.

Ministry	*Application*
Housing, Physical Planning & Environment	Requests for rent allowances
Traffic and Water Authority	Permits for houseboats. Accreditation for garages as official car inspections
Education and Science	Requests for study grants for minor and part-time students
Finance	Establishing fiscal obligations as to income tax and value added tax
Welfare, Health and Culture	Contributions of parents whose children are raised outside the home

Social Security and Employment	Assessment of requests for overtime work Finally, the following ministries use some information systems which assemble at least part of the necessary data in an automated way:
Finance	Import declaration
Defense	Draft
Welfare, Health and Culture	Determination and publication of prices of medicines

- Thus, the improvement in terms of case management processes are of varying degrees. The earlier systems automated the administrative processing of cases. Later on, systems were developed which assessed cases without interference from officials (e.g., rent allowance) or which selected cases on the basis of their complexity and directed them to specialized officials (e.g., taxes). At the highest level were expert systems in which expert knowledge was codified to take over the decision-making from specialists in a certain area.
- *Re-engineering of Singapore's Trade Clearance Process.* Singapore has the strategy of acting as an international trading hub. International trade is characterized not only by the physical movement of goods across national boundaries, but also by the unwieldy, voluminous, and costly paper work that accompanies it, containing data that facilitate the physical good movement, show ownership and meet governmental requirements. The Singapore government requires that trade documents be prepared and submitted to a number of government agencies for clearance before goods may be imported or exported. There are 20 government agencies requiring documentation for specific categories of goods, although up to three agencies' approval is the norm for any one commodity. The documents are in paper form and are often hand-delivered to, and collected from, the agencies in many geographically dispersed locations. Moreover, even though much of the information contained in these

documents is common, each agency has its own format: with the consequence of entering the same information several times on different forms by the trader. As the average number of trade documents is about 10,000 per day, the whole process is complex, time-consuming and may be even irritating both for the trader as well as the government. To overcome this problem, the Trade Development Board (TDB), which is the government agency for promoting international trade, re-engineered its trade clearance with the help of TradeNet, an EDI system that allows traders to send trade documents *electronically* to TDB as well, as other government agencies simultaneously (Neo, 1994). With the re-engineered process, trade permits are now approved in 15 minutes rather than two days. Similarly, trade statistics are now available in two weeks (down from four weeks) for internal management reviews and four weeks (down from six weeks) for public release. Also, the number of staff in TDB's documentation department dropped from 134 in 1988 to 88 in 1992, though all this staff was redeployed for other work. This re-engineering of the trade clearance process became possible as TDB extended its own vision of not merely acting its traditional role of trade controller but also of trade facilitator.

- *Re-engineering of Customs Administration Process in the European Union.* Customs administration in most countries used to be a heavy handed instrument of government, very often militarily organized, to safeguard borders in order to make it difficult to import goods, and used mainly as a tool to fuel the government's budget. This strategy has now changed in general in the modern customs administrations in the countries when they changed to a free-market economy in European Union as well as in countries of Eastern Europe and former Soviet Union (who are now moving from a state-controlled economy into a free-market economy). Now, they are talking of a customs service as an instrument to develop the economy (for example, still levying a certain amount of duties to safeguard virgin firms or industries, or industries having higher labour costs than others), to safeguard the people, for instance, concerning health, weapons, drugs, and also to safeguard animal species, environment, etc.). With this change in the strategic role of customs departments, the customs administration process has changed too. In the past, every shipment to be imported had to be inspected in order to control the correct application of duties, which were different for the different kinds of merchandise, and to combat smuggling of unwanted items. Nowadays, this old process has been re-engineered into a more efficient process in most industrialised countries, because otherwise importations and therefore the international trade would come to a standstill (because of its immense growth during the last few decades).

- In the new customs administration process in European Union, instead of stopping a shipment for controls at the point of entry, viz., border, airport or seaport, customs depends on its clients' own declaration of goods required by international legislation for other purposes. The merchandise passes the border with a very simple formality done in seconds, only meant to check that the shipment is later really declared to customs. When the merchandise arrives at the factory or any other importers' premises within the country, customs is informed. If it does not want to inspect it, this is considered to be imported. The items then will have to be entered into the books of the firm and declared periodically to customs, who will audit the books from time to time to find out if everything has been done correctly. Another change made in the new process is the method of differed payment, in which the importer may take the merchandise away without paying the customs duty and sell it, and pay the duty later. This change is very important for those countries where credits are very expensive because the importer can pay the duty out of the payments received from the buyers. These changes in the new process are based upon new legislation and do not need use of information technology (IT).

With the use of IT, the customs administration process could be made even more effective. For example, IT-based systems are being used by the UK Customs Directorate for automatic compilation of trade statistics and generating single European market declarations. Use of EDI in these systems enables the establishment of an *integrated customs clearance system* with the following operational scenario. Customs wants to be in the possession of consignment data prior to the arrival of the actual goods. This is achieved by a pre-arrival cargo reporting facilitated by the EDI system. With a pre-arrival lodgement of the goods declaration, the customs procedure of clearance could start well in advance. Customs can then screen these data carefully against its own selection criteria within the automatic selectivity programme. Customs may then decide as to whether the cargo should be subjected to full examination, partial examination, or no examination upon arrival at its port of destination with a pre-arrival notification of customs status.

Critical Success Factors for PAR

A critical success factor (CSF) is an element that makes a vital contribution to the success of a project, if missing, it is likely to lead to the failure of the project. Ensuring that the critical success factors are all addressed might be considered an organizational prerequisite for a PAR exercise. The CSFs for a PAR exercise are:

- the desire to change the status quo – a willingness to rethink all aspects of the administration process,:

- sustained drive, commitment, patience and active involvement at the highest level;
- clear and consistent strategic focus and long-term vision shared across the organization;
- demanding goals – out of reach but not out of sight;
- good planning and management;
- participation with all those who have a stake in the successful outcome of the exercise;
- effective communication throughout the PAR project; continuous measurement of performance against targets.

Conclusion

This paper has extended the re-engineering concept to public organizations as public administration re-engineering (PAR), which is an approach to bringing about radical change. It provides public organizations with a means of delivering major improvements identified in their goals and objectives. We believe that PAR is certainly within reach for many developing countries, in particular India, if the public administration in the country can be properly motivated (or enlightened!). It is hoped that the paper will stimulate thinking in this direction among the public administrators and will enable them to reap the benefits of PAR.

References

Avegerou, C. (1990) "Computer-based Information Systems and Modernization of Public Administration in Developing Countries", in *Information Technology in Developing Countries*, by Bhatnagar, S. C. and Bjorn-Andersen, N. (eds.), Elsevier Science, pp. 243-250.

Bavec, C. (1992) "EDI Strategy in the Public Administration in Slovenia", *Proc. Fifty International EDI Conference*, Bled, Slovenia, September, pp. 179-186.

CCTA (1994) BPR in the Public Sector: *An Overview of Business Process Reengineering*, Her Majesty's Stationery Office, London.

Carr, D.K. and Littman, I.D. (1990) *Excellence in Government: Total Quality Management in the 1990s*, Coopers & Lybrand.

Gulledge, T.R., Sibley, E.H., Hill D.H. and Sullivan, L.M. (1994) "Functional Process Improvement Implementation: Public Sector Reengineering", *Proc. 13th IFIP World Computer Conference 94*, Vol. 2, Elsevier Science, pp. 475-480.

Katz, R.H. (1994) "Reengineering Government Through Information Technology: The Performance Review", *Proc. 13th IFIP World Computer Conference 94*, Vol. 2, Elsevier Science, pp. 373-379.

Morgan, C. and Murgatroyd, S. (1994) *Total Quality Management in the Public Sector*, Open University Press.

Neo, B.S. (1994) "IT-Enabled Business Reengineering: A Study of Singapore's Trade Clearance Process", in *Business Process Re-engineering: Information Systems Opportunities and Challenges*, by Glasson, B.C. et al. (eds.), North-Holland, pp. 433-422.

Osborne, D. and Gaebler, T. (1993) *Reinventing Government: How the Entrepreneurial Spirit is Transforming the Public Sector*, Penguin Books.

Parker, B. (1994) "Business Reengineering and Management Alignment: A Re-engineering and Management Alignment: A Review of Structural Reengineering in the Public Sector and the Problem of Management Alignment with Enterprise Objectives", in *Business Process Reengineering: Information Systems Opportunities and Challenges*, by Glasson, B. C. et al., (eds.), North-Holland, pp. 459-468.

Saxena, K.B.C. (1998) "Gaining Competitive Edge through Strategy-driven Business Process Reengineering", *Management Review* (March).

Saxena, K.B.C. (1996) "Reengineering Public Administration in Developing Countries", *Long Range Planning*, Vol. 29 No. 5, pp. 703-711.

Snellen, I. Th.M. (1994) "Automation Policy Implementation: Reengineering from within Public Administration", in *Business Process Reengineering: Information Systems Opportunities and Challenges*, by Glasson, B.C. et al., (eds.), North-Holland, pp. 545-556.

20 Creativity

Pradip N. Khandwalla

There are many definitions of creativity, each emphasizing a different facet of creativity. Those who emphasize outputs of creative effort, describe creativity as the discovery of something that is novel, but also useful or relevant or economical or elegant or valuable. Thus, a ballpoint pen that lasts forever, or at least much longer than current options, would be classified as an act of creativity. A novel hypothesis that explains, say gravity, would be a creative act. A poem that successfully combines both naturalism and surrealism, may also be considered as an act of creation. The merely trivial is not creative, nor the merely novel. The product or outcome of a creative effort must be both significant and strikingly different from the beaten track.

Some others have stressed the creative process. In this view, creativity is divergent thinking, the seeking of relationships between previously unrelated concepts or frames of reference, of exploring the under-known. The outcome of this effort may or may not be creative, but the effort reveals the characteristics of the creative process: wide search or exploration, leaps of imagination, incubation, sometimes strikingly fresh insights. Therefore, we say that the sciences and the arts are generally more creative pursuits than factory work or vocational training; or that research and development is a more creative activity than accounting and control. That is, problem solving in the sciences, the arts or R & D generally exhibits greater divergent thinking than problem solving relating to factory work, vocational training or accounting and control. (This does not, of course, mean that one cannot be creative in factory work or in accounting; only that, because of the routinized nature of the work, the individual is not required to be imaginative).

Still others identify creativity with certain states of being. For example, Abraham Maslow, the high priest of humanist psychology, has identified creativity with openness in expressing feelings, receptivity to ideas, concern for other's desire to grow as a person and actualize one's potential and so forth. Other psychologists have compared creative and non-creative persons from the same profession. They have identified a number of additional personality traits and abilities that distinguish the creative from the non-creative persons, like the greater love of complexity of the creative; their more bizarre fantasy life, but simultaneously, a high degree of practicality their greater independence of judgement. The ability to come up with many, varied and uncommon ideas or solutions also seems to distinguish the creative from non-creative persons.

Each one of these views of creativity is flawed. If one judges creativity only in terms of the novelty and usefulness or elegance of a product, one may sometimes find that this creative product may have been discovered or produced, either accidentally or by a non-creative process. Today, innovations are increasingly institutionalized. For example, many researchers discover something or the other, simply by taking a problem area and by applying to it the scientific method. Indeed, Maslow has contemptuously disposed off universities and scientific establishments as havens of the mediocre. If one judges creativity by the creative process instead of the creative product, the dreamer would be the champion creative, for the extent of imagination and divergent thinking, combinatorial play, the relating of remote ideas and so forth that characterize the creative process, are at their flood tide during dreaming. If creativity is to be judged, in terms of the characteristics of the creative person, such as lack of inhibitions, receptivity, curiosity, idea flow, etc., the child would outrank the Einsteins, Tagores, and Picassos of the world.

I suspect creativity has to do with the employment of a playful and exploratory, rather than a mechanical process of problem solving, by a person who is open, curious and imaginative, rather than by a person who is inhibited and conventional, to find solutions or designs that are novel (and yet useful) rather than merely run-of-the-mill.

Let us explore briefly creativity as a mental ability and distinguish it from another famous mental ability, namely, intelligence, as it is measured in contemporary IQ tests. The best way to appreciate the difference between creativity and intelligence is to do a test of each. Given ahead is a 5-minutes, 'test', that will give you a feel for the difference between intelligence and creativity, as they are measured now a days.

Test

1. Find the word that does not fit with the rest:

   MBAOBY DNOONL COWSOM ATR

2. Guess the word given the following four clues:

   Law Chair Bangle Sword

3. Write the 3-letter word that means the same as the words outside the brackets:

   PROHIBIT (- - - - -) DRINKING PLACE

4. Complete the following sentence humorously: One moonlit night, while strolling in a garden.............
5. Find the missing number

2	9	0	8
4	10	5	4
3	5	2	2
3	14	3	–

6. Give striking alternative titles to World War II.

Creativity Versus Intelligence

Notice that possible solutions are much fewer in the three IQ items, 1, 3 and 5; to solve them mostly logic and vocabulary rather than imagination are required; and that solutions once found, fit the problems rather snugly. In the creativity items, a number of other mental capabilities get exercised, such as associative thinking as in item 2, wide search as in item 4, and an enormous degree of compression of thought required in item 6 that must, however, be expressed aesthetically. Also there is no certainty at all that the solutions are the best possible or even good. As is obvious, the degree of convergent thinking needed is much higher for the IQ problems than for the creativity problems, while the degree of divergent thinking needed is much higher for tackling creativity as compared to IQ problems. They represent quite distinctive sets of abilities, and indeed, research suggests that those who are high IQ scorers are not necessarily creative and vice versa. The ranks of the uncreative and the stupid are alarmingly large, and rare indeed are humans that are both creative and intelligent. No more than one in ten thousand may be exceptionally creative and intelligent.

Creativity Abilities

Creativity is not one ability at all, but a whole cluster of abilities. These are described as follows:

The first is called ideational fluency. It measures a person's ability to come up with a number of solutions to a given problem. For example, if I ask a group of persons to list the number of uses of bricks, some might come up with five uses, others with 15 or 20. Those that come up with a large number of uses, would be called ideationally fluent persons. Ideationally fluent persons tend to come up with a greater variety of solutions, as well as with a larger number of unusual solutions, than persons that are ideationally not fluent.

The ability to provide a large variety of solutions, to respond to a problem from a variety of view points, and to use a variety of approaches in problem solving is another important ability. It is called flexibility. In the brick example, one person may have listed several uses of bricks, but all of these uses may be connected with its use as a construction material - build houses, build bridges, build wells, build walls, etc. Another person may list a large variety of uses, such as bricks as weapons, as stepping stones in mud, as doorsteps, as engraving material, as supporters for shelves, etc.

The third creative ability is originality, or the ability to come up with unusual but appropriate responses. For bricks, their use as hiding places for jewellery, or their use as dumbbells, or their use as substitutes for pillows by placing them under the mattress, may be considered unusual, and therefore, original responses. A related ability is the ability to come up with novel relationships between ideas or two frames of reference. This is the sense in which Koestler understands creativity. It is the faculty that helps an Edison leap to the realization that what you need to turn electricity into light is not a good conductor of electricity as his contemporaries thought, but a bad conductor - a new relationship between current, impedance and incandescence. Or the faculty that helps one see the possibilities for perspective painting, by measuring the angles subtended in the eye by objects. And finally, it is the faculty that helps a poet to see neckties as tethers of civilization, or rivers as arteries of God, or a dewdrop as the abode of Vishnu.

A fourth ability is to notice the unexplained, the unsatisfactory, or the incongruent – in other words, the ability to sense problems. Scientists often dismiss data inconsistent with their pet theories as 'noise'. It is the inquisitive scientist, curious about 'noise', that sometimes makes remarkable discoveries. Alexander Fleming, the discoverer of penicillin, is a case in point. Many scientists had observed that fungus forming in a bio-chemical culture inhibits the growth of bacteria. But they failed to grasp the significance of this 'noise' in their experiments. It was Fleming who wondered about this and ultimately saw the significance of this for treating infections.

A fifth ability is the ability to go to the roots of a phenomenon by unravelling its causes, and equally, to visualize its consequences. This, of course, is a vital ingredient of scientific creativity. But I suspect it may be equally important in artistic creativity, where the ability to discern the mental associations of an object, and its potential as a metaphor in a work of art may be vital – to see, for example, modern city life as a spiritual waste land, as in Eliot's *The Waste Land*. Or, since death reminds us of tears, and tears of dewdrops, to use dew to convey pain at the death of a child as in the following lovely haiku:

Dew evaporates
and all our world
is dew....... so dear,
so fresh, so fleeting.

The ability to elaborate on a theme has also been recognized as a significant creative ability. It is the difference between a legend and Shakespeare's dramatic version of it, or an insight that capitalist economics get stuck with recessions and the full-fledged Keynesian general theory of economic equilibrium, or the idea that man has considerable creative potential and a full-fledged training programme for increasing creativity, or the difference between the notes of raga and its alaap. The ability to elaborate is indispensable in putting a creative idea to work.

An ability of considerable importance, is the ability to go behind the surface features of a problem, and see what the 'real' problem is. A group of psychologists, called gestalt psychologists have held it to be mainly responsible for producing original insights. Consider the problem faced by an ambulance, blocked on a long narrow bridge by a flock of sheep. So long as one defines the problem as how to get the ambulance to overtake the sheep, there would be no really effective solution. It is only when one defines the problem, as one of getting the ambulance ahead of the sheep, that a solution at once dawns – the flock can be turned around and driven past the stationary ambulance.

Obviously, these abilities – ideational fluency, fluency, flexibility, originality, problem-sensitivity, the ability to grasp the causes and visualize the consequences, the ability to elaborate, the ability to restructure problems – are not generally found in equal measure in the same individual. The individual, who can ideate fluently, may not be very original, and vice versa. It is, therefore, inappropriate to categorise a person as creative or uncreative, without specifying the dimensions on which he has high ability and the ones on which he has limited ability. If we are comparing two individuals, we should be very careful before we brand one person as less creative than the other. The chances are that the former may well be superior in at least one of the creativity related abilities.

Techniques of Creativity

A number of techniques have been developed to stimulate creative thinking. Some of these are based on the idea, that if we can defer evaluation of the ideas we produce, that is; separate out the phase of idea-evaluation from the phase of idea-production, we can greatly increase the number of ideas we produce. Thereby, we increase substantially, the chance of coming up with a really brilliant idea. Some other techniques are based on the idea, that if we can subject the mind to certain kinds of constructive strain, it is likely to leap to an original insight or idea.

The most widely used technique for generating creative ideas is the one called brainstorming. It was the brainchild of one Alex Osborn, an advertising executive. The basic steps are:

1. A problem is presented to a brainstorming panel by the leader. The problem should be stated as clearly as possible, so that there is no misunderstanding about what it is. The more precise the problem, the better.
2. The leader requests one idea at a time, from each member of the panel. It goes on for several rounds.
3. During the idea-generation, the rule is that no one is to criticize anybody's idea. Hitchhiking, or basing an idea on someone else's idea, is encouraged.

Research has shown that ideas produced by this deferred evaluation technique, are not only more numerous but also of better quality, than the ideas produced by an equivalent sized group, in which the deferred evaluation principle is not used. In fact, research suggests that individuals brainstorming alone, tend to produce more and better ideas than a brainstorming group consisting of the same number of individuals. This technique is highly recommended as being eminently practical and productive.

A technique that combines the convergent thinking principle of forming categories, with the brainstorming principle of generating many alternative solutions, is the technique of attribute analysis, ascribed to Crawford. The steps are:

1. Given an object that we wish to design, be it a tangible object or an activity, we first identify its major attributes. If we are trying to design a better chair, for example, we may identify comfort, durability, ease of moving and attractiveness as, say, the major attributes.
2. Next, we take up each attribute and generate as many alternative ways of securing the attribute as, we can. For example, to make a chair more comfortable, we may consider upholstering it, make it adjustable as to length,

direction, level, etc., curving the back to provide support to the spinal column, giving it supporting handles or support for the feet, and so forth. It is easy to see that if we generate even four alternatives, for each attribute, we have generated $(4)^4$ or 256 alternative designs for a chair. After generating these alternative designs, of course, we need to evaluate them in terms of criteria such as cost, marketability, etc.

Both these techniques, that is, brainstorming and attribute analysis, guarantee the generation of many solutions. The problem then becomes one of choosing, one or a few solutions for more intensive testing. One simple technique is to establish criteria of evaluation, and then have each member of group of experts pick out, say, the three solutions he or she thinks are most promising. These votes are pooled and the solutions receiving the most votes are taken up for more intensive investigation.

A very unusual technique for solving many complex technical problems is the technique of synectics, invented by Gordon, an advertising executive and later a management consultant. The technique is based on the principle that constructive psychological strain can lead to original solutions to problems. This is another group problem solving technique. This constructive psychological strain is generated by a number of processes:

1. After the problem is explained to the group, members are asked to explain the problem as they understand it. For example, if the problem is one of estimating petroleum reserves thousands of metres underground, one member may state that the problem as he understands it is one of making rocks tell us how much oil they contain.
2. The leader invites social or biological analogies, pertinent to the problem as understood, if it is a physical or a technical problem, and analogies from the physical sciences, if it is a problem concerning a living system.

Thus, one may look into the structure of the whale to explore a problem connected with submarines, and the processes of the computer to understand better the brain. In other words, there is a deliberate attempt to gain insight, by searching into analogous but otherwise very different terrain.

3. To generate insights through empathy, the leader may request personal analogies. Thus, if one is looking into the causes of metal fatigue, the members are asked to imagine themselves to be metal in a jet plane flying at a high altitude, and report what they feel-see-hear-smell-taste. This subjectification of an object of enquiry, sometimes, yields discoveries.
4. Synectics problem solving, goes through phases of imaginative exploration, such as through various personal and other analogizing and phases of imaginative compression through book titles or symbolic analogies. After there has been a good deal of exploration, the leader may seek to crystallize the images and ideas generated, by inviting group members to come up with poetic or paradoxical phrases, that could serve the same function as book titles. Suppose the original problem had been the control of hurricanes and a very elaborate exploration of a war had ensued, in order to gain insights into what happens when air masses with different moisture contents and pressures collide. The leader, at this point, may request members to provide alternative book titles to a battle. A number of titles could be generated, such as, 'greatness decimated' or 'migration to hell', or 'vulture's paradise' or 'sin immortalized' or 'dicey chastity', or 'finished hate'. One or more such book titles could trigger further poetic exploration in search of a technical solution.

During the process, any evaluative remarks are, of course, taboo. The imagination is continuously stretched, by going from the familiar to the unfamiliar and from the strange and unfamiliar to the familiar. The technique has been successfully employed in finding solutions to a number of intractable technical problems.

Synectics is a difficult technique, but its principle of constructive psychological strain is most practical. Basically, it consists of mechanisms that bend and stretch the mind in every direction, through the stuff of poetry. It is a technique for churning the mind, so that novel visions and insights rise to its surface.

Another technique that can be usefully combined with any of the other three techniques described earlier, is the one of checklist of questions. This was also developed by Osborn, the creator of brainstorming. This consists in subjecting a tentative solution to a barrage of questions. Some of these are quite straight forward questions, such as, how can we modify the solution to make it more economical; or can we find other uses of the solution; or can we get to the solution through other cheaper means; or what could we add or delete from the solution to make it more elegant, more practical, etc. Some questions stimulate more for research, such as "how do we miniaturize or minify X" or "how do we magnify X many times" or "what is the opposite of X", etc., where X is the proposed solution. As someone has put it, questions are the creative acts of intelligence, for they could be so designed, as to force a dramatic shift of perspective.

To summarize the principles that underlie creative thinking techniques, they are:

1. Structure the problem so that it is well understood.
2. Separate the phase of idea production from idea evaluation. Do not evaluate or criticize ideas – whether of one's own or another's during the time they are being articulated.
3. Ideate copiously. Churn out a large number of ideas, both, because this heightens the possibility of hitting upon some

really good ones, and also, to let one idea lead to another and to still another, and so on, like a chain-reaction.

4. Create constructive psychological strain by continuously enticing the person to go from the familiar to the unfamiliar terrain and back to the familiar, such as by coming up with analogies, metaphors, and empathic statements.
5. Force wide shifts of perspective by asking such questions as "What could be the opposite of the current solution?", or "How could we magnify or minify the solution?", or "Is there a radically different way of looking at the problem?"
6. Having generated a large number of ideas or solutions, identify the ones with the greatest potential by some sort of an assessment and selection procedure, such as experts picking out the three most promising ideas.

The creative person pioneers, seeks to do new or novel things, in novel ways. These are intrinsically risky activities that often invite a good deal of criticism or opposition from those wedded to the status-quo. Hence, the creative person needs a good deal of courage, independence, and ability to take risks. Failures in such novel activities may be frequent. Therefore, persistence and self-confidence are needed. In doing something creative, one needs to be very open to ideas and one must seek a good deal of information. Thus, the creative person must be inquisitive. Finally, creation requires a high degree of psychological complexity - ability to visualize a new order of things, ability to intuit or grasp the basics, a capacity to be moved by higher emotions, the endless search for the elusively aesthetic or true or good.

21 Theories of Leadership: A Conceptual Overview

Asha Hingar

The need for effective leadership and motivational systems cannot be exaggerated in an organizational setting. A.M. Meerlo has emphasized that leadership stems from a man's desire to master his environment through group effort.[1] Leadership arises in the group where the members of the groups seek to satisfy their need through interaction. Leadership is one aspect of entire mechanism devised by the group for the fulfilment of its needs and goals. Through the device of role differentiation, groups make use of the various characteristics of the members to the advantage of all by assigning group tasks to those best qualified to perform them.

Research Efforts

A pioneering study in the field of leadership was conducted in the late 1930s by Ronald Lippitt and Ralph K. White with the assistance of Kurt Lewin.[2] The study was significant in the sense that it was the first serious attempt to analyse leadership through the use of scientific methodology. The analysis showed that different styles of leadership can have varying degrees of influences in the same groups.

The Ohio State Research Group identified consideration and initiation as two major functions of leadership.[3] Lester Coch and John French tried to testify the importance of participation in leadership.[4] Douglas McGregor also presented X and Y theories of leadership. Theory X represents the traditional and authoritarian type of management, while theory Y incorporates basic elements of human motivation, proper orientation and training.[5]

The Concept of Leadership

The concept of leadership has covered a wide variety of behaviours, many of which are unrelated with each other. In an unpublished review, V.J. Bentz has listed 130 definitions of leadership. These definitions were obtained through a review of literature published prior to 1949. Fred E. Fiedler has enumerated a dozen different definitions of leadership with varying connotations and degrees of emphasis. He has concluded that a leader is the individual in the group who directs and coordinates the group activities or who, in the absence of a designated leader, carries the primary responsibility for performing these functions in the group. Emphasis on coordination here seems to indicate that the task of leading is synonymous with managing.[6] But, essentially management is considered to be a much more broadly based function which also includes several activities other than leading.

Keith Davis has observed that "Leadership is the ability to persuade others to seek defined objectives enthusiastically. It is human factor which binds a group together and motivates it toward goals. Management activities such as planning, organizing, and decision-making are dormant cocoons until the leader triggers the power of motivation in people and guide them toward goals."[7]

The above definition stresses the role of leadership in eliciting behavioural responses which are beyond routine. But Robert Tannenbaum and Fred Massarik have underscored the influence system in the total leadership structures. They have summed up the relationship between leadership and influence/systems by stating that leadership is "interpersonal influence, exercised in situations and directed through the communication process, toward the attainment of a specified goal or goals. Leadership always involves attempts on the part of a leader (influencer) to affect (influence) the behaviour of a follower (influencee) or to follower in the situation.[8]

It may be pertinent to mention at this point that a definition of leadership should not be confined to one or two variables only but instead should incorporate all the crucial elements which collectively integrate themselves into the broader concept of leadership.

In social science literature, leadership is viewed with reference to three broad categories, viz., as the attribute of a position, as the characteristics of a person, and as a category of behaviour.[9]

This brief paper aims to examine whether all the three ingredients of leadership, viz., leader, situation and follower are included in a particular leadership theory or not.

Analysis is being attempted of the trait theories, sociometric theory, situational theories, general interaction theories, and idiosyncrasy credit theory.

Trait Theories of Leadership

The scientific analysis of leadership initially started with the concentration on the leader himself. The question arises as to what makes a person leader? The earliest trait theorists emphasized that leaders are born not made. This 'Great Man Theory' of leadership propounds that leadership traits are inborn, and generally cannot be acquired during one's life time. The Great Man Theory gave way to trait approach. But behavioural psychologists have observed through the use of scientific research methodology, that all traits are not completely inborn; some can also be acquired through learning and training. Thereupon, researchers began searching universal traits possessed by leaders. Numerous physical, mental and personality traits were researched between 1930s and 1950s. But the outcome of these researches were not consistent. Only intelligence seems to hold some degree of commonality among the various lists of trait on the basis of numerous empirical researches.

According to H.C. Warren, leadership depends on attitudes and habits of dominance in certain individuals and submissive behaviour in others. In view of these limitations and the absence of any causal relationship, Keith Davis has highlighted four traits which appear to have an impact on successful organization leadership. These factors are: (1) intelligence, (2) social maturity, (3) inner motivation and achievement, and (4) human relations attitudes. That seems to be a reasonable blend of traits which might be found in successful leaders. And if good leadership is defined according to some consensual yardstick these attributes gain significance. But a total reliance on the trait approach may not be a sound approach. Ben Solomon, who has suggested that certain specific qualities are obviously desirable in a leader but that more seems to be absolutely essential.

Trait theories of personality have certainly provided some insight into the traits of leaders, but in fact contain little analytical or predictive value.[10]

Sociometric Theory

A very large proportion of the research in leadership has made use of the sociometric method. This technique was developed by Jacob Moreno,[11] while the first sociometric study was made by Helen Jennings.[12] The approach provides an easily accessible and relatively objective means of assessing interpersonal attitudes within a group. The simple but important recognition that different choice criteria could be incorporated in the sociometric question has led to very significant insights into the leadership of groups. The sociometric method has also demonstrated that interpersonal designation of leader varies in any group, with the change in goals, tasks and internal structure of an organization.

Situational Theories of Leadership

Limited success attained by focusing upon the leader in the theories of leadership led to a new perspective stressing an analysis of situational influences in leadership growth. Situational theorists emphasize that leadership roles, skills and behaviour considerably depend upon external and internal environmental situations. Leadership is a function of interaction[13] between personality and situation.

Since 1940s several researchers have identified various situational variables which bear relevance to the conceptualizations on leadership. The general conclusion of such researchers is that depending on the situation, some leadership styles seem to be more effective than others. For example, Alan Filley and Robert House, in review of research literature on leadership found the following situational factors influencing leadership effectiveness:[14]

1. The history of the organization, the age of the leader and his previous experience;
2. the community in which an organization operates;
3. the work requirement of the group;
4. the psychological environment of the group which is going to be led;
5. the kind of job the leader holds;
6. the size of the group;
7. group member personalities; and
8. the time required and allowed for decision-making.

The list underscores the abundant impact of the situational factors on leadership. However, most of the variables enumerated in the above list have not been duly verified by further research. Nevertheless, their heuristic value remains.

General Interaction Theory

Basically, leadership under this conceptual scheme, is a function of personality and social system in a dynamic interactional situation.

Some aspects of interaction theory have been systematically elaborated and investigated into by Fred Fiedler and his associates. Fiedler combines the trait and situational approaches to come up with an overall theory or at least a model, of leadership effectiveness.[15] To understand his model, it is necessary to have a resume of his research techniques and findings.

Fiedler chose to measure, as indicators of leadership effectiveness "assumed similarity between opposites" (ASO) and "esteem for the least preferred co-worker" (LPC). ASO calculates the degree of similarity between the leaders' perception of his least and most preferred co-workers. LPC calculates the degree to which the leader favourably perceives his worst co-worker. The two measurement which can be used interchangeably, relate to leadership style in the following manner:

1. The human relation oriented leader who does not distinguish a great deal between the most and the least preferred co-worker which gives a relatively favourable description of the LPC.
2 The task-oriented leader sees a great difference between his most and least preferred co-workers (ASO) and gives very unfavourable description of the least preferred co-workers.

Fiedler's Contingency Model of Leadership

To test his hypotheses, Fiedler developed contingency model of leadership which contained the relationship between leadership style and the favourableness of the situation. This favourableness was described by Fiedler in terms of three propositions:

1. the leader-member relationships,
2. the degree of task structure, and
3. the leader's position power obtained through formal authority.[16]

Situations are favourable to the leader if all three of the above dimensions are high, and if these dimensions are low, situations become unfavourable to the leader. Fiedler observes that the favourableness of the combination with the leadership's styles determines effectiveness.

Fiedler discovered that under very favourable and unfavourable situations, the task-oriented type of leader was not effective, and the situation was only moderately favourable; employee oriented leader was most effective.[17]

The question arises why the task oriented leader is successful in very favourable situations. Fiedler explains that in very favourable conditions in which leader has power and informal backing and a relatively well structured organization, the group is ready to be directed, for it expects to be told what to do.[18]

Fiedler's contingency model has so far stood the test of research but much more needs to be done. In general, Fiedler's contingency model suggests that the effectiveness of group performance can be affected by changing the leader's style and/or the situation in accordance with the described relationships.

Fiedler and Meuwese have also demonstrated that a leader's ability scores corelate highly with group performance only if the leader is sociometrical accepted or liked.[19]

Hollander's Idiosyncrasy Credit

It is noteworthy that both the trait and situational theories make a contribution to understand leadership behaviour. But they are only partial theories. They neglect or underemphasize the followers role in leadership behaviour despite the fact that followers form the central part of leadership.

Probably the best word for the definition of leadership is, 'influence'. The leader influences his followers but perhaps equally or important is the fact that followers influence the leader. Edwin P Hollander and James W. Julien use the concept of 'exchange' to explain this leader-follower interaction process.[20] Situation, group, and leadership style can be integrated with an overall influence system of leadership.

Conclusion

The popular idea that leaders are born not made, highlights the importance of individual traits of leaders but ignores other equally relevant factors. The characteristics of social group which is going to be led is also an important variable in understanding situations. The presence of certain basic personality traits and behavioural characteristics is helpful but neither necessary nor sufficient for the success as a leader.

In conclusion, the most appropriate leadership technique is probably the one which recognizes the importance of systematic interaction among style, group and situation. The administrator should attempt to adopt a style which is compatible with the needs and expectations of subordinates and is appropriate in the given situation. One should recognize that this style may vary from group to group or even from individual to individual and from situation to situation.

Notes

1. A.M. Meerlo, *Leider en geleide; bijdrage tot de psychologie van het leiderschap. (Leader and Follower. A Contribution to the Psychology of Leadership)* (Mensch en Maatschappiji, 1934), pp. 196-210.
2. Ronald Lippitt, Ralph K. White and Kurt Lewin, "Patterns of Aggressive Behaviour in Experimentally Created Social Climates", *Journal of Social Psychology*, May 1939, pp. 271-276.
3. Ralph M. Stogdill and Alvin E. Coons (eds.), *Leader Behaviour: Its Description and Measurement* (Columbus, Ohio State University, Bureau of Business Research 1957).
4. Lester Coch and John R.P. French, "Overcoming Resistance to Change", *Human Relations*, Vol. 1. No. 4, 1948, pp. 512-532.
5. Douglas McGregor, *The Human Side of Enterprise* (New York, McGraw Hill Book Company, 1967).
6. Fred E, Fielder, *A Theory of Leadership Effectiveness*, New York, McGraw Hill Book Company, 1967.
7. Keith Davis, *Human Behaviour at Work*, 4th ed, (New York, McGraw Hill Book Company, 1972, pp. 103-104.

8. Robert Tennenbaum and Fred Massarik, "Leadership: A Frame of Reference", *Management Science*, October 1957, p. 3.
9. Daniel Katz and Robert L. Khan, *The Social Psychology of Organization* (New York Wiley, 1966).
10. L. Jacob, Moreno, *Who shall Survive Foundations of Sociometry, Group Psychotherapy and Sociodrama Sociometry,* Monograph No. 29 (Beacon, N.Y.: Beacon House, 1935).
11. On this point, see, "Leader Behaviour and Member Reaction in Three Social Climates", in Dorwin Cartwright and Alvin Zander (eds.) *Group Dynamics: Research and Theory*. (New York, Harper and Row, 1953) pp. 385-611,
12. Helen, Jennings, *Sociometry of Leadership Based on Differentiation of Psycho-group and Sociogroup Sociometry,* Monograph No. 14 (Beacon N.Y.: Beacon House).
13. J.C. Wofford, "Managerial Behaviour, Situational factors, Productivity and Morale", *Administrative Science Quarterly,* March 1972, pp. 10-37.
14. Alan C. Filley and Robert J. House, *Managerial Process and Organizational Behaviour* (Gleenview: Scott, Foresman and Company Gleenview, 1969), pp. 409.
15. Fred E. Fielder, *A Theory of Leadership Effectiveness* (Now York: McGraw Hill Book 1967),
16. *Ibid.*, pp. 143-144.
17. *Ibid.*, pp. 133-153.
18. *Ibid.*, p. 147.
19. Fred E., Fiedler and Meuwese. W.A.T. "Leaders Contribution to Task Performance in Cohesive and Incohesive Groups", *Journal of Abnormal and Social Psychology,* 1967, pp. 86-87.
20. Edwin P. Hollander and James W. Julian "Contemporary Trends in the Analysis of Leadership Process", *Psychological Bulletin,* May 1969, p. 390.

22 Good Governance and the Desideratum of Sustainable Efficiency: The Indian Experience

Ramesh K. Arora

Any thesaurus would tell us that the word 'efficiency' carries numerous synonyms. Some of these are: ability, capability, adeptness, competence, economy, effectiveness, efficacy, power, productivity, proficiency, and skilfulness. In common parlance, efficiency denotes the quality of being able to do a task successfully and without wasting time or energy. It has been closely, linked to the ratio between cost and benefit input and output, effort and result, expenditure and income. As Herbert Simon comments, the criterion of efficiency dictates that choice of alternatives which produces the largest result for the given application of resources.[1] Administrative theory, as evolved during past twelve decades or so, has underscored efficiency as a cardinal goal as well as technique of good administration.

It may be recalled that Woodrow Wilson in his seminal essay, published in 1887, had underscored the significance of promoting efficiency in government systems which was possible only when public systems gained substantial autonomy in their functions. Later, Taylorism was responsible for catapulting the notion of efficiency to the highest level of concern and priority in administrative analysis as well as in organizational practice. It was on account of the orthodoxy emanating from Taylorism that efficiency experts mushroomed and dominated the whole industrial and commercial scene throughout the United States in the early part of the twentieth century. Little wonder, there was an enormous demand for applying the principles of Taylorism even in the government sector. The President's Committee on Economy and Efficiency, set up in 1910, was a clear signal that efficiency had arrived as the most eminent concern of government systems. Almost at the same time two other scholars were also according primacy to the notion of efficiency in organizational analysis. Max Weber, in his ideal-typical model of bureaucracy had visualized characteristics such as hierarchy, specialization, recruitment on merit, written rules, etc., as requisites to making bureaucracy the most efficient administrative system vis-a-vis its counterparts of traditional and charismatic authority systems. In fact, his notion of efficiency and the concept of rationality were intertwined, for both focussed on cost-benefit relationship. Weber's analysis of Protestant ethics and the rise of capitalism underscores the value of efficiency. He averred that whosoever was most efficient would be most successful in business. And, in France, Henri Fayol was also crystallizing his principles of administration in the context of their relevance to organizational goals, including efficiency.

The classical organizational theory considered efficiency as a 'goal' and looked at it as an outcome of the traditional principles of administration such as hierarchy, specialization unity of command, span of control, coordination and decentralization. There was no fundamental deviation from this perspective in the Human Relations School, for the human relationists also considered efficiency as the most important indicator of administrative effectiveness, though they had discovered that formal structure alone was not sufficient to achieve efficiency. Informal organization played a complementary role in advancing its cause. Almost all theorists in Management Sciences have treated efficiency as a key variable of administrative analysis.

In administrative theory, there have been two parallel foci: the separation of politics and administration and concern for efficiency. While there have been a number of views and counterviews on the relationship between politics and administration, the acceptance of efficiency as a dominant criterion of evaluating an administrative system's performance has had a remarkable consistency during the past one hundred years or so. Nowhere is the 'transplantation' of the core value of private administration to the field of Public Management has been more prominent than in the adoption of the criterion of efficiency as the key measure of the success of an organization.[2]

Efficiency: A Continuing Concern of Administrative Reform

Efficiency has been the key concern of most administrative reform measures in India. Five days before independence, a report was submitted by Girija Shankar Bajpal, as the Chairman of the States Reorganization Committee suggesting procedural changes in the secretariat of the Government of India. In 1948, the Economy Committee, headed by Kasturbhai Lalbhai an industrialist, recommended measures to check government expenditure, including what was incurred on staff. In 1949, N. Gopalaswami Ayyangar, a minister in the Central Government, presented a report on the reorganization of the government machinery, recommending regrouping of ministries, improving the competence of the personnel and creation of an O&M Division in the Government of India. In 1951, Gorwala in his *Report on Public Administration in India* recommended introducing effective organizational procedures in various government organizations. He stressed upon efficiency, economy, integrity and discipline as the basic attributes of good public administration. Gorwala advocated reorganization of the government for facilitating efficiency, effectiveness and responsibility. In 1952, R.A. Gopalaswami submitted a memorandum to the Cabinet Secretary on improving efficiency in the secretariat and on creation of an O&M Directorate. Paul Appleby in his *Public Administration: Report of A Survey* (1953) commended India as "among the dozen or so most advanced governments in the world" and then went on to call it "archaic, feudalistic and unimaginative". He made several recommendations for improving work procedure and for enhancing the capability of administrative organizations. He also advocated for the creation of an O&M Division, which was set up in 1954, in the Cabinet Secretariat. Further, he stressed upon the need for specifying tasks and responsibilities for better implementation of plans and programmes and their continuous monitoring and evaluation. In 1954, Ashok Chanda recommended the adoption of officer-oriented system in the government organizations.

In 1975, L.P. Singh and L.K. Jha both seasoned civil servants who had served as members of the Indian Civil Service, presented to the Government of India a *Note on Improving Efficiency in Administration* which contained recommendations, among others on improving work conditions and office environment, enforcing punctuality and discipline and strengthening O&M to minimize delays, making assessment of staff requirement, house-keeping and staff welfare.

In 1976, in the conference of State Chief Secretaries, it was resolved to delegate greater financial powers to the secretariat departments and HoDs, improvements and simplification of rules, strengthening the administrative coordination system and making performance appraisal system more rational.

Perhaps, the most comprehensive set of recommendations, including those on administrative efficiency emerged from the reports of the Administrative Reforms Commission which during its working of four and a half years (1966 to 1970) presented 20 major reports. ARC's seven major concerns in this respect were:

1. A more rational distribution of work in the secretariat and among the executive agencies; a regrouping of subjects.
2. Improving coordination.
3. Reduction in and staff.
4. Strengthening top management and integrating specialists and technical experts into the administrative hierarchy.
5. Reduction in levels of consideration to reduce delays and promote quick decision-making adoption of desk officer system.
6. Integration of the secretariat with field agencies.
7. Delegation of power.

The most relevant among the 20 reports for our purpose is the report on "The Machinery of Government of India and its Procedures of Work". The ARC recommended the regrouping of subjects among ministries - a recommendation that was rejected since the government did not find it feasible to impose any, hard and fast pattern on the number of ministries and departments and the business allocated to them.

An important recommendation of the ARC pertained to the reduction in the number of hierarchical levels generally involved in decision-making in government. The Commission observed: "There should be only two levels of consideration below the minister, namely, (i) under secretary/deputy, secretary, and (ii) joint secretary/additional secretary. Work should be assigned to each of these two levels on the lines of 'desk officer' system. Each level should be empowered to dispose of a substantial amount of work on its own and be given the necessary staff assistance.[3]

Desk Officer System

As pointed out already, certain earlier committees also made the suggestion for the adoption of desk officer system but the system was adopted only on an experimental basis in a few organizations. The Government of India, reacting to the recommendation of ARC, commented that there could not be a rigid formula fixing the number of levels of consideration at two only, though efforts should be made to reduce the number of levels of decision-making. While the principle of desk officer system was considered to be good in principle, it could not be applied uniformly to all secretariat wings. Hence, the decision to adopt it was left to the individual ministries and departments, keeping in view its feasibility.

The government observed that while adopting the desk officer system, the personnel should be carefully selected and the pace of the adoption of this reform should be adjusted to the capacity of the total machinery to absorb the staff that may have to be transferred out of the reorganized wings. However, whenever a new unit is set up in the government, efforts should be made to adopt the desk officer system. Despite the recommendation of the ARC, the desk officer system has not been adopted in most of the ministries and departments of the Government of India.

It may be worthwhile to mention that at the state level also, certain experiments were conducted in the adoption of the desk officer system. The nomenclature of this system varied from state to state. However, this innovation was not welcomed extensively because of the following main reasons:

1. Frequent transfers of officials did not give them long enough tenure in a department to understand the intricacies of functioning, particularly if the department happened to be a technical department.
2. There was a resistance on the part of the secretary of a department to decentralize authority to his subordinates, apprehending that his grip on the department would be loosened.
3. The system was not applied uniformly in all departments, thus a pattern of functioning and an administrative style could not develop among officers who moved from one department to another.
4. There were hardly any transfers at the level of the lower staff functioning in the government departments.

Resultantly, the 'memory' of official decisions continued to be with the *babus* who became the custodian of information in the department, while the senior officers who had a very short tenure on a particular position, could not match the intensity of knowledge and understanding of the lower level bureaucracy.

5. The senior officers found it convenient to cling to the traditional system as it provided them with a secure base for decision-making. In the desk officer system, they could be made directly and solely responsible for any lapses committed in decisions made by them, but in the traditional section system, they could easily have all alibi that they made their judgment on the advice or information provided by the lower and middle level functionaries.

The above 'reasons' have been considered as sufficient to prevent the expansion of the desk officer system in the Indian government system. Thus, what has proven to be a time-tested efficacious pattern of work performance in Britain has been treated as irksome in the Indian context. Hence, what is needed is a big push to this desk officer system through political and administrative will. The speed and quality of governmental decisions is bound to improve through this structural device.

In order to make the desk officer system successful, a precaution will have to be taken to follow a rational system of placement and transfer of senior and senior-middle officers and normally give them at least a neat three-year tenure on a particular position. Only then their understanding of and commitment to a particular department will strengthen.

Recent Initiatives

In the nineties, in the wake of structural reforms in governance throughout the world, adoption of liberalization in India and a growing stress on improving governmental performance, a series of efforts have been made to introduce reforms in the Indian administrative system. At the level of the Prime

Minister, Cabinet Secretary, Chief Ministers and the Chief Secretaries, brainstorming has taken place and an Action Plan has been prepared by the Department of Administrative Reforms and Public Grievances which, in turn, is based on the recommendations of the conference of Chief Secretaries held on "An Agenda for an Effective and Responsive Administration" in November, 1996. This Action Plan focuses on Citizens' Charters and an administration; effective and speedy public grievance redressal system; empowerment of local bodies; decentralized delivery system; review of laws, rules and procedures; transparency and right to information; code of ethics for public servants; combating corruption; and stability of tenure of civil servants.[4] Reading between the lines, one can discern the centrality of efficiency in the visualized reform process. In fact, no agenda on good governance can fructify unless optimum standards of efficiency are attained.

The debate on the issue of good governance was initiated vigorously by, the advocacy for 'reinvesting government'[5] although the recent initiatives of the Government of India and the state governments seem to be influenced by the maxims of good governance postulated by the World Bank.[6] Among the seven requisites of good governance as per the World Bank perspective, one that is most pertinent to our theme is as follows:

A sound administrative system leading to efficiency and effectiveness. This, in turn, means the value for money, and cost effectiveness. The effectiveness includes the degree of goal achievement as per the stated objectives and also the administrative system which is able to take secular and rational decisions and the system which is self propelling to take corrective measures.

Themes and Issues for Analysis and Action

There has been a spate of ideas on improving efficiency of the governance system in the Indian context. Reports of various committees and commissions, deliberations of seminars and other published sources are full of useful ideas on enhancing governmental efficiency. Hence, it may not be necessary to reproduce or summarize them. However, an attempt is being made in the following pages to discuss certain themes and issues that are germane to the notion of administrative efficiency and which cumulatively present an instrumental perspective in this context.

Rightsizing the Government

Lately, in tune with the cross-national trends, there has been a visible emphasis on the need for downsizing or 'rightsizing' governments in India. It is significant to note that the size of the government has been increasing at a fast pace over the years. This has resulted into over-staffing at all levels. The Central Government has more than 3.4 million people on its rolls. This has resulted into a proliferation in the budget for emoluments paid to the bureaucracy. The government's wage bill is going up by 14.3 per cent every year. At the state level as well, there has been an abundant increase in the size of bureaucracy with the number of senior positions increasing to accommodate officials in all-India and state services. There are more than 6 million people employed by state governments. Even at the lower level, there has been an uncontrolled growth in the number of personnel. According to World Bank Report, India: Sustaining Reform, Reducing Poverty (2003), of the total 9.4 million employees, nearly 93 per cent are class III and IV employees. It is only recently that serious attention is being paid to the issue of downsizing. The concept has gained currency particularly after the report of the Fifth Pay Commission which had recommended a 30 per cent decrease in the staff of the Central Government over a period of time. However, the compulsions of a welfare state have prevented the implementation of this recommendation, for there could be seriously adverse political implications if such a suggestion was to be carried through. At the state level also, the position is not markedly different.

It is obvious that a radical or drastic plan for downsizing may not be feasible either from a political or from an administrative angle. Instead, there has to be a phased action programme to implement this strategy. The following could be a feasible strategy in this regard.

1. An attempt should be made to transfer to the private sector or to NGOs certain functions, which are peripheral to the core government systems. Either these functions could be contracted out or transferred through a formal arrangement.
2. Those agencies which are performing such peripheral functions, ought to be wound up in a phased manner and their personnel transferred to other departments where they can be more productive.
3. While, making all transfers, appropriate training should be imparted to the staff so that they do not find their newer responsibilities too complex to be performed satisfactorily.
4. There should be a ban on recruitment at the lower level bureaucracy, with more and more responsibilities for decision-making entrusted to the senior officials in tune with the spirit of the officer-oriented systems.
5. Zero-based budgeting ought to be adopted in most departments in order to analyse the staff needs of various organizations. In this respect, the techniques of work study should supplement the process of staff need-assessment. It may not be possible to retrench all the surplus or less useful staff forthwith, yet a plan of action could be drawn to rightsize public organizations in a systematic and phased manner.
6. A rational system of Voluntary Retirement Scheme (VRS) should be implemented not only in public sector enterprises but also in government departments.
7. Rigorous manpower planning should be undertaken to assess the future requirements of personnel.

It may be underscored that overstaffing causes complacency, blurring of responsibilities, role-conflict, wastage and inefficiency. Hence, without curbing it, efficiency would be inconceivable.

Minimizing Bureaucratic Delays

Bureaucracy has become a synonym for red tape. Ever since Harold Laski dwelt upon the demerits of bureaucracy and ever since the explanation of 'bureau pathological' traits of organizational systems have been explicated by Victor Thomson and other scholars, there has been a general down sliding in the image of public bureaucracies. In this context, the most popular insinuation against bureaucracy has been its stifled with 'red tape'. Normally, red tape refers to an inordinately long time taken by bureaucratic organizations in performing their most basis tasks. It is commonly accepted that public bureaucracies are not 'free agents', and their goals are contingent on the purposes, goals and activities of other official actors.[7] This interdependence of bureaucratic organizations and the imperatives of coordination further lead to delays in the decisional process. Thus, the biggest challenge before administrative analysts is to distinguish between delays that are 'optimal' and those which are avoidable.

Optimal red tape is riot basically dysfunctional. Wintrobe argues that it is useful to conceptualize red tape in terms of its advantages.[8] Red tape often serves as a necessary check on discretion which, in case left uncontrolled, can lead to the advancement of personal over organizational interests. Besides, red tape exercises a desirable check on the unreasonable discretion exercised by decision-makers. Wherever coordination and monitoring are required, discretion becomes necessary, thus unintendedly resulting into red tape. While rules and procedures are essential elements of an ideal type bureaucracy in the Weberian framework, these may also hamper efficiency. For instance, Robert Merton[9] and Victor Thompson[10] view red tape as a cause of organizational pathology. However, a more realistic approach could be to examine the consequences of red tape in terms of promoting stability and objectivity in organizational dynamics. Hence, in the Indian public systems, certain form and size of red tape can be accepted as 'optimal', while the undesirable and dispensable red tape ought to be clipped and slashed.

Technological Basis of Efficiency

Use of modern technology has led to enhancement of efficiency in a variety of governmental organizations. There has been a perceptible revolution in transportation and communication sectors. Faxes and e-mails and telecommunication advances have dramatically added to the speed of communication. Computerization of services in educational administration, admissions, examinations, recruitment through Public Service Commissions, reservations in airways, railways and roadways, and in postal services have made a noticeable difference in the status of efficiency and objectivity in government systems. The need is to expand computerization in as many delivery systems as possible. The IT revolution should cover the rural scene, more particularly that of land records management. Further, in the areas of planning, project management, manpower planning and financial forecasting, technological efficiency can prove to be functional.

Human Resource Management

A few critical aspects of human resource management need to be examined in the context of their relevance to efficiency enhancement.

Amendment of Article 311

An opinion has been voiced in many circles that Article 311 of the Indian Constitution, subscribing to the due process of law, protects even the incompetent and the corrupt from termination of service. The process of inquiries entailed under the safeguard is dilatory and cumbersome. Consequently, the government system continues to suffer the burden of unwilling, inefficient and corrupt personnel.

Since the Constitution of India is being reviewed, it would be correct to examine the possibilities of amending Article 311 in a manner that would pave the way for summary trials and, if warranted, termination, of personnel who have proven unworthy of the constitutional security of service.

Prudent Placement and Rational Transfers

There is rampant ad hocism in placing bureaucrats at different positions in government. Their experience, orientations and talent are rarely considered as critical factors in determining their placements. Sound manpower planning demands the placement of right person on the right job. Past records, professional experiences, personal interviews, performance and potential appraisals can help decide about appropriate placements.

Regarding transfers, there has to be a more rational policy at the state and lower levels. There ought to be adopted a transfer policy and transfer rules and, even a legislation, to ensure that normally, a person works on a position for three to five years and he is transferred only as per norms and rules or in exceptional personal or professional circumstances. Proper placement and transfers will enhance motivation and curb wastage of human and financial resources.

Training in Decision-Making

Various researches in the identification of training needs have consistently revealed that in Indian governmental systems, middle level and senior officials are not adequately equipped with decisional acumen. Although they may be aware of the logical sequence of the decisional process involving the Simonian categories of intelligence, design, choice, implementation and feedback, yet when it comes to the applied world of complex decision-making, they find themselves wanting in this realm. There are two obvious reasons for this paradoxical situation: first during the foundational and field training there is hardly any exposure to the complex process of, decision-making and second, most senior administrators do not devote attention to the grooming of their juniors in the decisional process. The old ICS tradition of developing the juniors faded away immediately after independence. It needs to be revived.

Back to Basics

The concept of efficiency had evolved with the classical administrative theory, but it has smoothly gained a respectable status in all succeeding theories. Efficiency in the classical approach is a function and consequence of a set of structural attributes of organizations. Of these attributes, supervision and control are most critical. Without optimum supervision and control exercised by legitimate sources of authority, efficiency is least likely to be generated and sustained. However, a glaring weakness of the Indian government system is the absence of optimum supervision and control mechanisms in organizational dynamics. There prevails in public systems either over-control or under-control, more probably the latter. Prakash Tandon, in the early seventies, had pointed out that there would be no need for any drastic administrative reforms in case their seniors exercised optimum and effective supervision over government functionaries. Non-fulfilment of expected roles leads to the need for extraordinary measures. But ad hocism and episodic reforms can never be good substitutes of consistent and constant regulation of a system in a rational and effective manner. The need is therefore to evaluate the performance of middle and higher level administrators in terms of their success in leading, guiding and supervising their juniors and subordinate agencies.

Innovation and Creativity

Government organizations in India are known for their archaic methods of functioning. Institutional innovations and structural redesigning are generally inspired by international organizations, funding agencies and occasionally by political leadership. Reform Commissions and Committees have been instrumental in giving ideas for introducing innovations in structures and procedures. A good number of chief executives such as Secretaries, Commissioners, Managing Directors. Directors and Collectors have provided leadership in introducing innovations in a number of public organizations. Some of these have been chronicled in different sources. However, the limitations of most innovations and initiatives in public systems are that these are inspired by individual administrators and not systemically generated. Consequently, the critical element of sustainability is mostly conspicuous by its feeble presence. The need remains of generating a culture of innovation and of rewarding creative teams and their leaders appropriately. Efficiency is bound to accelerate in all innovative and creative environment.

Refocusing on the Babu Bureaucracy

A.D. Gorwala had christened Indian bureaucracy as the Babu bureaucracy. It implied two things: First, the babu dominantly, though imperceptibly, influences the decisional process in the governance system, and second, the mind-set of the Indian senior officials as well as that of a babu, favours performing the routine tasks of administration in a regulated manner and is used to interpreting the written laws, rules and codes in a conventional manner. While the orientation of senior bureaucrats is intended to be transformed through in-service training and conference and seminars, there is hardly any attempt made to change the attitude of the babu. The problem assumes gigantic proportion when these babus who enter the government service as lower division clerks, get promoted steadily to higher echelons. For instance, in the Rajasthan Secretariat, which is manned at the middle and the senior-middle levels by the Assistant Secretaries and the Deputy Secretaries, is mainly run by officials who started their careers as LDCs and reached the position of Deputy Secretaries through sheer promotions by seniority. With inbreeding ruling the roost, the chance of fresh perspective influencing the decisional process in the secretariat are woefully meagre. The babu mentality of obstructing, counter-questioning, doubting, objecting and procrastination does not allow decisions to be made rationally and swiftly, unless of course, the political or administrative leadership of a department asserts effectively, but that does not happen very often.

There should therefore be direct entry to all government posts at least up to 50 per cent of the sanctioned positions. Besides, a person should not be placed in a department for more than five years at a stretch. Moreover, there should be regular training for the lower and lower-middle level functionaries in information, skills and attitudinal change. It is paradoxical that the senior officials of the state government are trained in basics of computers, while the lower level functionaries have no motivation or compulsions to learn information technology. In order to move towards reducing paperwork and to plan for paperless offices, the plan of action must take into account the needs and capacity-building of lower level bureaucracy.

Efficiency as Value

In developing countries, efficiency takes a great deal of effort to establish itself as a key component of administrative culture. In these societies, there is a very high level of tolerance for inefficiency, ambiguity and indecisiveness. In fact, efficiency in public system is an exception rather than the rule. Little wonder, expectations of the common man from the government institutions and functionaries are generally not high. And, when the government organizations are found to be inefficient, it is accepted as natural. Those who are politically, socially or economically resourceful can 'buy' efficiency. The rest remain complacent and continue to believe in their incapacity to get things done. The situation does not apply to administrative system alone. In fact, it is all-pervasive, government educational institutions, hospitals, transport corporations, airlines, scientific laboratories and art academies – all of them show symptoms of inefficiency.

There is, however, episodic efficiency discernible in public systems from time to time. During the President's rule in a state, and during the general elections, census, communal riots etc., one can see commendable level of administrative efficiency. But, in normal times, the law of inertia reinforces itself. Things come back to their original state of slowness and procrastination. Hence, efforts should be made to inculcate a culture of time-consciousness among all enlightened sections of society. Lessons on self-management, self-discipline and time-management should become integral parts of the curricula and training systems. A comprehensive socialization programme in these areas can help transform a climate of indolence and complacency into a culture of Karma Yoga. The journey will be long but in the right direction. This will help establish efficiency as a value rather than just a technique.

Promoting Work Culture

It is common knowledge that the overall work culture in public systems in India is relatively low when compared to the prevailing work climate in the private sector in India and in other government systems, more particularly in the developed world. There have hardly been any empirical studies to identify the levels of productivity in government, but on the basis of whatever broad qualitative analyses are available, it can be surmised that there is a distinctly low level of productivity in most sectors of the Indian socio-economic order. In the government administrative system, the situation is woefully disquieting. There are a number of reasons for a dissatisfying level of work culture in government. Some of the factors responsible for this state of affairs are as follows:

1. There are no specific norms for productivity and work-performance in government systems.
2. Job descriptions and job assignments are unspecific, leading to ambiguity in roles and responsibilities of government employees.

3. There is an over-centralization in organizational designing with most of the powers for decision-making concentrated at the top. This leaves very little autonomy and scope for initiative at the middle and lower levels of bureaucracy.
4. Since well-intentioned decisions, which incidentally have proven to be wrong, are generally not defended in government, there is an obvious hesitation among the middle and lower level functionaries to give unambiguous and independent opinion on decisions, which contain a risk element. This generates a tendency among the middle level officials of passing the buck to higher authorities.
5. Over-cautiousness in decision-making, on account of the compulsions of accountability, leads to delays in the disposal of government business. Unfortunately, the accountability and control system in India is either too lax or too rigid. Sometimes, the overbearing and suspicious attitude of the controlling authorities leads to a state of 'timidity' in decision-making which, in turn leads to avoidable delays in government functioning.
6. There is hardly any reward for the good work done in public organizations. It is true that the efficient and honest workers in government are given their due promotions, but it is only for an extraordinary performance that someone is recommended for a prestigious award.
7. Paradoxically, those who are less efficient also continue to get their normal promotions. Playing safe and not taking any initiative helps them in steering through a long government career without any problem. In fact, there is hardly any punishment for low performance in government. Little wonder, a typical bureaucrat likes to remain anonymous and impersonal, for that appears to be the most secure course of action to take.
8. The performance appraisal system prevalent in government system is a routine affair, with hardly any scope for evaluating the outstanding traits of individuals, despite there being specific columns for identifying them.

It is very rarely that the performance appraisal reports are used for identifying training needs, making proper placements and even recommending out-of-turn promotions. The annual performance appraisal reports are filled in at the end of the year and therefore for most of the year a person can be sure that he is not being evaluated concurrently for his performance at work. Alls' well that ends well!

Work culture can improve only when initiative, enterprise, efficiency and integrity are rewarded, while indolence, indecision, inefficiency and dishonesty are punished. Besides effecting modification in rules, the mindset of key policy and decision-makers should also undergo transformation.

Continuity and Consistency in Administrative Change

In 1954, the O&M Division was set up in the Cabinet Secretariat in the Government of India. Later, in 1964, it became a part of the Department of Administrative Reforms, which is currently functioning as the Department of Administrative Reforms and Public Grievances within the wider framework of the Ministry of Personnel, Public Grievances and Pensions. An important responsibility of the Administrative Reforms Wing is to undertake O&M activities including revamping of government offices through modern office aids, reduction in paper work, records management and minimizing levels of consideration in the disposal of work. It is also expected to conduct research studies on administrative structures and procedures.

Experience has shown that the Department of Administrative Reform (and its later manifestation) has not functioned as a catalyst to rigorous administrative transformation in the Central Government. There is hardly any radical initiative which goes to the credit of this department. When the reform process gets routinized, it loses its vitality. Same is true of the Administrative Reforms Departments working at the state level.

The need is to examine and explore constantly, through rigorous specialized research, the alternatives to the traditional modes of administrative structures and procedures, incentive systems for promoting innovations, strategies for rightsizing the government, methods of changing the mindset of government functionaries, evolving designs for making the performance evaluation system more rational. The Department should scan the cross-national initiatives and experiments in administrative reforms and test their viability in the Indian conditions. Micro-level experiments can pave the way for wider application of newer structures and strategies for administrative effectiveness.

Another area that needs to be highlighted is that of 'Ergonomics' – the study of how working conditions, machines and equipment call be arranged in order that people can work with them more efficiently. There is much to learn from multinational working in India as well as from recently established banking institutions in creating congenial ambience for work performance that could also help promote client-orientation in government organizations. The Lakhina model in the reorganization of collectorates must be given a fresh look and lessons from this successful experiment be utilized for other pubic system functioning at the cutting edge level.

There should be undertaken periodically SWOT analysis for each major government unit. This exercise could help facilitate decentralization with accountability for performance, develop resilience and challenge-taking capacity and develop personnel to prepare them for achieving organizational goals.[11] SBI and LIC among others, have gained considerably through the adoption of these strategies.

India can also take a lesson from the American initiative in cutting red tape and paper work. The Paperwork Reduction Act of 1980 (which replaced the Federal Reports Act of 1942)[12] can provide some guidelines for action in this respect. The central and the state governments in India should take unit-wise analysis of paperwork and rationally reduce it to the minimum.

Value for Money

Government systems can learn a great deal even from private entrepreneurs. Sir Derek Rayner, who had eliminated much of paper use in the management of Marks and Spencers, the well-known departmental store, while studying government organizations in the early eighties, had suggested that we ask a pertinent question in case of every organization: "What does the organization do: at what cost and to what purpose?" This 'value for money' analysts was instrumental in saving for the British government about $ 500 million a year, and 3,000 different types of government forms were done away with.[13] This was the beginning of the 'Value for Money' movement which, transcending the traditional budgeting and accounting principles, evolved indicators for measuring government performance in various functional areas like health, welfare, education, environment and even crime control. Value for money advocates have pushed for three objectives, namely, the elimination of unnecessary government activities, the reduction of public spending and costs, and the increase of public sector productivity.[14] They attack the symptom of laziness, non-performance and indifference towards the people and underscore the reinforcement of efficiency in administration. Their techniques of increasing productivity are not new, what is new is a renewed emphasis on the basics of good governance.

There is a clear need in India to a transplant movement such as the Value for Money and make the business of government business-like without compromising its humanizing orientation. Efficiency is a precondition as well as an upshot of good governance and this equation is not likely to lose its authenticity in the foreseeable future.

Notes

1. Herbert Simon, *Administrative Behavior*, 3rd edition (New York: Free Press, 1976). p. 179.
2. Robert Denhardt. *Theories of Public Organization* (Monterey, Cal: Brooks/Cole, 1984). p. 62
3. Government of India, Administrative Reforms Commission, *Report on the Machinery of Government of India and its Procedures of Work* (New Delhi, 1968), p. 56.
4. For details. see M.C. Gupta and R.K. Tiwari (eds.), *Restructuring Government* (New Delhi: IIPA, 1998). Also refer. P. K. Dave, "The Citizen and the Administration" in V.A. Pai Panandiker and Subhash C. Kashyap (eds.), *Political Reforms Asserting Civic Sovereignty* (New Delhi: Konark, 2001), pp. 93, 121
5. The classical source is David Osborne and Ted Gaebler. *Reinventing Government: How the Entrepreneurial Spirit is Transforming the Public Sector* (New Delhi: Prentice-Hall 1992).
6. See, among others, Peter Blunt, "Cultural Relativism, Good Governance and Sustainable Human Development", *Public Administration and Development*, Vol. 15 (1995). pp. 5-7; and the whole special issue of *IJPA* on "Towards Good Governance", Vol. XLIV (July-September. 1998).
7. Stuart, L. Bretschneider and Barry Bozeman, "Understanding Red Tape and Bureaucratic Delays", in Arie Halachami and Geert Bouckaert (eds.). *The Enduring Challenges in Public Management* (San Francisco: Jossey-Bass, 1995), pp. 81-92
8. R. Wintrobe, "The Optimal Level of Bureaucratization within a Firm", *Canadian Journal of Economics*, Vol. 15 (1982). pp. 649-668), cited in Ibid.
9. Robert Merton, "Bureaucratic Structure and Personality", *Social Forces*, Vol. 18(1940), pp. 560-568
10. Victor Thompson, *Modern Organizations* (New York: Knopf, 1961).
11. Note, for instance, the, restructuring experience of SBI. See Pradeep Khandwalla, *Organizational Design for Excellence* (New Delhi: Tata McGraw Hill. 1993), p. 177.
12. See Gerald Caiden, *Administrative Reform Comes of Age* (Berlin: Waiter de Gruyter, 1991), pp. 105-106.
13. Padma Ramchandran, *Public Administration in India* (New Delhi: National Book Trust, 1996), p. 224.
14. Caiden, *Administrative Reforms Comes of Age*, pp. 300-307.